KAZI SYED KARIMUDDIN

LIFE AND LIBERTY

MOIN QAZI

Grandson of Kazi Syed Karimuddin

The increasing tendency towards seeing people in terms of one dominant 'identity' ('this is your duty as an American', 'you must commit these acts as a Muslim', or 'as a Chinese, you should give priority to this national engagement') is not only an imposition of an external and arbitrary priority but also the denial of essential liberty of a person who can decide on their respective loyalties to different groups (to all of which they belong)

– Amartya Sen, The Idea of Justice.

INDIA • SINGAPORE • MALAYSIA

ISBN

Hardcase 979-8-89724-252-8
Paperback 979-8-89724-251-1

CONTENTS

1. KAZI SYED KARIMUDDIN – SPANNING AN ILLUSTRIOUS CAREER

A family biography

Vidarbha, in the north-eastern region of the Indian State of Maharashtra, has always been fertile soil for many social reformers and intellectuals. It has played an active role in the nation's destiny, and its social, cultural, and political rivulets have flowed into and enriched the great sea of national civilization. One such luminary who emerged from Yavatmal was Kazi Syed Karimuddin. He rose to be a great criminal lawyer in the region and played a critical role in the drafting of the Indian Constitution.

Kazi Karimuddin was born on July 19, 1899, at Darwah in the Yavatmal district of Maharashtra, to Kazi Syed Nasiruddin and Dayanath Begum. He received his education at Mohamedan High School, Amravati. He graduated from Morris College, Nagpur, and obtained his postgraduate degree in economics from Aligarh Muslim University. He later qualified for law. He married Qadirunnisa Begum on May 24, 1926.

Kazi Karimuddin was active in Yavatmal's social, legal, judicial, and political circles. He was Vice-Chairman District Council (1924-28), Sub-judge (1928-31), President of Anjuman Middle School (1932-37), and Public Prosecutor (1939-45). A criminal lawyer par excellence, he was a prominent member of the Congress party. His younger brother, Kazi Syed Gyasuddin, was also a famous criminal lawyer (LLB from Aligarh) and a Congress MLA from Akola, holding several ministerial positions in the Maharashtra Assembly (1951–62).

He participated in the Constituent Assembly that framed the Constitution for independent India from 1947 to 1950 and was a member of the Madhya Pradesh Legislative Assembly until 1952 (at that time, Madhya Pradesh was named Central Province). Following that, he was a member of the Rajya Sabha (the upper house of the Indian Parliament) from 1954 to 1958. He moved an amendment along the lines of the American Constitution to make the right to privacy a fundamental right, but Dr. B.R. Ambedkar only gave it reserved support.

He had three sons, Quazi Syed Shahabuddin, Nooruddin Javed, and Ejazudin Tariq Kazi, and he had three daughters. The two elder sons died early. The youngest son is settled in the UK and is an accomplished technocrat. His sons-in-law excelled in their respective fields: Nizamuddin Ahmed (LLM), Syed Mukassir Shah, Justice M.M. Qazi, and Dr. Mirza Basheer Baig were notable professionals in law, administration, and medicine. Though a staunch opponent of the Uniform Civil Code, Karimuddin was a progressive and forward-looking Muslim who ensured his children received premier education. Kazi had five daughters. Since Yavatmal lacked adequate facilities for higher learning, he sent his daughters to Hyderabad to pursue postgraduate courses at Osmania University.

Kazi passed away on September 14, 1977. His life and contributions serve as a beacon to modern-day Muslims and others, highlighting the importance of balancing tradition with vision and the role of individual rights in shaping a democratic society. As a college student, I always accompanied him during my vacations in his trials. He was a familiar face on the court campus, where crowds would flock to him to seek his blessings. His health had become frail, but the embers in his growing ashes would still sparkle with the sinking glory. The judges would extend great respect in the courtroom. The whole space would give an idea of his glorious era, which I miss because I was still in school and not at an age when I could grasp the nuances of his erudition. I still remember my days with him, and this book is a homage to his marvellous intelligence and humanitarian services,

A high-flying legal eagle

From the triumphs and errors of those who came before us and the course of history that their efforts helped shape, we learn about how our own choices can shape the history that is in the making and the r minor role we may play in its unravelling its potential. This is no less true for the lives of lawyers than it is for any other player in a democracy's evolution. And it is certainly true for the life of Kazi Syed Karimuddin.

He used 'sketches' to contrive his biography because there are far too many stories to tell. In covering this range of subjects in a limited number of pages, the biography ends up losing its steam. There are so many momentous legal proceedings mentioned that the sheer significance of each is that each has a spread of quotes sparingly carrying his comments. The writing treads lightly on Kazi's personal life, neither exploring the full richness of the family and professional relationships he shared nor entering into any controversies on private matters.

For readers from the legal community, the pages have many sparkling pointers on how to develop one's practice in Court. One learns about the importance of having a broad set of sources for clientele, listening to a judge's questions carefully, treating one's juniors courteously, and maintaining a degree of independence from one's clients. He is cutting a striking figure as a legal professional whose ability is so formidable and integrity so sound that there are no controversies to surround him. He has been criticized in public and confronted in Court. Another image that emerges is of a lawyer who showed earnest concern as a crusader for human freedom and constitutional rights and fought for liberty and free speech in times when these were under siege.

My writing may seem more concerned about these professional aspects than about more significant socio-political questions or moral dilemmas. Still, the book, written in clear, accessible and engaging prose and littered with many anecdotes spanning a considerable canvas, should be of great interest to readers from any field, especially if they are interested in India's pre-and post-Independence history or at all curious about the workings of its legal system. It gives remarkable insight into the fascinating process that involved Kazi and his peers in the making of the Constitution out of the ashes of Partition.

Kazi Karimuddin was the most active critical persona with Hasrat Mohani in the deliberations on the Uniform Civil Code in the Constituent Assembly. He argued, "The people outside and the members of the Constituent Assembly must realize that a Muslim regards the personal law as part of the religion, and I really assure you that there is not a single Muslim in the country—at least I have not seen one—who wants a change in the mandatory provision of religious rights and personal laws. If there is anyone who wants a change in the mandatory principle or religion as a matter of personal law, then he cannot be a Muslim."

Kazi's phenomenal acclaim as the leading criminal lawyer of Central India has been admired and exemplary because he operated from a small district of Yavatmal as his base. The courtrooms in places where he held his trials overflowed with both lawyers and non-lawyers who would be enthralled witnessing the legendary lawyer tear away witnesses who would helplessly surrender to his psychological brainwashing. Experts in various fields also found their brilliance inadequate to cope with his versatile range of inquisitive questions, which tickled and cornered them into acknowledging their limited abilities to stand up to a colossus. Kazi Karimuddin was not constrained to being a mere intellectual icon. He was victorious even in electoral politics on account of his brilliance, which complemented logical exposition, as well as his popularity, which was the outcome of his ethical conduct.

A versatile genius

Constitutional India was born from the ethos of the deep and prosperous civilization that he lived through, which was the soul inside him. He believed that the Constitution was a product of its times and a living document containing a prescription for national leadership. Imbued with the spirit of the Constitution, he and his fellow architects and political philosophers strove hard to infuse the embodied ideals of Indian civilization.

Kazi's character stood out for its independence, unwavering integrity, and staunch commitment to constitutional principles, setting a high standard for others to follow. His passing is particularly poignant at a time when dissenting voices face challenges in a shrinking space.

Throughout his long and impactful professional and personal life, Karimuddin n engaged deeply with the public sphere, especially during the formative years of the making of India's Constitution. His lifelong mission was to uphold constitutional principles, with a particular focus on the right to dissent in a diverse nation. Notable for his aggressive and confident style as the leader of the Bar, Kazi Syed Karimuddin's charisma stemmed from a direct approach to the law. His commitment to secular values and liberal ideals left an indelible mark on modern India. Although he ceaselessly strove for the protection of minority rights, he remained a committed nationalist. He opted to choose to stay back in India when hordes of Muslims were trekking and boarding trains to Pakistan after Partition.

An architect of the Constitution

Kazi and his fellow members of the constituent assembly decided that Political freedom and civil liberty should be the keystones of the Indian Constitution. Our Constitution is primarily shaped and moulded for the common man. The only persons who would be disappointed with our Constitution are those who believe in outdated ideologies, which can only result in levelling down and not levelling up. His great fellow makers of our Constitution clearly intended that we should preserve the integrity of the Constitution against any hasty or ill-considered changes, "the fruits of passions or ignorance". The essential purpose of our Constitution is to ensure the freedom of the individual and the dignity of man and to put fundamental human rights above the reach of the State and of transient politicians in power.

Kazi was a man of many parts—a chiselled mind, a daunting opponent and a skilful wordsmith whose presence one felt the moment he walked into Court. When he stood up, there was silence; when he spoke, Judges listened with rapt attention. One could disagree with him, but one never stopped admiring him. He was a professional to the core with the innate ability to persuade even a hostile bench to listen and ponder. His greatest attribute was his ability to stand up and remain counted. He was unafraid to speak his mind.

Renowned for his unwavering belief in judicial independence, human rights, and the rule of law, Kazi Syed Karimuddin's career reflected a deep commitment to these principles. Kazi, a mentor to countless young lawyers, was admired not only for his legal brilliance but also for his dedication to constitutional principles. Throughout his life, Kazi stood for secularism, democracy, integrity, and professional ethics, consistently speaking out against the erosion of constitutional principles. His enduring legacy continues to inspire legal professionals to champion the values of the Indian Constitution and strive for excellence in the field of law.

In a problematic case, there are a number of competing principles that need comparison, and one preference is warm out over another. Kazi collaborated to assist the judiciary in putting justice first, and precedent came lower down in the scale of importance. Justice has been realized by applying the principles of equity, where necessary, and adapting the law to modern conditions. His attitude to the law was positive, and he exercised all the powers of a judge to do right.

Kazi had great learning, which enabled him to skirt around awkward precedents with skill and ingenuity and produce a result which accorded with morality and natural justice. He believed that people would not be disposed to obey the law unless they felt convinced that it was, on the whole, just and justly applied. It was necessary to explain. To convince, and he was renowned for his clarity of expression: simple words and short sentences. His style was lively and entertaining, and he was a storyteller. Simplicity and clarity of language made the law more accessible to the layman. He saw the danger of treating logic as the only basis for law.

Troubleshooter for negative perceptions of the Constitution

Wily politicians have sedulously propagated the myth that the Constitution stands in the way of the nation's economic progress and the uplift of the masses. This is the most significant fraud ever perpetrated on the people. The truth of the matter is that it is the wooden-headed and disastrous economic policies of the Governments at the Centre and in several States which are genuinely responsible for the miseries of the seventeen million unemployed and the many more millions who, though employed, are still living below the minimum subsistence level due to the erosion in the value of the rupee. There is not a single sound economic policy or scheme for the social development of the masses, which is, to the slightest degree, hampered or hindered by any of the provisions of the Constitution. The legacy of the late includes his unwavering commitment to minority rights and secularism, emphasizing the Constitution's defence in its current form against the many challenges in an ideological state. Kazi was a valued member of the India Business Law Journal's editorial board for several years. The role of the guardian of the Constitution is essential to maintaining the integrity of democratic governance. By ensuring that constitutional ideals are acknowledged and upheld, the Court protects individual rights, upholds the balance of power, and advances the rule of law 5 days ago. He spoke clearly but politely, and during cross-examination, he respected the dignity of the witness. He specifically avoided pressuring the wines with aggressive postures. He aimed to arrive at the truth without browbeating or using strategies or gestures with the client.

Breach of any of the constitutional provisions, even if made to further a popular cause, is bound to be a dangerous precedent. Disrespect to the Constitution is bound to be broadened from precedent to precedent, and before long, the entire Constitution may be treated with contempt and held up to ridicule. That is what happened to the Weimar Constitution. The fundamental issue arising for decision in these cases is of far greater significance than it appears at first sight. The question of whether the Rulers can be de-recognized by the President is of secondary importance. What is of utmost importance for the future of our democracy is whether the executive of this country can flout the mandates of the Constitution and set at nought legislative enactments at its discretion. If one holds that it can, then our belief that we are ruled by laws and not by men and women must be erroneous. To generations who have passed their lives in the law, Kazi was a colossus who strode the judicial landscape in the second half of the last century, shedding lambent light on ticklish legal corners and illuminating the legal and judicial landscape with his effulgence. He was unique. He expanded the universe of criminal law. Indisputably made him the best-known criminal lawyer of his era, which he spanned for almost eighty years,

It was not just the magnitude but the manner of his contribution to jurisprudence that made Kazi unique. In many leading cases, he captured the courtroom's attention by an opening paragraph setting the scene with simple but colourful language.

A spiritual philosopher

He was known to speak his mind with unflinching courage. Kazi Syed Karimuddin His sharpness and brilliance as a criminal law were widely acknowledged. He continued to be among the best criminal lawyers. Apart from his grip over criminal law and its philosophy, he was well-versed in constitutional law and could dissect any situation with clarity. He has always maintained a calm composure and made the witness comfortable without targeting him for soliciting favours.

Despite possessing a different political persuasion, Soli steadfastly believed in Voltaire's famous dictum that he would disagree violently with anyone but defend to death that person's right to disagree with him. While his extraordinary brilliance, legal skills, court craft and commitment to human rights make him a legend, he is also noted for his compassion, empathy, generosity, wit, curiosity and mischievousness, often almost naughtiness. But above all, he was a human being par excellence.

Kazi was a warm, genteel, intellectual practitioner of the law of a different era where facts and the interpretation of the statutes were the overriding considerations. His presentations overflowed with wit, polish, and erudition, which kept the courtroom glued to his presentation. For him, the law was a calling, and money was never the prime motive, as it is for many leading lawyers today.

Kazi was considered such a good lawyer that the courtrooms where he argued his cases often overflowed with audiences, and colleagues sometimes yearned to join in standing ovations for the eloquence of his arguments. Young lawyers gathered around him to hear how he handled celebrated cases. He often laced his court presentations with wit, and he spoke with few notes — an approach he likened.

In public life, he was not given expressions even of just indignation. There were moments of significant irritation and even flashes of exasperation, but he never fit his temper. Kazi Syed Karimuddin believed in (as eminent philosopher Ludwig Wittgenstein said once about the task of philosophy) "showing the fly the way out of the fly bottle". He was committed to the basic principles of law and justice, but all his life, he regarded principled pragmatism as a virtue of democratic lawyering and justice.

Inside the courtroom, Kazi, I also took on responsibility for our mistakes and always apologized charmingly to the Court if the brief or facts came undone. What happened outside and in the late evenings remains legally privileged! A stickler for detail: Once you choose law as a profession, you don't retire till you die.

A genteel personality

Kazi trusted the fallibility of judges and accepted every judgment with grace and dignity. Judicial activism must not be confused with judicial showmanship or judicial adventurism. Judicial activism does not warrant a trigger-happy approach of striking down laws which are unpalatable to the personal predilections of judges. Judicial activism does not warrant venturing into fields where the judiciary does not have the requisite expertise. What is the solution? Alas, the real problem is that justice is not dispensed by slot machines but by human beings. Perfection is not an attribute of shared humanity, and judges are, after all, human beings. They are not celestial bodies endowed with the gift of infallibility. Therefore, judicial aberrations do occur occasionally. But that is no reason for wholesale condemnation of the active exercise of judicial power.

The rule of law is not a one-way traffic. It places restraints both on the Government and individuals. If the underlying principles of the rule of law are to become a reality in governance and our lives, no doubt laws are necessary, but they alone are not sufficient. In addition, fostering of the rule of law culture is imperative. The only proper foundation on which the rule of law can rest is its willing acceptance by the people until it becomes part of their way of life.

Therefore, we should strive to instil the rule of law temperament and the rule of law culture at home, in schools, and colleges. We should strive for the universalization of its basic principles. Our effort should be to constantly aim at the expansion of the rule of law to make it a dynamic concept that not merely places constraints on the exercise of official power but facilitates and empowers progressive measures in the area of the socio-economic rights of the people. That, indeed, is the moral imperative for the civilized world. He considered legal practice a spiritual art.

He rightly pointed out that they "are neither satellites nor agents of the Centre" and "have as important a role to play in the political, social, educational and cultural life of the people as the Union". However, there is genuine concern about misuse by the Centre of Article 356 on the pretext that the State Government is acting in defiance of the essential features of the Constitution. The real safeguard will be full judicial review extending to an inquiry into the truth and correctness of the basic facts relied upon in support of the action under Article 356, as indicated by Justices Sawant and Kuldip Singh. If, in some instances, that entails evaluating the sufficiency of the material, so be it. The line between the existence of material and its relevance is not a rigid one and is susceptible to flexible fluctuation depending on the facts of a particular case.

Throughout his career, he has had a substantial impact on the country's judiciary. Known for his contributions to the field of law, He became one of the highest-paid lawyers in India due to his ability to turn around the hardest of cases. He defended many high-profile personalities, including politicians and gangsters, throughout his career.

Kazi, who was known for his straightforward nature, never hesitated to point out issues, even if they discredited his party. While his political career does not comprise his fondest memories, his contributions to the field of criminal law helped redefine the legal system of the country.

A spiritual philosopher

One of Kazi Syed Karimuddin's defining traits was his unwavering commitment to defending civil liberties and individual rights. He firmly believed in the principle that everyone, regardless of their standing in society, deserved a fair trial and competent legal representation. His passionate advocacy for the marginalized and downtrodden earned him widespread respect and admiration.

Kazi's brilliance was not just in the courtroom alone. He was also a prolific commentator and politician. His lectures on legal matters are revered as authoritative texts, offering invaluable insights into various aspects of Indian law and jurisprudence. Additionally, his stint in politics added another dimension to his multifaceted persona, as he fearlessly voiced his opinions on matters of national importance.

Throughout his illustrious career, Kazi Syed Karimuddin was never one to mince words or shy away from controversy. He was known for his outspokenness, often courting controversy with his candid remarks and fearless critique of the establishment. His sharp intellect, combined with his no-nonsense approach, made him a reckoning force both inside and outside the courtroom.

Despite his advancing age, Kazi remained as active and spirited as ever, continuing to take on cases and champion causes close to his heart. His passion for the law and unwavering commitment to justice served as an inspiration to generations of aspiring lawyers, reminding them of the noble ideals that lie at the heart of the legal profession.

History is replete with instances of violent upheavals and breaches [es] of peace on account of intolerance leading to the oppression of minorities and other unpopular groups. Violent conflicts, which we are witnessing today, are also the result of intolerance. What we need urgently and should aspire to is the practice of tolerance. It is noteworthy that the Preamble to the Charter of the United Nations proclaims that to achieve the goals of the Charter, we need "to practice tolerance and live together in peace with one another as good neighbours.

A suave handler of dissent

Tolerance entails a positive attitude that permits and protects not only the expression of thoughts and ideas that are accepted and acceptable but also accords an accommodation that is hospitable to the thought we hate as that assured to the orthodoxies of the day. Disagreements with the beliefs and ideology of others are no reason for their suppression because tolerance recognizes that there can be more than one path for the attainment of truth and salvation.

Intolerance stems from an invincible assumption of the infallibility of one's system, the dogmatic conviction about the rightness of one's tenets and beliefs and their superiority over others. When intolerance reigns, reason takes a back seat. Intolerance thrives on prejudice. It fosters feelings of ill will and enmity between different classes and communities. Intolerance eventually leads to forcible imposition of one's ideology and dogmas on others and results in violent conflicts and breaches of peace.

An intolerant society does not brook dissent. An authoritarian regime cannot tolerate the expression of ideas in the form of writings, plays, music or paintings that challenge its doctrines and ideology. Consequently, censorship is an indispensable instrument for a totalitarian regime. An intolerant, authoritarian regime and censorship are indeed natural allies.

Our Supreme Court has accorded a high place to tolerance in our polity. A fine example is its landmark decision in *Bijoe Emmanuel vs. the State of Kerala.* The educational authorities expelled three students of the Jehovah's Witnesses faith because they refused to sing the Indian national anthem even though they respectfully stood up in silence to the rhythm of the singing of the anthem. The High Court of Kerala upheld the action of expulsion. In appeal, the Supreme Court accepted the plea of the students that they be forbidden on account of their religious beliefs to sing the national anthem of any country. The Court held that their expulsion was violative of their fundamental right to freedom of expression, which includes the right to remain silent. The Court concluded with a ringing note: "Our tradition teaches tolerance; our philosophy preaches tolerance; our Constitution practices tolerance; let us not dilute it."

In its celebrated judgment in *S. Rangarajan vs. P. Jagjivan Ram*, our Supreme Court emphasized that "freedom of expression protects not merely ideas that are accepted but those that offend, shock or disturb the State or any sector of the population. Such are the demands of pluralism, tolerance and broadmindedness, without which there is no democratic society." that tolerance. We cannot legislate tolerance. We must develop the capacity for tolerance by fostering an environment of tolerance and a culture of tolerance. We must not penalize the right to dissent and must protect the dissenter against coercive action by the State or non-state actors, especially fanatical, intolerant groups. Education has a vital role to play in this connection. Indeed, the highest result of education is tolerance.

The press, too, has a vital role to play in highlighting the necessity of tolerance and condemning instances of intolerance. It should ensure that prejudices and stereotypes about specific communities and classes are not popularized and thus perpetuated. The press should incessantly preach the message that no group or body has the monopoly of truth and wisdom, and we must respect the point of view of the 'other minded.'

Our priority should be to promote tolerance in our multi-religious, multi-cultural nation, thereby strengthening our pluralist democracy and ensuring that freedom of speech and expression and freedom of the press become living realities. Our Constitution prescribes a list of fundamental duties to be performed by citizens.

A promoter of tolerance

To his mind, the practice of tolerance is imperative and should be the foremost fundamental duty of every citizen. If done conscientiously, it would bring salutary change to our society and also bring about harmony in relations between peoples of the world.

In the pantheon of legal luminaries, Kazi occupies a place of honour, and his contributions to the legal field serve as a testament to his unparalleled brilliance, courage, and unwavering commitment to the cause of justice. As the legal fraternity reflects on his remarkable legacy, one thing remains abundantly clear: Kazi was not just a lawyer; he was a legend.

Kazi's illustrious career spanned over seven decades, during which he handled a multitude of high-profile cases that propelled him to national and international fame. Here are some of the landmark cases that played a significant role in cementing his reputation as one of India's most celebrated lawyers:

He was the leading lawyer of the time, both civil and criminal. Later, as a senior advocate, he became known as the defender of indefensible cases but succeeded in a large number of them. With his legal acumen and skill in

He was an aggressive and skilled attorney who was committed not only to zealously defending your rights but also focused on how the outcome of your case could affect your future. Not every case is the same, and not every client is the same.

A collaborator with judges

There is nothing novel about judges creatively adapting the language of the Constitution so as to apply its values to new situations. Has aptly stated that by the statement that what the Constitution meant at the time of its adoption, it means today, the significant clauses of the Constitution must be devoted to the interpretation which the framers, with the condition and outlook of their time, would have placed upon them, the statement carries its refutation". Neither the Constitution nor the Bill of Rights is a self-executing instrument. It is what the judges say it is. Whether the judiciary is the protective sentinel of our rights under the Constitution will depend upon its interpretation of the Constitution and, in particular, of the Bill of Rights. A most generous Bill of Rights can be reduced to arid parchment promises by narrow and insensitive judicial interpretation. It is well to remember the dicta of our Supreme Court that "a Constitution is not an ephemeral legal document embodying a set of legal rules for the passing. It sets out principles for an expanding future and is intended to endure for ages to come and consequently has to be adapted to the various crises of human affairs." Therefore, according to our Supreme Court: "a constitutional provision must be construed, not in a narrow and constricted sense, but in a wide and liberal manner so as to anticipate and take account of changing conditions and purposes so that the constitutional provision does not get atrophied or fossilized but remains flexible enough to meet the newly emerging problems and challenges"

A committer to ethical values

Kazi was committed to establishing an inclusive and supportive culture in which all staff and students feel welcomed, accepted and given a voice, irrespective of individual and group differences. We each have a responsibility to create an environment where everyone feels equally valued.

He expected all intellectual members to treat others with dignity and respect. We recognize that we differ from each other in backgrounds, beliefs, and cultures and that such differences can lead to conflicting expectations and interpretations of each other's behaviour, as well as misunderstandings. We need to be open-minded and aware of our implicit assumptions and work together constructively to improve our understanding of different perspectives and beliefs.

Kazi Karimuddin's vast experience and insights gave him an uncanny knack for unravelling the anatomy and pathology of crimes. He was always apprehensive about the pervasive scope of the intrusive lens of the state and private agents. He considered privacy as one where no one violates privacy, a vital constituent of a healthy constitutional polity since India's enormous right of the people to be secure in their persons, houses, papers and effects against unreasonable searches and seizures.

A sharpshooter

Kazi coupled legal scholarship with courtroom wit to decimate the prosecution's cases against mafia bosses. Kazi, who unapologetically vowed to "do anything that the law will allow to defend the crooked politicians and other miscreants he represented for more than four decades as a savvy criminal lawyer.

More often than not, Kazi combined cogent legal scholarship with shrewd courtroom theatrics to vindicate a roster of high-profile criminals. The gregarious Kazi not only represented but befriended clients in the legal profession. Kazi won great acclaim for his courtroom acumen. "He was the best criminal lawyer of his generation," What distinguished him most was he not only knew his case inside out and could plan an excellent defence strategy, but he was so disciplined." Kazi subjected prosecution witnesses to withering cross-examination, peppering them with sarcastic zingers that undermined their credibility and charmed juries.

Kazi could move a jury emotionally and also had a total command of the law: "It was an extraordinary combination. His style was unique because of his ability to speak to juries with an eloquent passion, which made them want to believe him. He was never ashamed of representing all those mobsters because a criminal lawyer represents criminals. Kazi argued that he was no more aggressive in defending his clients than the Government was in prosecuting them. Clients hire me "because I'll do anything that the law will allow, without concern for how it's gonna make me look.

Kazi once said he was appalled that there were offenders of minor crimes who got charged with profound changes. Still, he insisted that defence lawyers should not be motivated by whether the defendants they represent were guilty. A lot of clients told him they're innocent because they think I'll work harder for them. That's not true. It's irrelevant. The question is: Can the State prove its case?"

He was involved in defence of collars of every colour: white-collar, grey-collar, blue-collar to represent doctors, lawyers, politicians, state senators, congressmen." He was also a notable contributor to numerous books and law journals and provided insightful commentary on legal issues for outlets, including the Daily Beast and CNN. His law school peers remember his knack for working with clients.

Kazi had an instinctive grasp of the law," friend and fellow alumnus Geraldo Rivera '69 once said. "He knows what the law is. He can relate to the client and make a legal rather than moral judgment about it." Recognized for his intense preparation, studied tactics, and dramatic presence in the courtroom, Kazi

A humane reformist

Kizi's gifts as a lawyer were many, but what distinguished him most, in my view, was he never let himself get distracted from his defence. He refused to make objections simply because he could or to fight ancillary battles just because the opportunities presented themselves at trial. He was laser-focused on the defence he brought into the case. That made him so effective, and it is also why judges loved having him in their courtrooms. Kazi's sedate style, coupled with his tactical approach, earned him accolades. Kazi has an instinctive grasp of the law," friend and fellow alumnus. He can relate to the client and make a legal rather than moral judgment about it."

Kazi was the most intelligent man several had ever met, a true gentleman who spent almost seven years working for the near-universally esteemed counsel. But as time passed, Lichtman said, "I began to realize I was a lot more like Jimmy," i.e. a pugnacious, sarcastic, nasty, and fearless spark plug of a man who once said it was not his job to prove the innocence of his clients but rather "to attempt to stop the prosecution from proving their guilt."

Renowned for his unwavering belief in judicial independence, human rights, and the rule of law, Kazi's career reflected a deep commitment to these principles. Life offers invaluable insights into his experiences and thoughts on the Indian legal system. A mentor to countless young lawyers, Kazi was admired not only for his legal brilliance but also for his dedication to constitutional principles throughout his life. Kazi stood for secularism, democracy, integrity, and professional ethics, consistently speaking out against the erosion of constitutional principles. His enduring legacy continues to inspire legal professionals to champion the values of the Indian Constitution and strive for excellence in the field of law.

Courts, legislatures, and officials at every level of Government have created so many protections for police officers and other government officials at every stage of litigation that a person who has had their life shaken to the very core by government misconduct can have the courthouse doors shut in their face. These barriers exist because of the fear that an easy path to relief for civil rights plaintiffs would overwhelm courthouses, enrich undeserving plaintiffs, bankrupt officers, and ultimately leave lawless danger in the wake of understaffed police departments (p. xv). Schwartz challenges that narrative, both from her own experience as a civil rights lawyer and her body of research (pp. xv–xvii). The Supreme Court labours under the impression that civil rights lawsuits have the power to motivate government officials to clean houses when bad actors within police departments are unsheathed· Kazi proposed that the barriers the Court and political actors have erected are so significant that civil rights lawsuits act as neither a vehicle for individual relief nor a motivation for reform.

Even when lawyers are available, and the judge and jury are at least not hostile to a civil rights plaintiff's claims, Schwartz highlights several doctrinal barriers to relief. Onerous pleading standards can keep claims out of Court for lacking information that a plaintiff needs the discovery process to obtain and fosters legal inquiry and argument that is fast-paced and timely — a complement to the long-form, in-depth analysis that has filled our pages for over a century. We hope the ideas presented through this new platform will generate debate, uncover new questions, challenge our readers, and inspire continued exploration.

Criminal reformer

Kazi was a giant among legal theorists of criminal law and procedure. Criminal justice is in crisis across the world in several countries. Prisons are overflowing with a lack of hygienic space, and there is the confidence that policing has plummeted, and race- and class-based biases distort every aspect of the system. American democracy is in crisis, too, as the chasm of loathing and incomprehension that divides political factions grows ever broader and more profound. Legal scholar and former prosecutor David A. Sklansky argues that these crises are deeply intertwined. And if the failures of American criminal justice are near the heart of our political divides, then reforming the system is essential for repairing our democracy.

"Justice" is one of the most popular, offering an introduction to moral and political philosophy and exploring critical analysis of classical and contemporary theories of justice, including discussion of present-day applications. Students learn the fundamentals of political philosophy, absorbing a more profound sense of the philosophy that underlies modern issues such as affirmative action, same-sex marriage, and equality. They also develop the ability to articulate better and evaluate philosophical arguments and ask philosophical questions, as well as gain an understanding of social justice and criminal justice and the roles they play in the modern justice system.

Kazi was a warm, genteel, intellectual practitioner of the law of a different era where facts and the interpretation of the statutes were the overriding considerations, and arguments overflowed with wit and erudition. For Sorabjee, the law was a calling, and money was never the prime motive, as it is for many leading lawyers today. A Parsi Lawyers in India never retire; they drop dead", remarked Fali Nariman. They are then hardly spoken about or remembered, save in rare cases where while we grieve at their departure, we recall and extol their lives and careers.

Kazi was certainly among such notable exceptions - one of the all-time greats both as a lawyer and a human being. His passing has created a great void and unkindly reminded us of the proximity of death to life - one so complete, rich and meaningful. He loved quoting Carlyle, saying that tradition is an enormous magnifier, but traditions are not like instant coffee, and each generation would have to imbibe and cherish them.

He did and taught others to do so. Teachers and seniors should lead and teach by example. Soli lived this; his chamber was a nursery for training a large number of distinguished men of law. In his long and eventful career, he appeared in a number of landmark cases and helped lay down the law.

When he took over, he said that he did not see his role as that of a 'hatchetman' of the Government of the day. His mentor, Palkhivala, who was greeting him on his appointment, had said the same thing about his role - the guardian of public interest and the protector of human rights. He could be critical of the Government whose principal law officer he was, much like his eminent predecessor, Motilal Setalvad.

Kazi was a sound lawyer and a skilled advocate. He was deeply rooted in legal theory. He was always very polite but firm. Gentle in manners, unfailingly courteous, he was grace personified.

Great liberality of thought and catholicity of outlook combined with sturdy independence, total fairness, objectivity and impartiality were his hallmarks. Hero of many battles and celebrated causes, he was a noble warrior who bore his scars and honours with philosophic indifference.

A moral giant

He brought to bear a moral eminence on a highly mercenary and, at times, unprincipled legal profession. He could take a principled stand on any question or case. He was a strong and outstanding ethical pillar of the Bar.

With his departure, the tribe has further dwindled. He believed that to preserve fundamental values, everyone - whether he be a public functionary or a private citizen - should display a degree of vigilance and willingness to sacrifice. He was an exemplar.

In an atmosphere where the pursuit of the higher and nobler ideals of the legal profession is becoming increasingly complex and where half-baked ideas reared by accident have sway, Kazi belonged to a refreshingly different genre.

He was a cultivated man to use Frankfurter's felicitous expression. Literature and music were his soulmates. The man was as great as the lawyer - an incredibly gracious person. His claim to eminence rests as much on his great humanity and urbanity.

A monk dedicated to the service of the leprosy afflicted had sought Sorabjee's help in some legal matter. When he went to meet and thank the lawyer, Soli gave him a cheque for a munificent sum as his contribution to the noble cause.

He has been, to his colleagues, a very dear and revered friend, philosopher and guide for about four decades. Carlyle wrote that a well-written life is almost as rare as a well-spent one. Kazi's life was genuinely well-lived.

Kazi agonized about the moral decay he witnessed in India. He believed the nation was suffering from "a fatty degeneration of conscience, and the malady seems to be not only persistent but prone to aggravation." He blamed it on the lifestyle of politicians and businessmen who single-mindedly pursued money, insisting that "such an obsessive pursuit impoverishes the mind, shrivels the imagination and desiccates the heart."

India's politicization. The India he knew has become deeply politicized. While envisioning a completely depoliticized society requires a big leap of imagination, there can still be doubts as to the degree to which modern societies may or should bc politicized in different dimensions. This book gives a range of answers to this question using selected examples from contemporary history and the present time, and it outlines the process of politicizing society, together with the tools and means used for that. It does not attempt an exhaustive coverage of the topic of politicization. Still, it serves as a reference for persons interested in the discussed issues, including students of political and social sciences.

A preserver of glorious pat

The old system's strength lay in dealing with conflicts between language groups, religions, regions, and castes, ultimately evolving a rough consensus through endless palaver. Its weakness was in solving economic problems. The palaver could grow exasperating—mainly when it took the place of action to relieve the hunger and poverty of ordinary Indians. But there was something extraordinary, too, about this new democracy struggling so earnestly to work out its staggering problems within the relatively unconstrained forms of Western liberalism. It was an endlessly fascinating struggle and one which was unimaginable with the talk.

Indeed, talk—what a cynical Indian friend calls "fearless gossip"—is the last remaining safety valve among those which once permitted the straining engine of Indian democracy to survive nearly apocalyptic pressures. All the other valves—a free press, the parliamentary opposition, regional parties, and an unfettered judiciary —have now been largely shut off.

One might be willing to sacrifice even the glorious if that would make some difference in the lives of ordinary Indians. One official told him bluntly, "It is only foreign reporters like yourself and your counterparts among the Indian upper middle class who worry about such things as freedom of expression. What most of our people care about is filling their bellies. We are tired of being the workshop of failed democracy. The time has come to exchange some of our vaunted individual rights for some economic development."

First, we had 5,000 years of civilization behind us — a civilization which had reached 'the summit of human thought' in the words of Ralph Waldo Emerson. We inherited excellent skills and a diversity of -splendid intelligence since genes evolved over five luminous millennia. We had a superb entrepreneurial spirit, honed over a century of obstacles. A few years ago, a World Bank report on India mentioned two very favourable factors — an unlimited reservoir of skilled labour and an abundance of capital available for investment in new projects. The trader's instinct is innate in Indian genes. An Indian can buy from a Jew and sell to a Scot and yet make a profit! Secondly, whereas before 1858, India was never a united political entity, in that year, the accident of British rule welded us into one country, one nation. When independence came, we had been a unified nationality for almost a century under one head of State. Thirdly, our founding fathers, after two long years of laborious and painful toil, gave us a Constitution which a former Chief Justice of India rightly described as "sublime".

The substance of the Universal Declaration of Human Rights, adopted by the United Nations on December 10, 1948, is embodied as Fundamental Rights in our Constitution. The unique feature is that all the rights to be given equality before the law to non-citizens alike. All religions have equal tolerance, and citizens have equal reverence. The religion of a citizen is no bar to his holding any office, however exalted, in politics or the judiciary. In this respect, we are more secular than the United Kingdom, where a Roman Catholic cannot be the monarch or the lord chancellor.

In another respect, our Constitution may claim to be more progressive than that of the United States of America. Equality of the sexes is a guaranteed right in India, whereas the attempt to incorporate a similar right in the United States Constitution faced resistance.

A true patriot of constitutional values

We can proudly say that our Constitution gave us a flying start and equipped us adequately to meet the challenges of the future. Unfortunately, over the years, we have dissipated every advantage we have started with, like compulsive gamblers bent upon squandering an invaluable legacy. I am afraid India today is only a caricature of the noble democracy which our forefathers strove to bring to life and freedom in 1947.

As early as January 1987, The Economist rightly remarked that socialism as practised in India has been a fraud. Our brand of socialism did not result in the transfer of wealth from the rich to the poor but only from the honest rich to the dishonest rich.

We built up state-owned enterprises called the public sector in India. The sleeping sickness of socialism is now universally acknowledged — but not officially in India. The union government runs more than

240 public sector enterprises, and state governments run more than 700. These public sector enterprises are the black holes, the money guzzlers, and they have been extracting an exorbitant price for India's doctrinaire socialism. There is a tidal wave of privatization sweeping across the world from Bangladesh to Brazil, but it has turned aside in its course and passed India by.

The most persistent tendency in India has been to have too much Government and too little administration; too many laws and too little justice; too many public servants and too little public service; too many controls and too little welfare. No democracy has ever paid all things considered, a heavier price for an adult franchise than India. I am not aware of any great democracy which started as a republic on the basis of an adult franchise: all of them started with a more restricted system and then graduated to an adult franchise. When the Constituent Assembly was in session, two of our greatest politicians — C Rajagopalachari and Sardar Vallabhbhai Patel — recommended that we should not start with the adult franchise but educate our people first to make them worthy of discharging their duties as citizens of a great democracy; but they were out-voted.

He often asked one question: How does India, with its extraordinary human potential and natural resources, manage to remain poor? The correct answer is very unflattering and hardly the type of answer which an ambassador of any country may give: We are not poor by nature but poor by policy. You would not be far wrong if you called India the world's leading expert in the art of perpetuating poverty.

Most of our politicians and bureaucrats, untainted by knowledge of development in the outside world, have no desire to explore new ideas which deserve to be called "a high-yielding variety of economics". We have smugly reconciled to low yield from high ideals.

India is rattling — and rattling violently with spare human capacity. Several million are on the roll employment exchanges. According to objective estimates, there must be at least thirty million more unemployed people who are not registered.

A fighter for reforms against moral decay

The picture that emerges is that of a great nation in a state of moral decay, of which corruption and indiscipline are two of the several facets. In the land of Mahatma Gandhi, violence is on the throne today. Mobocracy has too often displaced democracy. The contribution of modern India to sociology has been a Bandh — the closure of an entire city by militant rowdies.

One may apply to India the words used by the late Benigno Aquino about the Philippines — “Here is a land in which a few are spectacularly rich while the masses remain abjectly poor, where freedom and its blessings are a reality for a minority and an illusion for the many, a land consecrated to democracy but is a land of privilege and rank, a republic educated to equality but mired in an archaic system of caste.”

The most significant problem of India is that its finest men — men of calibre and vision, knowledge and character — are not in politics and stand little chance of getting elected with regard to the murky atmosphere of our political life. I was one of the foolish people who told Hari Nanda to stand for Parliament. He stood for Parliament from the seat which was supposed to be the safest for him — Faridabad. He was not only defeated, but he forfeited his deposit!

He said that if he were to name one curse which deserves to be the greatest curse of India, he would say it is casteism. Unfortunately, divisiveness has become an Indian disease. Truly, divisiveness is a disease that is spreading fast and wide, preys on the public mind, and is without a cure in sight. Communal hatred, linguistic fanaticism, regional fealty, and caste loyalty are gnawing at the vitals of the unity and integrity of the country. To the growing army of terrorists and professional hooligans, caste or clan, creed or tongue, is a sufficient ground to kill their fellow citizens. National integration is born in the hearts of the citizens. When it dies, there is no army. No government can save it. Inter-faith harmony and consciousness of the essential unity of all religions is the very heart of our national integration.

The soul of India aspires to integration and assimilation. Down the ages, Indian culture — a tremendous force of power and beauty — has been made richer and deeper as a result of absorbing what is best in outside influences and integrating those various influences to grace and enrich its own identity. Ambassador John Kenneth Galbraith remarked that while he had seen poverty in many countries of the world, he found one unusual attribute among the impoverished of India — "There is richness in their poverty."

Hundreds of millions who have no standard of living still have a standard of life. The ancient civilization survived and will survive when the raucous and fractious voices of today have gotten lost in the silence of the centuries. Nature has been kind to India in one respect. It has endowed the country with the gift of producing great leaders in the darkest hour — leaders with the gift of grace who can arouse the trusting millions to lofty heights.

There is an introductory lesson on Indian history. Our people have always taken their moral standards from their rulers; the people have risen to great heights when they have basked in the glow of noble kings or leaders. The present generation is waiting for a leader who will make it relearn moral values and who will inculcate in the people, as Gandhiji did, a sense of responsibility that falls on every citizen of a free society.

Eternally vigilant for liberty

Eternal vigilance is indeed the price of liberty. But it is true, in an even more profound sense, that eternal responsibility is also part of the price of freedom. Excessive authority without liberty is intolerable, but excessive liberty without authority and responsibility soon becomes equally unacceptable.

De Tocqueville made the profound observation that liberty cannot stand alone but can prosper with companion virtues: freedom and morality, liberty and law, liberty and justice, liberty and the common good, and liberty and civic responsibility. One last thought, and shall have done it. Today, the unity and integrity of India seem to be at stake. But "even this shall pass away". Indian society will, over time, acquire the requisite political culture — the attitudes and habits of tolerance, mutual respect, and goodwill- which alone can make democracy workable. The day will come when the states of India realize that, in a profound sense, they are culturally akin, ethnically identical, linguistically knit, and historically related.

The primary task before India today is to acquire a keener sense of national identity, to gain the wisdom to cherish its priceless heritage, and to create a cohesive society with the cement of Indian culture. We shall then celebrate our Republic as the dependence of the states upon one another, the dependence of our numerous communities upon one another, the dependence of the many castes and clans upon one another — in the sure knowledge that we are one nation.

Our people have always taken their moral standards from their rulers; the people have risen to great heights when they have basked in the glow of noble kings or leaders. The present generation is waiting for a leader who will relearn moral values and who will inculcate in the people, as Gandhiji did, a sense of responsibility that falls on every citizen of a free society.

Reformer for criminal laws

Criminal reformsCriminals are humans, too. It seems very obvious to say, but in America, this is actually a radical idea. If it weren't a radical idea, how would we justify the inhumane and degrading conditions of prisons and jails, the disregard with which we speak to the accused, or the post-release disenfranchisement of convicted felons? I am not here to argue for anarchy, but I am here to say for humanity, and this is why I have chosen to write this column on criminal justice reform. First, every human being is a human being. This simple fact arouses my empathy for the human condition. I know what it feels like to be cold, and so does almost every human being. I know how it feels to be hungry, and so does virtually every human being. I know what it feels like to be lonely, and so does almost every human being. The fact that I am human makes it intolerable for me to see other human beings as though they are not. This is not to say that no one should be penalized, but punishment in its current form in our country destabilizes my understanding of what it means to treat humans as humans.

Second, every human being has the capacity for change. I emphatically believe that no human being is permanently lost, permanently irredeemable. Looking at data on recidivism in the US doesn't prove that people can't change — it shows that the way we punish is not rehabilitative. Repentance, rehabilitation, and reentry, I believe, are possible if we only recognize our flaws and our ability to change and apply our understanding of our ability to slip up to those whose flaws may be more than our own.

Whether we believe that every human being is made in the image of the Divine, that every human being has inherent worldly value, or that we should treat others how we wish for ourselves, Human beings deserve humane treatment. Over this semester, this column will explore inhumane aspects of the criminal legal system, sometimes proposing alternatives and sometimes just bearing witness to these practices and spreading awareness of them. I hope you will join me.

2. LIFE AND LIBERTY IN INDIA BEYOND 75 YEARS

Two hundred years ago, the principles of liberty, equality and fraternity were radical, challenging and iconoclastic. In modern societies, although there are many differences in interpretation and approach, it has become hard to find people who do not accept the ideas to some extent. Many of the ideas around liberty, equality and fraternity are radical in the sense that they represent a challenge to existing patterns of social relationships. Social welfare provision depends on a complex constellation of political, economic and legal provisions, conventionally described in terms of 'welfare states'. The focus is on three principles — liberty, equality, and fraternity.

India has long been the torch bearer of these great searchlights. It has gained an enormous momentum. Its population has surpassed China's, making it the most populous country in the world. Its economy may become the world's third-largest in the next few years. It seems positioned to take today's geopolitical tensions and turn them into its

The birth of India and Pakistan as independent states in 1947 was a key moment in the history of Britain's empire and its army. However, the process of partition saw mass migration and ethnic violence that has left a bitter legacy to this day.

His long campaign for Indian independence, which had begun with the Indian Mutiny (1857-59), grew in intensity following the Second World War (1939-45). Indians increasingly expected self-government in return for their wartime contribution. But this was accompanied by serious inter-communal violence between Hindus, Sikhs and Muslims.

The new British government, elected in 1945, was determined to grant independence at long last and hoped to leave behind some form of united India. But, despite repeated talks, the mainly Hindu Indian National Congress and the Muslim League could not reach an agreement on the shape of the new state.

Partition meant that millions of people found themselves on the 'wrong' side of the border. Ten million became refugees in what was the most significant population movement in history. Muslims travelled to Pakistan, Sikhs and Hindus to India. Up to a million of these refugees were killed in a series of horrific massacres in the border regions. Some of the worst atrocities took place in the Punjab. Despite the efforts of the 55,000-strong Punjab Boundary Force, nearly 200,000 people lost their lives in the arson and. violence that followed the aftermath of the Partition.

It was Mountbatten rushed the partition process and failed to tackle the migration and communal violence that attended the birth of the new nations.

The very structure of British imperialist rule aggravated our problems and did not solve any of them," wrote Jawaharlal Nehru, a leader of India's independence movement and the country's first prime minister in 1938. Although achieving independence would be "a hard task," India, with its "vital spirit" awakened, "will no longer be merely a passive instrument of destiny or another's will. While the protection of the liberties of the subject is one of the main aims (and boasts) of almost all constitutions,

FhumanIndian culture

India had early trade connections with the Persian Gulf. Still, it remained unknown to Mediterranean peoples until the extension of the Persian empire to the Indus and the voyage of Darius' admiral Scylax down the Kabul and Indus rivers and perhaps around Arabia to Suez. Even so, India remained a land of fable and The conquests of Alexander(the

Great (327–325) brought more accurate knowledge of NW India as far as the river Hyphasis (Beas) and vague information about the Ganges valley and Sri Lanka, and the voyage of Nearchus informed the Greek world about the sea connection with the Persian Gulf.

The ancient Indian medical system of Ayurveda, which is rooted in nature-based healing methods, was widely taught at Nalanda and then migrated to other parts of India via alums. Other Buddhist institutions drew inspiration from the campus' design of open courtyards enclosed by prayer halls and lecture rooms. The stucco produced here influenced ecclesiastical art in Thailand, and metal art migrated from here to Tibet and the Malayan peninsula.

Those of us who have lived through the earlier days, when the entire nation is looking forward with zeal and fervour and with a sense of national pride, cannot but look upon the present times with deep anguish and distress.

The only achievement of Indian democracy has been that it has survived unfractured for so many. Nine hundred fifty million people — more than the combined population of Africa and South America — live together as one political entity under conditions of freedom. Never before in history, and nowhere else in the world today, has one-sixth of the human race existed as a single free nation. Professor Rostow of Texas University regards the survival of Indian democracy as the most important phenomenon of the post-war era.

The achievement is all the more creditable since no other democracy has had such diversity in unity or was such a mosaic of humanity. All the great religions in the world have flourished in India. We have 15 major languages written in different alphabets and derived from different roots, and, for good measure, our people — whom you can never call taciturn — express themselves in 250 dialects.

The English language, which is not one of the 15 significant languages listed in the Constitution, continues to be the only link language for the whole country; it is the only tongue in which the South can communicate with the North.

The epochal story

Having shaken off the yoke of the British Empire, the country embarked on m the world's most radical democratic experiment. Never before had a nation with such a low per capita level of income extended universal voting rights to its citizens in varied topography, unparalleled ethnic and religious diversity, the inheritance of a socially rigid and unequal caste system, and the fact India resides in a fractious geopolitical neighbourhood, and its flourishing democracy looks, even more, remarkable wondering whether it is possible to build a united and progressive nation out of the seemingly infinite diversity that makes up the fabric of Indian life.

We live in an age of inequality, or so we're frequently told. Across the globe, but especially in the wealthy economies of the West, the gap between the rich and the rest has widened year after year and become a chasm, spreading anxiety, stoking resentment, and roiling politics. For decades, policymakers and scholars have been training the West and elsewhere to think of the countries of the Indian subcontinent as part of a coherent region: South Asia. Home to around a quarter of the world's population, the area consists of eight countries:

Afghanistan, Bangladesh, Bhutan, India, the Maldives, Nepal, Pakistan, and Sri Lanka. Its diverse peoples speak hundreds of different languages and follow numerous other religious traditions, but they have shared histories, including the experience of British colonialism and shared cultural connections on the democratic front; India's success was immediate and came with astonishing speed. Over time, India became the first underdeveloped country in the world to be a full-scale democracy. There was--and is--success enough here. There was a short-lived hiccup in the 1970s when there was a brief attempt to change the system, but when the Government sought endorsement in a general election for those changes, it was driven out of office by the voters.

Of the many tropes that have cluttered foreign policy analysis in recent decades, few are as widespread or as enduring as the inevitability of India's rise. Built on a foundation of liberal democracy, fueled by a population of more than a billion people occupying a vast territory and enabled by the United States' desire to find a counterbalance to an expansionist China, India has been inching toward the geopolitical spotlight. Now, a confluence of recent events has convinced some observers—and arguably India's leadership—that its moment has finally arrived. There have been regular and orderly elections, and the ruling parties have vacated office when defeated in general elections rather than calling in the army. India has also had other essential features of a democracy, in particular, continued freedom and vigour of the media and independence of the judiciary, with the Supreme Court often disallowing decisions of those in the governmental office on constitutional grounds.

So, democracy has indeed flourished in India, and that has been the case since India became independent after two centuries of authoritarian British colonial dominance. India's democratic success is sometimes seen only as a consequence of British rule. However, that is a comparatively recent history shared by a hundred or more other countries that also emerged from the empire, none of which has had quite the effortless success that India has had with democracy.

The struggle for India's independence was a pivotal moment in its history, a journey marked by the unity and dedication of individuals from all walks of life. Among the many communities that actively participated in this fight for freedom were the Muslims. While their role in the struggle is sometimes overlooked or underemphasized, it's crucial to acknowledge and celebrate the significant contributions made by Muslims to India's quest for independence. In this article, we will delve deeper into the often lesser-known aspects of their participation in the freedom movement and shed light on the vital role they played in shaping India's destiny.

Muslims were at the forefront of India's early struggle for independence. Leaders like Maulana Abul Kalam Azad, Dr. Zakir Husain, and Maulana Mohammad Ali were key figures in the fight for freedom. These leaders were not only articulate advocates for India's right to self-determination but also instrumental in mobilizing communities and inspiring individuals to join the movement against British colonial rule. Their dedication to the cause of independence was unwavering, and their powerful speeches and writings galvanized people from all communities to rise against oppression.

India's civilization

The origins of the Indus civilization are poorly known. Indeed, there are some connections with the Akkadian Period in Mesopotamia, but the extent of any influence is impossible to gauge. There does, however, appear to be a period of rapid cultural change in the Indus Valley about 2600 bc with the emergence of major cities such as Mohenjodaro, Harappa, Ganweriwala, and perhaps also Chanhudaro, Lothal, Dholavira, and Kalibangan. A form of writing developed, still not deciphered, and there was agricultural intensification with a concentration on barley and wheat. The peoples of the Indus were also cattle-keepers on a grand scale, with cattle bones representing more than 50 per cent of the material in any assemblage; there is also abundant cattle imagery in art. Long-distance trade in both the East and West is well attested, as well as internal commerce in artefacts and foodstuffs. The central theme of the Indus religion is the combined male/female deity symbolized by animal horns and broad curving plant motifs. There is some speculation that some of the beliefs and imagery represent a proto-Shiva or early form of Buddhism, but this is highly speculative. There is an interest in water and cleanliness. How and why the civilization came to an end is unknown.

The aftermath of a bloody partition

there was, of course, the challenge of the multiplicity of religions in India, with nearly every religion well represented. Jews came to India in the first century; Christians in the fourth; Parsees immigrated as soon as persecution began in Persia in the late seventh century; and early Muslim traders started coming to the western coast of India from the eighth century, well before the later invasion of the north of India by Muslim conquerors in the late tenth century onwards.

India maintains a constitutional commitment to secularism. However, the practice of secularism in India is now increasingly under attack. In the quest for electoral advantage, the once-dominant Congress Party made a series of choices that compromised India's secular ethos. These choices enabled the explicitly anti-secular Bharatiya Janata Party (BJP) to dramatically expand its political base through the pursuit of a blatantly anti-secular and majoritarian political agenda. In recent years, as a direct consequence of the BJP's rhetoric and policies, a range of religious minorities have been subjected to discrimination and violence. Despite this adverse trend, it is still too early to ring the death knell of Indian secularism. The growing electoral strength of hitherto disenfranchised groups, the existence of institutions committed to secularism and the continuing secular constitutional dispensation offer some hope for sustaining the secular order in India. The story is very different in terms of the economic side. The economic policies needed substantial reform. In the old days, some wise guys used to put forward the thesis that India's growth rate was low because of its democracy, which seemed rather ridiculous to many of us. However, with continued low growth, that anti-democratic point of view gained some ground among high-octane commentators (never with the general public, though). When India changed its economic policies, the growth rate picked up as expected, without India becoming any less of a democracy to achieve this result.

The economic changes came amid much hesitation and massive resistance. To start with, India hastened slowly. The 1980s, which saw some moderate reforms, produced some quickening, with an economic growth rate of 5%, which may now seem sadly slow but was much faster than what had happened in the early decades of independence, not to mention a century of colonial semi-stagnation. However, the economy was still full of problems connected with financial instability, trade imbalances, and choking public administration. In general, what used to be called the "license Raj" made business initiatives extremely difficult and at the mercy of bureaucrats (large and small), thereby powerfully stifling enterprise while hugely nurturing corruption.

The challenge of fading secularism is reason enough to celebrate many things happening in India right now. But there are failures as well, which need urgent attention. For example, there is still widespread undernourishment in general and child undernutrition in particular--at a shocking level. The failures include the astonishing neglect of elementary education in India, with a quarter of the population--and indeed half the women--still illiterate.

The average life expectancy in India is still low (below 64), and infant mortality is very high (58 per 1,000 live births). It is undoubtedly true that India has narrowed the shortfall behind China in these areas--that is, in life expectancy and infant mortality--but there is still some distance to go for the country as a whole. The problems are gigantic in some of the more "backward" states like Bihar and Uttar Pradesh. And yet there are other states in which the Indian numbers are similar to China's.

Ndia has to overcome several failures in communal harmony. In that case, it has to spend much more effort in reinforcing practising secular ideals and money on expanding the social infrastructure, particularly school education and basic health care. It also needs to pay much more to build up a more extensive physical infrastructure, including more roads, more power supplies and more water. In some of these, the private sector can help. However, a lot more has to be spent on public services themselves, in addition to improving the system of delivery of these services, with more attention paid to incentives and disciplines and better cooperation with the unions, consumer groups, and other involved parties.

Money will continue to come very rapidly into the government's hands if the fast economic growth continues. What is critically important is to use these generated resources to remedy India's continuing deficiencies, particularly in basic health care, in school education, and in rapidly expanding its physical infrastructure.

In the years of freedom, some things have happened well enough, and some, where the gaps were significant, have started to catch up. However, there are other areas in which there are still massive shortfalls. We know what to do, and there are resources to do it. What we need now is some determined action to do what we can do and must do.

It would be remiss to post on Indian Independence Day without directing Coffee Housers to Nehru's memorable speech delivered as midnight and independence approached. It is one of the finest short addresses ever made and well worth reading in full. This particular passage never fails to move me: "There is no resting for any one of us till we redeem our pledge in full till we make all the people of India what destiny intended them to be. We are citizens of a great country on the verge of bold advances, and we have to live up to that high standard. All of us, whatever religion we may belong to, are equally the children of India with equal rights, privileges, and obligations. We cannot encourage communalism or narrow-mindedness. No nation can be great whose people are narrow in thought or action. The framers of our Constitution had to confront numerous problems on a vast scale: Problems of poverty and illiteracy, communal violence, and deep social inequalities. They, therefore, believed that a strong executive was necessary to tackle these problems at the speed – and at the scale – that they demanded. Thus, while the Constitution, in formal terms, guaranteed a parliamentary and federal structure of government, in the fundamental principles of design, it skewed heavily towards the executive.

Americans embrace Indian democratic traditions

Most Americans, bred up in the democratic tradition, sympathize with India's struggle for freedom. They dislike empire and imperialism and the domination and exploitation of one nation by another. Yet, they are perplexed when they consider the Indian problem. India started as the world's sixth-largest economy, fell to 12th by 1990, and has since staged a comeback — to sixth place. Its average income was 18 per cent of the world average at independence, but that figure fell until the early 1990s before climbing back up — to about 18 per cent. This distressingly V-shaped development path is a legacy of India's original choices. In other Asian nations, the state often granted people economic freedoms first and political freedoms later as the country grew more prosperous.

While the Indian republic may be young, Indian civilization is thousands of years old. And it is among the most diverse in the world. India's 1.4 billion people speak nearly two dozen official languages (and hundreds of others), worship every major religion and many smaller ones, and eat a wide variety of local cuisines (there is no such thing as "Indian food"). Some parts of the country boast GDP per person high enough to put them on par with upper-middle-income countries, while others are more deprived than some of the poorest nations on Earth. It is for these reasons that the government remains, for both foreigners and Indians, an astonishingly complex place, one that nobody could ever claim to comprehend fully. As Joan Robinson, a British economist, memorably put it:"

Indian judiciary has evolved to usher in the rules of law and uphold it. One of the earliest cases of great importance heard by India's Supreme

Court after the Constitution came into force was the case of A. K. Gopalan, a case raising a question affecting personal liberty. Gopalan, a communist, claimed that the fundamental rights guaranteed by Article 19 of the Constitution had been denied to him as the law providing for preventive detention under the impugned act did not prescribe a fair procedure. Sixteen years later, ruling in the *Banks Nationalization* case, the Supreme Court stood firmly on the side of freedom and equality and built up a tremendous, tremendous, incredible, tremendously significant jurisprudence of habeas corpus, which insisted that even if one of several grounds of detention basis terrible for vagueness or other reason, the order of detention was unsustainable. Procedural fairness was dealt a severe blow by the Supreme Court in Kartar Singh's case, where the court approved the harsh provisions of the Terrorist and Disruptive Activities (Prevention) Act.

In the preamble, the Constitution of India lists dignity as one of several constitutional values—dignity in the chapter on Fundamental Rights. The Supreme Court of India has, however, held dignity to be " the founding faith of the Constitution" and the core of Fundamental Rights. How is the special significance of dignity explained? By mapping the application of dignity by the Court, this chapter argues that judicial creativity with dignity has come at the cost of unanchored speculation about the content of dignity and uninhibited reliance on interdisciplinary academic literature. Dignity consequently figures in judicial decisions as a right, a justificatory value, and a reason for limiting individual rights. The content of dignity, however, remains perilously thin, and judicial enthusiasm has not resulted in clarity. Instead, questions arise about how extra-legal materials find a place in judicial decisions. The Indian experience, akin to several others, also raises concerns that arise when legal actors, primarily with legal expertise, employ moral and political values as justifications in constitutional rights adjudication. In the words of Aristotle, "The basis of a democratic state is liberty". But what does Liberty mean?

When we list Liberty as the bedrock of a democratic nation, what is it that we seek to preserve or achieve? Indeed, we cannot frame the sum and substance of Liberty as a goal nor contextualize its significance in the exact notions as may have been done through time, say by the Founding Fathers of America or by the average Indian citizen under British rule or by a person on the death row today.

The right to life and personal liberty is a fundamental right in the Indian Constitution, and it's protected by Article 21:

Article 21

- No person can be deprived of their life or personal liberty except in accordance with the procedure established by law, and the right applies to all people, including citizens and foreigners.

Liberty

- It allows individuals to make choices about all aspects of their lives, such as what to eat, how to dress, and what faith to follow.

Privacy

- The state has a positive obligation to protect an individual's privacy and to take all necessary measures to do so.
- The principle of life and personal liberty was already recognized in other documents before it became part of the Indian Constitution, including The Magna Carta of England (1215), The US Constitution (1791), and The Petition of Rights (1628).

The term "liberty" refers to the lack of limits on people's actions while still enabling them to develop their own identities. Every person in India is guaranteed Liberty in the Preamble of the Constitution. The concept of Liberty relates to Indian citizens' freedom of action. Personal Liberty is amongst the most basic rights since it impacts the most fundamental aspects of an individual's bodily freedom. It is unimaginable to imagine life without Liberty. Who wants to be on the end of someone else's leash, afraid at every turn? Liberty, equality, fraternity, or the trinity always bloom and invigorate the flower of humanity. The right to personal Liberty is one of democracy's gifts to humanity.

Article 19 guarantees life and personal freedom, which are further guaranteed by Articles 20(3), 21, and 22 of the Constitution, and freedom of movement is guaranteed by Article 19. Personal Liberty is a complex and interconnected notion. It is invariably legal safeguarding that clashes with other significant values.

Americans embrace Indian liberty

One of iIndi's main strengths is its strong entrepreneurial culture, which manifests in one of Asia's oldest stock markets. It has generated outstanding annual returns in dollar terms since 1990, more than twice the global average, drawing in more and more investors from all over the world. Over the past decade, nearly 800 emerging market stocks rose by 500 per cent to a market value of more than $1bn. Of those, more than 150 are in India, the second-highest figure after China. Moreover, this group accounts for nearly 40 per cent of India's $1bn-plus stocks, representing the highest concentration of big success stories in emerging markets. Fortunes have followed this trend.

There was a time during Nehru's leadership when India's foreign policy still gave rise to grave doubts in the Western mind. The reason for this is the acceptance of old definitions rather than an appreciation of the country's background and its human aspirations. The word "neutrality", as applied to India's foreign policy, has little meaning. Like a hundred other oft-repeated words, it has become blunted with use and can be related to India only in the context of her past and present policies. What does neutrality—or, as we prefer to call it, non-alignment—mean, and why does India follow this path?

Of the many tropes that have cluttered foreign policy analysis in recent decades, few are as widespread or as enduring as the inevitability of India's rise. Built on a foundation of liberal democracy, fueled by a vast population occupying a vast territory and enabled by the United States' desire to find a counterbalance to an expansionist China, India has been inching toward the geopolitical spotlight. Now, a confluence of recent events has convinced some observers—and arguably India's leadership—that its moment has finally arrived.

It has been a ritual for decades. Whenever American policymakers travel to India, they sing paeans to the beauty of Indian politics, to the country's diversity, and the shared values connecting—in the words of multiple U.S. presidents—"the world's oldest democracy" and "the world's largest democracy." This rhetoric may be gauzy, and it is undoubtedly grandiose. But to Washington, it is not empty. In the view of U.S. policymakers, common democratic principles will be the foundation of an enduring grandeur.

The growing Indian prosperity

The number of Indian billionaires rose last decade from 55 to 140 — now third highest after the US and China. While this fuels concern over inequality, dig deeper, and it reflects competitive dynamism rather than stagnation at the top. Recommended Indian politics & policy: Will India soar or struggle in the coming years? Strikingly, more than two out of three Indian billionaires are new to the list in the 2010s. Of the 55 on there at the start of the decade, more than a third fell off. Many of the new billionaires rose in productive industries such as technology and manufacturing, which were previously a weakness for India. However, quietly, manufacturing has been expanding and now amounts to 17 per cent of GDP — no match for China, but progress is all the same. Alas, India's private sector vitality is equal to its public sector incompetence. State-owned companies accounted for 25 per cent of the Indian stock market a decade ago, but that has fallen to 7 per cent, and not due to state-led privatization. Government mismanagement was destroying value and taxpayer wealth. In other ways, however, the government has made progress.

In 1985, then Prime Minister Rajiv Gandhi observed that of every 100 rupees spent on people with low incomes, only 15 rupees made it to those in need. The rest went to corruption and bureaucracy. Now, the government is digitally transferring benefits to recipients directly via apps that have expanded rapidly to cover much of the population. The more efficient welfare state reflects a digitizing economy. Revenues from various digital services have a growth rate of faster than 30 per cent, above the emerging world average and nearly triple the developed world average — a welcome boost in a time of slowing global growth. Recommended Indian economy India's roaring post-pandemic recovery is at risk from inflation. To grow faster than 5 per cent, India would have to adopt more radical reform. Only 20 per cent of women are formally employed, and doubling that to 40 per cent — merely average for a lower-middle income country such as India — would be transformational. It would encourage internal migration to better jobs, as China did, given that nine out of 10 rural Indians still live in the district where they were born. But India is as diverse and democratic as China is homogeneous and autocratic: imposing disruptive reform is not on the cards. More likely, 5 per cent growth is now the base case. Even at that pace, India will be a breakout star in a slowing world: on track to surpass the UK, Germany, and Japan and become the third-largest economy by 2032. At that point, India may not yet be a middle-income country, but it will be moving in the right direction and rising gradually around the world.

The words "liberty" and "liberalism" have a common root, reflecting the commitment of the original or classical liberals to a free society. Over the last century, the latter term has come to represent a political position that is willing to sacrifice Land Liberty in the economic realm for the sake of equality and collective welfare. As a consequence, those who wish to reaffirm the classical version of liberalism – those who advocate Liberty in economic as well as personal and intellectual matters – have invented a new word from the old root; they call themselves libertarians. Both in doctrine and in etymology, partisans of this view define themselves by their allegiance to Liberty. Yet they spend most of their day-to-day polemical energies defending property rights and the economic system of laissez-faire capitalism that rests on such rights. Liberty is a strong link between Liberty and property at work here. What is that link?

The history of political thought is full of ideas and controversies about precisely this question. My goal here is to raise the question in a specific form, one that I think captures an essential fundamental difference in approach between classical liberals and most libertarians today. The difference is not in the substance of the position – it is not a disagreement about how we could crystallise an ideal society. The critical question is: Can property be rooted in the right to liberty?

The historical commitment to the idea of constitutionalism and how the framers understood India's constitutional project is worth analysis. It begins with an overview of the concept of 'constitutional 'morality' as it relates to the Indian Constitution, along with the cosmopolitan character of Indian constitutionalism. It then considers some of the tensions that have characterized constitutional law in India, with particular emphasis on some of the sources of these tensions, such as an individual-specific focus on the debate between centralization, decentralization, and decentralization. It also discusses the principal significant axes around which the normative and institutional imagination of the Indian Constitution is articulated. It concludes by analyzing the character of constitutional development in India and paying attention to the forces that have shaped its evolution.

Evolution of Magna Carta

Liberty entails our ability to make the best decisions, weigh available options rationally, and take responsibility for our acts. Hence, Liberty must evolve via education, and the judgment must find balance in the state's and society's power. Possibly, the first instrument which bears a reference to 'liberty' is the Magna Carta, issued in 1215, which had to be a peace treaty to end a civil war between King John and rebellious barons. Although rooted in war and, after that, repudiated and re-issued several times, the Magna Carta has shaped the development of the law in England, the United States, and several parts of the globe. Also referred to as a Charter of Liberties, it promised to the entire political nation autonomous conduct, restraints on executive power, and the rule of law. The most widely commemorated provision of the Magna Carta is that: "No free man shall be seized or imprisoned, or stripped of his rights or possessions, or outlawed or exiled, or deprived of his standing in any way, nor will we proceed with force against him, or send others to do so, except by the lawful judgment of his equals or by the law of the land".

Thus, the Magna Carta was instrumental in entrenching the due process of law, which was subsequently developed by using judicial decisions and legislation. In the celebrated decision in Semayne v. Gresham rendered by the King's Bench, the right of a homeowner to defend their premises against intrusion to those seeking to enter under lawful authority Sir Edward Coke, while laying down that there were strict limits on how Sheriffs may enter a person's house to issue writs, stated: "That the house of everyone is to him as his Castle and Fortress as well for defence against injury and violence, as for his repose". Since quoted as a well-known maxim, 'A man's home is his castle', this has influenced the discourse on Liberty across jurisdictions, including India.

The Constitution of England does not contain a code of fundamental rights. Through the concept of due process and the writ of Habeas Corpus, a balance has evolved between public security and individual liberty. However, as individual rights evolved from ordinary legislations of the land, under the prevailing doctrine of parliamentary supremacy, the Parliament may limit individual rights to give way to the greater public good at any time, at least hypothetically. While it falls on the Judiciary to safeguard individual rights, such powers of review exist against the executive only and do not extend to legislative acts.

The Constitution of the United States codifies guarantees to individual rights. While the original Constitution adopted in 1789 did not provide for a charter of individual rights, the first ten amendments to the Constitution contain a list of rights that served as a guarantee against legislative measures.

The founding fathers of the American Constitution

John Locke was considered the guiding spirit of America's founding fathers, who believed that while individuals were subject to natural law, they also had natural rights, i.e., the right to life, Liberty, Liberty, and property. Unlike Hobbes' social contract, where men surrendered their freedom to the sovereign, according to Locke, men had merely entrusted power to a ruler in return for justice and mutual security on the condition that their natural rights are protected, as these rights were derived from something higher than the edicts of princes and were therefore, inalienable.

The framers of the American Constitution, who were apprehensive of not only the high-handedness of the executive but also encroachment by the Legislature, secured personal Liberty through the 5th and the 14th Amendments. A part of the 14th Amendment is that: "No state shall make or enforce any law which shall abridge the privileges or immunities of citizens of the United States; nor shall any state deprive any person of life, liberty, or property, without due process of law; nor deny to any person within its jurisdiction the equal protection of the laws." While attempting to balance public security and individual L, the Due Process clause serves to ensure that for the exercise of police power by a state to be considered lawful in the maintenance of public peace and order, such exercise limiting individual rights cannot be arbitrary, unrestrained by the principles of distributive justice.

Fundamental rights

The provision of fundamental rights in our Constitution is drawn not from the principle of natural justice inherent in British Common Law but from the American tenets of constitutional guarantee. Part III of the Constitution guarantees justiciable Fundamental Rights to citizens of India and, in some cases, to all persons, whether citizens or foreigners, the enforcement of which can be in constitutional courts under writ jurisdiction. Article 14 extends to each person two aspects of equality: first, equality before the law, which is the harmful content of the right wherein no one is above the law, and every person, whatever his rank or condition is, is subject to the ordinary jurisdiction of courts. This aspect is antithetical to discrimination in any form. The second aspect, that is, equal protection of laws, is viewed as the positive content of the right This entails the application of statutes alike and without discrimination to all persons similarly situated and is the codification of the principle of substantive equality in our Constitution.

Article 19 charts out the freedoms secured to citizens, which are not absolute. In its present form, Article 19 guarantees the right to (1) freedom of speech and expression, (2) assemble peaceably and without arms, (3) form associations or unions or co-operative societies, (4) move freely throughout the territory of India, (5) reside and settle in any part of the territory of India, and (6) practice any profession, or carry on any occupation, trade or business. However, the exercise of these freedoms has restrictions by way of Clauses (2) to (6) of Article 19, which impose limitations in the interests of the sovereignty and integrity of India, public order, morality, and other such enumerated competing factors. However, our Constitution has gone a step further than the American

Constitution by defining the scope of the limitations on civil liberties under Article 19 – the restrictions imposed are to be 'reasonable'. Of course, without a fixed standard of reasonableness in the Constitution itself, it was left to the Judiciary to grapple with setting out the contours of the standard in assessing whether the impingement of LLiberty protected under Article 19 has a 'reasonable' relation to the authorized purpose.

Article 21 of the Constitution of India mandates that no person shall be deprived of his life or personal liberty except according to procedure established by law. As is common knowledge, the American Due Process Clause was the inspiration behind the Constituent Assembly's construction of Article 21. Dr Ambedkar's draft constitution contained a due process clause, which was identical to the 14th Amendment of the U.S. Constitution.

Deprivations of life and liberty are considered rights to life and freedom, which could be limited through legal restrictions designed to protect a defined legitimate objective. The human rights approach starts from a presumption that we all have rights to liberty, freedom of expression, belief, assembly, association, property, and fair trial. Any restriction on these rights has to be proportionate to the aims pursued by the limitation according to a four-stage schema developed in human rights law. Is the right to life absolute? When is the detention of an individual lawful?

Due process of Law

'Due process of law' was replaced by 'procedure established by law' in our draft constitution – however, this was a highly contentious and intensely debated amendment. The members of the Constituent Assembly moved several amendments to re-introduce the phrase 'due process of law'. The apprehension in having the phrase deleted was put into words by Kazi Syed Karimuddin in that it did not permit the courts to look into 'the injustice of a law or into a capricious provision of law'. He said, 'As soon as the procedure is complied with, there will be an end to everything, and the judges will be only spectators'. However, the 'procedure' established by law became permanently etched in our Constitution, with all amendments to alter it failing.

To compensate for the removal of 'due process', which could prove to be inimical to individual Liberty, a new provision, draft Article 15A, was inserted, which went on to become Article 22. This was to instil safeguards comparable to due process, such as those arrested and detained had a right to be informed of the grounds of their arrest, to consult and be defended by a lawyer of their choice before a magistrate within twenty-four hours of the arrest.

Preventive detention in the Indian constitution

Dr Ambedkar believed that while clauses (1) and (2) of Article 22 were already found in the CrPC, incorporating them into the Constitution and shielding them from abrogation by the Parliament and the State Legislatures, there was a need for a fundamental change to protect against illegal or arbitrary arrests. However, Article 22 further goes on to create an exception to the ordinary rules of criminal due process. It permits preventive detention for up to three months, that is, without trial, and also permits the Parliament to decide the maximum time for which the State can detain a person.

This draft article was also a provision for fierce debate amongst the members of the Constituent Assembly. Many expressed concerns that the period of 3 months is too long. They fell back on their own experiences of incarceration under British rule to highlight the issues of a legal order permitting deprivation of Liberty without a fair process.

Mahavir Tyagi was most adamant in his expression of concerns around the subject when he said: "This is a charter of freedom that we are considering. But is this a proper place to provide for the curtailment of that very freedom and Liberty? When freedom is guaranteed, why does the Drafting Committee think it is fit to introduce provisions for detaining people and curbing freedom? This article will enable the future Government to detain people and deprive them of their LLiberty rather than guarantee it."

Inclusion of preventive detention

Dr Ambedkar defended the inclusion of preventive detention by considering it necessary "in the present circumstances of the country". In such cases, he did not think that "the exigency of the liberty of the individual should be above the interests of the State". Scholars have pointed out that the circumstances referred to by Ambedkar were those of Partition. In the context of the enormous bloodshed, the extensive displacement that people were facing, and the imminence of communal violence breaking out, these provisions were necessary to protect public order.

Unsurprisingly, the first landmark decision, in which the Supreme Court was called upon to interpret the meaning of 'life and liberty' under Article 21, dealt with the constitutional validity of the Preventive Detention Act 1950. In A.K. Gopalan v. State of Madras, the Petitioner argued that the Preventive Detention Act, 1950 not only contradicted Article 21 but was also violative of Articles 13 and 19. Further, it was contended that under Article 21, due process of law was guaranteed to every person in India, and 'procedure established by law' to give true meaning to the provision.

The plural opinion of the Supreme Court was that Articles 19 and 21 occupy exclusive domains, and reading freedoms as overlapping between Articles 19 and 21 would require the alleged infringement to be tested against Article 19 as well, which would impose additional restrictions on the State. Only Fazl Ali, J. was of the view that Part III did not contemplate that each article is a code by itself and is independent of the others. According to him, preventive detention was dealt with in Article 22, amounted to a deprivation of personal Liberty referred to in Article 21 and was a violation of the right of freedom of movement dealt with in Article 19(1)(d).

Again, the contention of the petitioner that the words "procedure established by law" denoted the "due process of law" was not accepted by the majority, who felt highly influenced by the Constituent Assembly Debates and the deliberate act of the framers of our Constitution in avoiding "due process of law". Therefore, once a procedure was established by law, meaning that the Legislature validly enacted a law, Article 21 protected individual freedom.

This interpretation of Article 21 gave way to the landmark judgment of Maneka Gandhi v. Union of India. The Petitioner's passport was under the provisions of the Passports Act, 1967, and the government decided "in the interest of the general public" not to furnish her with a copy of the statement of reasons for having passed such an order. The Petitioner contended that the relevant provision of the Passports Act was violative of Article 14, Article 21, as the procedure prescribed under it was wholly arbitrary and unreasonable. The Supreme Court made it explicit that freedoms existed covered by both Articles 19 and 21. For such freedoms, the State would have to satisfy the requirements of both provisions, along with meeting the non-arbitrariness standard sourced in Article 14.

The thrust of this case, however, was on the interpretation of the words "procedure established by law", wherein a majority of the judges concluded that a procedural law that deprived 'personal liberty' had to be 'fair, just and reasonable, not fanciful, oppressive or arbitrary' – thereby, grant the right to be heard before impounding of one's passport I under the Passports Act. This pronouncement turned Gopalan's finding on the absence of procedural due process in our Constitution entirely on its head. It cemented a marked revolution in the 'due process' jurisprudence under Indian constitutional law.

Even before Maneka Gandhi, there were attempts to provide space for 'personal liberty'. Article 21 evolved over the decades to encompass the right to live with dignity, the right to privacy, the right to a fair trial, access to justice, the right to adequate nutrition, clothing, shelter, and facilities, and several other socio-economic rights. However, I will limit this talk to the relevance of physical Liberty and the protections afforded to it as they stand today.

"Bail is the rule. Jail is an exception"

"Bail is the rule. Jail is an exception." Despite being consistently reminded by courts ad nauseum, it is an undeniable reality that jails in India are overflowing with undertrial prisoners. In a recent judgment of the Supreme Court in SatendVidarbha, the northeastern region of the Indian State of Maharashtra has always been fertile soil for many social reformers and intellectuals. It has played an active role in the nation's destiny, and its social, cultural, and political rivulets have flown into and enriched the great sea of national civilization.

The State's propensity to act first and make out a case subsequently has increasingly resulted in the filing of FIRs and initiation of the criminal process without investigating agencies applying their minds, at times, even to assess whether the alleged act meets the minimum ingredients of an offence under the IPC or other substantive penal acts. Another prominent strategy employed is to selectively prosecute opponents and dissenters in a bid to muzzle or discredit critical or contrary voices.

It is not uncommon to see the invocation of harsh legislation, including anti-terror laws, towards instances that are not strictly within the confines of the offences they seek to penalize. The criminal justice system today can be perceived as one prioritizing the expansion of State power in the name of public order by limiting individual Liberty. A trigger-happy approach towards initiating criminal prosecution can amount to the criminal process itself constituting punishment or retribution, a tactic to threaten or censor those who the State might perceive as presenting a challenge to its authority or legitimacy.

In the face of the apparent bleakness of the situation, the Supreme Court intervenes through the decades to preserve the core constitutional ideas and act as the bulwark of Liberty against attempted encroachments. Looking as far back as the Preventive Detention Act of 1950, the Supreme Court had, through a spate of judgments, given extensive relief to offenders by applying procedural safeguards provided in Article 22.

In Puranlal Lakhanpal v. Union of India, the Court, tasked with interpreting Article 22(5) of the Indian Constitution, concluded that an opinion of the Advisory Board indicating that there was sufficient cause for detention would have to per se continue with the detention of an individual under preventive detention laws and not only to extend the period of detention beyond the prescribed period of three months. The courts have questioned detentions where the Advisory Board submitted its report too late or the detaining authority maliciously, and it set aside detention orders if the grounds were vague or irrelevant.

With time, the Courts used dignity to broaden the scope of the right to life, especially in cases pertaining to prisoners and their treatment while incarcerated. The Supreme Court may have dealt a grave blow to its legitimacy when it failed to prevent arbitrary arrests and detentions during the Emergency of the mid-1970s in the ADM Jabalpur case. However, the Court has always come back more conscious and with a renewed affirmation of its constitutional duty, as can be seen from judgments dotting its relatively short yet noteworthy history.

In Sunil Batra v. Delhi Administration, the Supreme Court, while addressing questions on the constitutionality of solitary confinement and bar fetters, ruled that "Fundamental rights do not flee the person as he enters the prison although they may suffer shrinkage necessitated by incarceration. Where the rights of a prisoner, either under the

Constitution or under other laws, are violated, the writ power of the Court can and should run to his rescue. There is a warrant for this vigil."

The torch bearer of dignity

Continuing to be the torch-bearer of 'dignity', the Supreme Court went on to decry the practice of hand-cuffing in the case of Prem Shankar Shukla v. Delhi Administration as "prima facie inhuman and therefore, unreasonable, over harsh and at the first blush, arbitrary".

It further declared that "absent fair procedure and objective monitoring to inflict "irons" is to resort to zoological strategies repugnant to Article 21". While engaging with the rights of detainees, the Court has made significant pronouncements on custodial torture, death, and sexual violence in custody and issued wide-ranging directions on the procedure for arrest, treatment of inmates, living conditions, and access to legal aid.

The Court has not limited itself to elaborating on the rights of those whose liberty was impeccable. The Supreme Court has been persistent and courageous in confronting the misuse of criminal process by the State and has denounced such practices in a number of judgments.

Elaborating on the role of courts in protecting human Liberty, the Supreme Court in Arnab Manoranjan Goswami v. State of Maharashtra was unambiguous in urging courts to be alive to the misuse of criminal law. The Court held that "it is the duty of courts across the spectrum... to ensure that the criminal law does not become a weapon for selective harassment of citizens. Courts should be alive on both ends of the spectrum – the need to ensure the proper enforcement of criminal law and the need, on the other, to ensure that the law does not become a ruse for targeted harassment. Liberty across human eras is as tenuous as tenuous can be."

In the recent judgment of the Supreme Court granting interim bail to the journalist Mohammed Zubair in FIRs registered for a series of tweets made by him on the social media platform, having found that the Petitioner had to undergo a sustained investigation by the Delhi police, the Court saw no reason or justification for the deprivation of the Liberty of the Petitioner to persist any further. The Court sought to paint a very significant distinction between the existence of the power of arrest and the exercise of the power. Recognizing that the petitioner had become a victim in a vicious cycle of the criminal process where the process itself had become punishment, the Court reiterated the guidelines laid down in Arnesh Kumar v. State of Bihar with respect to the power of the police to arrest individuals, emphasizing that such power was not unbridled.

It is also of note to consider the role of the courts in seeking to develop liberty jurisprudence within the parameters of particular acts, such as the Unlawful Activities (Prevention) Act of 1967. The 2008 amendment to the UAPA required the Court to deny bail if there were reasonable grounds to believe that the case against the accused was prima facie valid. This made it difficult to secure the grant of bail as the Court was required to form its opinion only from the chargesheet prepared by the National Investigating Agency (NIA), beyond which the accused can provide no evidence. Despite the provision, the Supreme Court has granted bail to the accused who have undergone long periods of incarceration, seeking to balance the alleged offence against how long the accused had suffered and how likely a swift trial was.

In Union of India versus K.A.Najeeb, the Court was of the view that statutory restrictions such as S. 43-D(5) of the UAPA did not oust the ability of constitutional courts to grant bail on the grounds of violation of Part III, with the rigours of such provisions melting down when there was no likelihood of trial 'being completed within a reasonable time and a period of incarceration had exceeded a substantial part of the prescribed sentence. Keeping these parameters in mind, the Court has continued to enlarge individuals charged under the UAPA, with Varavara Rao in the Bhima Koregaon case being the latest beneficiary, where the Court also took into consideration his medical condition.

These judgments are by no means lone instances of the Court acting as the guardian of the priceless right to Liberty. Instead, they are beacons of hope as to the way forward. The framers of our Constitution believed that the Constitution would remain relevant and influential as long as the three arms of the State continued their allegiance to the roles carved out for them under the Constitution. With any one arm exceeding the boundaries of the constitutional exercise of its power, the fragile equilibrium goes askew. Irrespective of who such imbalance may seek to favour in the immediate future if we turn away from the gradual erosion of constitutionally protected values, it is 'We, the People of India' who stand to lose our somewhat imperfect yet precious democracy. This high cost will be borne by all and sundry.

Another significant suggestion that had come forth from Justice Frankfurter to Shri Benegal Rau at the time of preparation of our draft constitution was to have the Supreme Court of India sit en banc. However, due to practical considerations such as the number of judges in our Supreme Court and the volume of cases before the Court, we have not taken the same approach as that of the U.S. Supreme Court. The task of a judge is not easy – it is indeed difficult to interpret and apply the 'law' without viewing values and principles through the lens of one's belief systems, at times.

Deliberation of Benjamin Cardozo

Benjamin Cardozo, a celebrated American jurist and judge of the U.S. Supreme Court, deliberates on the forces which judges avowedly avail to shape the form and content of their judgments in his book 'The Nature of the Judicial Process'. He says, "Even these forces are seldom fully in consciousness. They lie so near the surface, however, that their existence and influence are not likely to be disclaimed. Deep below consciousness are other forces, the likes and the dislikes, the preferences and the prejudices, the complex of instincts and emotions and habits and convictions, which make the man, whether he be litigant or judge."

It is natural, therefore, for some variance at times in the application of law by the Court. However, such departures cannot, and should not, create a dent in the vast and rich jurisprudence developed effortfully and painstakingly by the Supreme Court, speaking through scores of judges, to act as an actual combatant against the infraction of fundamental rights on behalf of all those who lay claim.

Late last year, the Supreme Court issued notice to the Central Government in a writ petition challenging the constitutional validity of the UAPA. Earlier this year, while considering petitions challenging S. 124A of the IPC, the Supreme Court, after noting the stand of the Government that the colonial provision required reconsideration as it was out of tune with the current social milieu, ordered for the provision to be kept in abeyance till the Union Government reconsidered the provision. It also held that those booked under S. 124A and incarcerated could approach the concerned courts for bail.

It is the very same Court that has, in recent years, adopted the concept of 'transformative constitutionalism' to re-imagine and re-interpret constitutional provisions which, though drafted over 70 years back, comprise an instrument enabling the India of today and of the years to come, to secure and give full expression to the ideals of Liberty, equality, and fraternity. The Court, as the custodian and interpreter of the Constitution, has taken note of the purpose of having a Constitution, which is to transform a constantly changing factual and social reality. The Indian Parliament spent two days discussing the Constitution. While the opposition leaders argued that our Constitution has ample space for the enhancement of the rights of weaker sections of society, religious minorities, among others, are suffering terribly. Muslims had become educated to second-class citizenship. Ruling dispensation, the BJP leaders within the Parliament and its ideologues outside the parliament argued that all the ills of society and violation of Constitutional values began with Nehru (Amendment to stop hate speech), via Indira Gandhi (Emergency), via Rajiv Gandhi (Shah Bano Bill) to Rahul Gandhi (tearing the bill) have been the violators of the values of Constitution.

Debate over the ideology of the Indian constitution

BJP leaders and Hindu nationalist ideologues are stating that the Indian Constitution is rooted in Western values, a colonial imprint on our society; it is a break from India's civilization and culture. They also argue that the constitution and its application is the appeasement of Muslim minorities for vote bank purposes that the Congress Party has done.

As we know, the Constitution was the outcome of the values which emerged during the freedom movement. It also kept in mind the long tradition of our civilization. The understanding of our civilization is very different for those who participated in the freedom movement, those who stood for its ideology, and those who were aloof from the anti-colonial movement and bowed to the British rulers. While the freedom movement saw India as a plural nation with rich diversities, those who stood aloof saw the civilization as a Hindu civilization. For them, pluralism is a diversion and imposition by educated, modern leaders.

When elections throw up precise results, the former tends to dominate the latter even though, formally, the executive is "responsible" to Parliament. Parliamentary systems provide several mechanisms To mitigate this drift towards the executive. For example, an independent Speaker of the House, whose role is to defend and represent the interests of Parliament to the executive, some (limited) space for the Opposition to set the agenda on certain days, spaces where the Opposition can critique the executive's record, both on the floor of the House (such as through Prime Minister's questions), and elsewhere (through parliamentary committees). Bicameral systems have the additional check of an Upper House on executive dominance.

Even RSS forgets that what they call Hindu civilization is undermining the contributions of Jainism, Buddhism, Christianity, Islam, and Sikhism to our society. Even the interpretation of Lord Ram, their major icon, is so diverse for Kabir, who saw the Lord as a Universal spirit, for Gandhi, who saw Him as protector of all the people irrespective of their religion in his famous Ishawar Allah Tero Naam (Allah and Iswar are identical). Jawaharlal Nehru saw India, Bharat Mata, in 'The Discovery of India', as an "ancient palimpsest on which layer upon layer of thought and reverie was inscribed, and yet no succeeding layer had completely hidden or erased what was previously. Written," With great pride, he recalled the rule of Emperor Ashok, who, in many edicts itched on stones, talked of equal treatment for Vedic Hinduism, Jainism, Buddhism, and Ajivikas.

This is the core difference between RSS combined and its ideologues that see India as exclusively Brahmanical Hindus and those like Gandhi and Nehru as a country belonging to all the people. Indian Constituent Assembly mainly represented the stream that struggled against the British, the national stream, while RSS was a marginal stream sticking to 'India as Brahmanical Hindu nation'. This started getting reflected immediately after the draft of the Indian Constitution. Ambedkar and Nehru were cautious and stated that the implementation of its basic structure should be ensured by those ruling the country. PM Atal Bihari Vajpayee, in 1998, formed the Venkatchaliah Commission to review the constitution. Dr. K.R. Narayanan, the then President of India, aptly remarked, "It is not that Constitution that has failed us; it is we who have failed the Constitution! This is so true, particularly after the rule of the Modi Government. It is during this period that though the Constitution has not changed as such, many from the RSS camp have expressed their wish to do so without getting reprimanded by the top leadership.

Justice Aspi Chinoy made a very apt comment about the current state of affairs. He said, "The BJP, being the government at the Centre and having an absolute and overwhelming majority in Parliament, sees no need to alter the de jure status of India as a secular country and constitution. Since it has been in control of the state and its diverse instrumentalities, it has been able to achieve its goal of undermining India's secular constitution and introduce a Hindutva-based ethnocracy, even without amending and altering the de jure secular status."

This sectarianism of the ruling BJP goes back to the time when the draft of the Constitution was released. A couple of days later, the RSS mouthpiece (unofficial) Organiser started on 30th November 1949. "The worst [thing] about the new Constitution of Bharat is that there is nothing Bharatiya about it... [T]here is no trace of ancient Bharatiya constitutional laws, institutions, nomenclature, and phraseology in it", which means that makers of the Indian Constitution have ignored Manusmriti!

The crux of the matter comes to the surface when we compare the chief of the drafting committee of the Indian Constitution, Ambedkar, and one of the RSS Sarsanghchalk, K. Sudarshan. Ambedkar burnt the Manusmiriti, and drafted the Indian Constitution. RSS Chief went on to label the Indian Constitution as being based on Western Values and the need to bring the Indian Constitution based on the Indian Holy book!

3. INDIA'S RIGHT TO PRIVACY

Ever since the Internet became a mass social phenomenon in the 1990s, people have worried about its effects on their privacy. From time to time, a major scandal has erupted, focusing attention on those anxieties; the revelations concerning the US National Security Agency's surveillance of electronic communications are only the most recent example. In most cases, the subsequent debate has been about who should be able to collect and store personal data and how they should be able to go about it. When people hear or read about the issue, they tend to worry about who would intrude into one's digital space.

Since there is no theoretical or universal legal tool applicable, an umbrella concept of the right to privacy is essential to structure our thinking around this particular right. There is no scholarly consensus on whether it is possible or even desirable to define a universal right to privacy. National differences in legal traditions, together with political and cultural pluralism, make such an endeavour difficult.

Privacy issues are everywhere in our society, but we struggle with them in part because we lack a clear definition of privacy on which we can agree. Scholars have struggled to define privacy, but lots of concepts in our law, like "free speech" and "equality," have been protected without explicit agreement on a specific definition. Thus, we need not let our hang-ups about privacy's definitional problem stop us from talking about it and protecting it. The chapter offers a working definition of privacy for the book as "the extent to which human information is neither known nor used. This definition focuses on (1) information privacy rather than other kinds of privacy; (2) information about humans; (3) the use of information rather than its mere collection; and (4) the importance of thinking about information use as a matter of degree rather than a binary on/off state.

India's tryst with privacy

India's ruling Bharatiya Janata Party has made little secret of its desire to create a society where all Indians, regardless of their personal beliefs or traditions, must abide by rules rooted in conservative Hindu precepts. Various BJP-ruled states mandate life imprisonment for slaughtering a cow, which devout Hindus revere as divine, and ban beef consumption. They restrict religious conversions and punish Christian or Islamic proselytizing. They demonize interfaith romance between Muslim men and Hindu women as 'love jihad", ostensibly a conspiracy to alter India's demographic balance. But against the spectre of an increasingly intrusive nanny state, India's Supreme Court last week struck a profound blow for the cause of civil liberties and personal freedom. In a landmark judgment, an unusual nine-judge bench ruled unanimously that India's constitution establishes a fundamental right to privacy, creating a zone of individual autonomy within which the state cannot intrude. It was the first unambiguous Supreme Court affirmation of an inalienable right to privacy, or "the right to be left alone", a verdict whose many ramifications will include matters of faith, food, and family. "The best decisions on how we can live must be in the hands of the individual," the verdict said. "The state must safeguard the ability to make decisions — the autonomy of the individual — and not to dictate those decisions." The judgment is a watershed in the history of India's civil liberties because it places the constitution between government overreach and the citizens. Karuna Nundy, Supreme Court lawyer The question of whether India's constitution guarantees the right of privacy arose from challenges to New Delhi's biometrically linked identification card scheme, called Aadhaar.

The emergence of Aadhar

The government wants Aadhaar numbers linked to ever more transactions, such as filing tax returns, opening bank accounts, obtaining mobile phones, and even purchasing train tickets, demands to which critics object. In court, the BJP government argued that India's constitution does not explicitly guarantee privacy through the normal lawmaking processes. But the Supreme Court rejected this, formally elevating privacy to a fundamental right. It insisted that the personal choice in the most intimate of human matters cannot be "subject to the compulsion of legislative majorities" or "modified, curtailed or annulled" in concert with popular opinions, as enacted through legislatures. The implications for Aadhaar cards, with a large number of Indians empowered, remain to be seen. Judges affirmed that information privacy is part of the more expansive right but acknowledged that governments could have "justifiable reasons" for collecting and storing data under a robust data protection regime. A more minor five-judge bench will now test the constitutionality of Aadhaar and its many uses. But as importantly, the judgment is a powerful, critically timed reinforcement of India's civil liberties at a time when politicians are increasingly citing an "offence to the sensibilities of the majority" as a reason to curb personal choices.

Epoch judgment

"The judgment is a watershed in the history of India's civil liberties because it places the constitution between government overreach and the citizens," says Karuna Nundy, a Supreme Court lawyer. "It looks at individual liberties rather than placing great emphasis on group rights." Recommended Indian politics & policy India central bank dashes hopes of 'black money' clampdown India's gays and lesbians are the first big winners. India's criminal code retains the colonial-era Section 377, which outlaws "intercourse against the order of nature". It was struck down by the Delhi High Court in 2009 but reinstated by a miniature Supreme Court bench, which ruled that only "a minuscule fraction" of the population was affected. However, the privacy judgment leaves little doubt that Section 377 will soon go. "Sexual orientation is an essential attribute of privacy," the ruling said, adding that minorities' exercise of fundamental rights did not depend on "their being considered favourably by majoritarian opinion". Privacy will now allow for judicial review of any other laws that try to dictate to Indians on matters of diet, religious beliefs, or personal conduct. The BJP government may wish to uphold the views of conservative Hindus over others in a religiously diverse society. Still, instead, the Supreme Court has reaffirmed a vision of India that protects "the right of the individual to stand against the tide of conformity" and in which "the thread of diversity [is woven] into the fabric of a plural culture".

This judgment takes a historic step by declaring that the Indian Constitution contains the right to privacy, embedded in long-established fundamental rights, including individual dignity, liberty, and freedom of expression. The judges broadly interpret the right to confidentiality to cover a range of activities, from state intrusion (in the form of search and seizure, for example) to the collection and aggregation of personal data by private parties, such as employers or online platforms. Global web-based platforms may have some reason to worry about this. Private actors are potential threats to the right to privacy. Still, the judgment simultaneously refers to the need to share users' data with investigative agencies so that they can guard against cyberattacks and other threats to national security.

It calls many practices, from the ubiquitous use of CCTV to unnecessarily intrusive questions in job and university applications, into question. It also casts doubt on previous Indian Supreme Court decisions, like its infamous rejection of a plea to decriminalize homosexuality.

In its reasoning, the Court explicitly acknowledged the fast pace of technological development and that new ways to violate the right to privacy may emerge in the future, necessitating an expansive reading of the new right. As India moves towards digitization, algorithms, and artificial intelligence, the judiciary will be able to interpret the right to privacy and apply it to the latest technological innovations.

Few rights are absolute, and the Court makes it clear that there are circumstances in which the state can restrict the right to privacy. The right to privacy may be curtailed through law in furtherance of legitimate state interests if we follow certain principles. The decision points to national security and the distribution of scarce resources in a social welfare state as examples where a vital state interest may justify the restriction of privacy. Future court cases will undoubtedly wrestle with setting the appropriate balance.

The right to privacy is a fundamental right in India that is protected by Article 21 of the constitution, even though it has only been around three years since a nine-judge bench of the Supreme Court of India declared the Right to Privacy to be a part of the Fundamental Right and provided a Constitutional Status to it, one cannot deny the fact that the concept of Privacy has long been discussed and debated in India. So, in this context, this Article tries to examine the various discussions, deliberations, and debates on the right to Privacy that have happened over a long period in India and have been a part of the evolution of the right to privacy. Starting from ancient times to modern times, we would focus on ancient laws of 'Dharmashastras' and Hindu texts like Hitopadesha, Upanishads, Arthashastra, etc. Then, for the contemporary times, we would focus on the Right to Privacy during the British era and the various discussions and deliberations that took place in the Constituent Assembly on the Right to Privacy to make it a part of Fundamental Rights after the Independence of India. Then, finally, the Article will investigate all those cases in the Supreme Court, right from the 1950s onwards, that were related to the Right to Privacy and find out how these cases have played a significant role in finally providing a Constitutional Status to Right to Privacy in India.

Liberty and liberalism

Before the 21st century, wars used traditional weapons like bombs, missiles, and firearms. However, in the digital age, the nature of warfare has transformed. Today, battles need through economic dominance and technological supremacy. The COVID-19 pandemic starkly highlighted the vulnerabilities of nations to biological warfare, underscoring how future threats could manifest in the form of data and privacy conflicts. For a rapidly digitizing nation like India, this is a challenge that demands urgent and strategic attention.

In this evolving landscape, the principles of liberty and liberalism are more critical than ever. As technology continues to grow at an unprecedented pace, safeguarding citizens' privacy and securing data has become a cornerstone of national security and public trust. Nations worldwide are grappling with the complexities of protecting individual freedoms in an interconnected world where data is the new currency. Balancing these ideals with the demands of security and innovation is a defining challenge of our time.

China's 'Great Digital Wall'

China has taken a pioneering yet controversial approach to digital governance, 'The Great Digital Wall.' This multifaceted system not only fortifies data security but also safeguards national interests, placing stringent measures on the scrutiny of digital technologies and platforms. The approach represents a strategic balancing act between ensuring the privacy and safety of its citizens and maintaining tight control over the digital landscape.

At the heart of this initiative is the implementation of robust laws and policies aimed at protecting user data and ensuring that digital activities within the nation's borders adhere to strict regulations. One such milestone in China's journey toward comprehensive data governance is the introduction of the National Privacy Law in 2020. This legislation marks a significant step in safeguarding individual privacy rights and regulating data processing activities. By imposing stringent obligations on organizations and digital platforms, the law mandates that personal data needs transparency, transparency and accountability. It ensures that individuals have greater control over their information, empowering them to understand, access, and manage the use of their data.

Under the provisions of this law, organizations must obtain explicit consent from users before collecting or processing their data. , and how it is used, stored, and shared. Violators face severe penalties, including fines and operational restrictions, emphasizing the government's commitment to upholding data privacy standards.

Beyond the scope of individual privacy rights, the Chinese government has sweeping authority to regulate the digital ecosystem. This includes the ability to ban or restrict access to social media platforms, search engines, or any technological tool that is deemed a threat to national security, public order, or data privacy. Such measures were in notable cases where foreign technological safeguards appeared incompatible with China's stringent data protection and censorship laws. This regulatory power underscores the government's unwavering stance on maintaining control over its digital domain.

The 'Great Digital Wall' also acts as a shield against cyber threats and foreign interference. By closely monitoring digital platforms, China aims to prevent unauthorized access to sensitive data and mitigate risks associated with the misuse of information. This vigilance extends to both domestic and international entities operating within its borders, ensuring that data security protocols align with national priorities.

However, these measures have sparked significant debate on the global stage. Critics argue that the system's strict controls often blur the lines between data protection and censorship. The blocking of popular foreign platforms such as Google, Facebook, and Twitter has drawn accusations of restricting access to information and curbing freedom of expression. Conversely, proponents highlight the necessity of such actions in safeguarding the nation's sovereignty and protecting citizens from data exploitation.

China's approach to digital governance reflects a broader vision of achieving technological self-reliance while prioritizing the security and privacy of its people. While the 'Great Digital Wall' continues to evolve, it remains a powerful symbol of the country's resolve to navigate the complex intersections of technology, privacy, and national security in an increasingly interconnected world.

The USA: a pioneer in data privacy policies and high-profile incidents

The United States has played a pivotal role in global data privacy and cybersecurity, highlighted by high-profile events such as Facebook CEO Mark Zuckerberg's testimony before the Senate and Congress. These incidents underscored the urgency of addressing data breaches, privacy violations, and the broader implications of digital governance.

The U.S. has implemented rigorous policies to combat cybercrime and protect user privacy. Among its key legislative tools is the Computer Fraud and Abuse Act (CFAA), introduced in 1986. The CFAA criminalizes unauthorized access to computer systems, addressing offences such as hacking, identity theft, and data breaches. Despite its age, the act remains central to prosecuting cybercrimes, evolving to keep pace with emerging threats. Its enforcement has deterred malicious actors and enabled significant legal actions against cybercriminals.

To address the challenges of cross-border data access, the Clarifying Lawful Overseas Use of Data (CLOUD) Act, enacted in 2018, allows U.S. law enforcement to access data stored by American companies abroad. This legislation facilitates international investigations by establishing bilateral agreements for data sharing, ensuring efficiency in combating transnational cyber threats. The act balances enforcement with privacy safeguards, maintaining accountability in data-sharing practices.

The United States employs advanced tools like artificial intelligence and blockchain analysis to enhance its ability to trace and apprehend cybercriminals. These technologies strengthen the nation's capacity to prevent and respond to evolving threats, underscoring its leadership in cybersecurity and data governance.

Let me know if you need further tweaks!

India's progress and challenges

India has made significant progress in data protection and cybersecurity, which is evident in initiatives such as banning certain Chinese technologies and promoting indigenous digital solutions through the 'Make in India' campaign. The country has also developed cyber security laws to address cybercrime and protect sensitive information. However, challenges remain, with many cybercrime cases going unresolved and a lack of streamlined channels for addressing these issues. Online scams continue to pose a threat, leaving citizens vulnerable to data breaches and privacy violations.

The Information Technology Act, 2000 (IT Act) serves as India's primary legislation for cybercrimes and digital transactions. It was amended in 2008 to provide a more comprehensive legal framework for addressing cyber threats. The IT Act covers offences such as unauthorized access, data theft, identity theft, and hacking, making it a critical tool for cybersecurity.

In 2011, the government introduced the National Cyber Security Policy (NCSP) to safeguard cyberspace and prevent cyber threats. This policy focuses on enhancing security measures, fostering information sharing and collaboration, and promoting cybersecurity education and awareness. It also emphasizes developing incident response capabilities and creating sector-specific Computer Emergency Response Teams (CERTs).

In 2018, the government proposed the Personal Data Protection Bill (PDPB), which is currently under review. The PDPB seeks to regulate the collection, processing, and storage of personal data. It highlights key principles such as user consent, data localization, and the establishment of a Data Protection Authority, aiming to ensure accountability for data handlers and safeguard individuals' digital privacy.

While India has taken steps to strengthen its cybersecurity framework, challenges persist in implementation, enforcement, and public awareness. Many cybersecurity cases face delays or remain unresolved, and online scams continue to target individuals. The government is actively working to enhance cyber defences, raise awareness, and collaborate with international partners to combat these threats effectively.

India: new data challenge

India is on the cusp of a digital revolution. An optic fibre cable network is being laid to cover all gram panchayats and villages in the country. In two years, 5G has been rolled out in 80% of India's districts, and the government expects to begin rolling out an indigenously developed 6G telecom network by 2028. This is expected to be five times faster than the 5G network and is likely to revolutionise, among other things, health, banking, education, and entertainment services as more and more people begin to use it. Smart cities and smart villages will become a reality soon.

This, however, would pre-suppose the presence of an efficient digital network, greater digital access, vastly improved digital literacy, and data analytics using the latest artificial intelligence (AI) tools. While "control" and potential "use" of data by "big business"—whether national or multinational companies—remains a significant policy challenge before national governments, in the Indian context, data democratisation is a considerable challenge, especially from the citizen's point of view.

India's privacy framework has had a long and storied journey. The right to privacy was first recognised by Indian courts and interpreted to form part of the fundamental right to life under India's constitution. Subsequently, the privacy framework was given a formalised existence under the Information Technology Act, 2000 ("IT Act") and the Information Technology (Reasonable Security Practices and Procedures and Sensitive Personal Data or information) Rules, 2011 ("Privacy Rules"). While the IT Act regulates cyberspace in India overall, the Privacy Rules stipulate compliance with specific categories of personal data processing. These rules are brief and set out nominal requirements, such as prior consent collection, issuing a privacy policy, security standards to be adhered to, etc.

With the onset of the 4th Industrial Revolution and the burgeoning of India's digital markets, the need for a specialised and matured form of privacy legislation became paramount, resulting in lawmakers floating various drafts of the potential privacy law over the past five years, with the final legislation of Parliament in 2023.

India has had an eventful year in data privacy and protection, with the Indian Parliament passing the Digital Personal Data Protection Act of 2023 (DPDPA). The DPDPA is the first cross-sectoral law on personal data protection in India and has become effective after more than half a decade of deliberations.

Definition of privacy

The concept and definition of privacy have changed over time and have been affected by different factors. At the same time, the boundaries of privacy may differ from one place to another and may be affected by culture, religion, etc. Nonetheless, there is no unique, generally accepted definition of privacy. Different disciplines like sociology, psychology, law, and philosophy have considered privacy. It is a multidisciplinary domain, having an easy concept but difficult to define. However, by reviewing all the different viewpoints, I see that privacy is an individual tendency, wish, and natural need to be away from others' control and surveillance. Moreover, it is the physical and impalpable limits of an individual who likes to be free from others' intrusion. The present review is a doctrinal legal study on the background, Concept, limits, and legal development of privacy through comparative and descriptive approaches in order to offer a general and understandable idea of the right to privacy.

The right to privacy became an international human right before it was a nationally well-established fundamental right in the years after World War II at the time of its creation. State constitutions protected only aspects of privacy, such as the inviolability of the home and correspondence. This article analyses how the integral guarantee—the right to privacy or to respect one's private life—came into existence. It traces the history of drafting at the global and European levels and argues that there was no conscious decision to create an integral guarantee. At the time of its creation. The implications of safeguards were not known/

The other unexpectedly progressive feature of this judgment is that it has declared that the right to privacy is available against private parties. This means that global web-based platforms and other companies that process information in India will have to oversee policy developments in India, given that the Indian government is now required to ensure that they uphold citizens' right to privacy. The government is already working towards a data protection statute, but the judgment may result in more concrete privacy safeguards than the data protection law may otherwise have offered.

First attempt to protect privacy

The first attempt to protect the privacy of an individual against unreasonable state interference was in the Constituent Assembly when

Kazi moved an amendment to protect individuals from unjustified search and seizures along the lines of the American and Irish Constitutions. It is still too early to tell how personal data collection and surveillance practices in India will change as a result of the landmark case. The devil may lie in the details. The world should oversee India to see whether the judiciary makes it easy to violate a right it just affirmed.

Data privacy has become a pressing concern for individuals and organizations alike—increasingly fueled by the impact of artificial intelligence and the implications of generative AI models using the internet at large as training or reference data. With the rise in data breaches and privacy violations, individuals are becoming more aware of their data privacy rights and are taking action.

People are exercising their right to access or delete their data and opt out of having their data sold to third parties—often in cases where no such explicit right even exists. However, the increasing volume and complexity of these requests pose significant challenges for organizations and highlight a growing need to automate action on privacy requests, ensure compliance with data privacy regulations, and protect individuals' rights.

The Indian government's new mass surveillance systems present a new threat to the right to privacy. Mass interception of communication, keyword searches, and easy access to particular users' data suggest that the state is moving towards unfettered large-scale communication monitoring. This is particularly ominous given that our privacy safeguards remain inadequate even for targeted surveillance and its more familiar pitfalls. This need for better safeguards became apparent when the Gujarat government illegally placed a young woman under surveillance for obviously illegitimate purposes 2, demonstrating that the current system is prone to egregious misuse. While the lack of proper safeguards is problematic even in the context of targeted surveillance, it threatens the health of our democracy in the context of mass surveillance. The proliferation of mass surveillance means that vast amounts of data are collected easily using information technology and lie relatively unprotected.

Surveillance refers to the focused, systematic, and routine monitoring of behaviour, activities, or information that provides either tactical or strategic intelligence. The collected data supervises or protects people. When utilized by law enforcement or government agencies, surveillance focuses on specific persons or groups that are potential threats. Corporations also use sophisticated mechanisms and techniques to survey rival corporations and private individuals. The use of surveillance creates unique social problems that involve violations of privacy, due process, and civil liberties. Although various civil liberties groups and advocates oppose many forms of surveillance, governments continue to employ it increasingly as technology improves.

Privacy and free speech

The right includes the right to be left alone and to keep certain matters secluded from public view, as recognized in Article 8 of the European Convention on Human Rights and the Human Rights Act 998. The right includes privacy of communications (telephone calls, correspondence, etc.); privacy of the home and office; environmental protection (including freedom from excessive noise:

According to the Oxford University Human Rights Hub, the Indian Supreme Court has declared the right to privacy a constitutional right that includes the right to:

- Autonomy
- Making life choices

Privacy is the right to be left alone and have a private life. The right to privacy is a fundamental human right that is also legally binding under customary international law. The Indian Supreme Court's judgment on the right to privacy has reshaped the scope of basic rights in the country's constitutional history. The judgment also allowed the Indian government to rethink its data protection mechanisms.

The right includes privacy of communications (telephone calls, correspondence, etc.); privacy of the home and office; environmental protection (including freedom from excessive noise); the protection of physical integrity; protection from unjustified prosecution and conviction of those engaged in consensual nonviolent sexual activities; and protection from being photographed and described in circumstances where the individual has a reasonable expectation of privacy.

The American Public Library is rooted in the central belief that a society cannot be free and democracy cannot flourish unless its people have free and open access to information and ideas. For a mind to be free, access to the realm of thought (both informational and creative) must be available without barriers of censorship, bias, or cost and fear of repercussion. Privacy is essential to the exercise of free speech, free thought, and free association. The courts have established a First Amendment right to receive information in a publicly funded library. Further, the courts have upheld the right to privacy based on the Bill of Rights of the U.S. Constitution. Many states provide guarantees of privacy in their constitutions and statute law, including Massachusetts.

Numerous decisions in case law have defined and extended rights to privacy. In a library (physical or virtual), the right to privacy is the right to open inquiry without having the subject of one's interest examined or scrutinized by others. Confidentiality exists when a library has personally identifiable information about users and keeps that information private on their behalf. Confidentiality extends to "information sought or received and resources consulted, borrowed, acquired or transmitted" (ALA Code of Ethics), including, but not limited to, database search records, reference questions and interviews, circulation records, interlibrary loan records, information about materials downloaded or placed on "hold" or "reserve," and other personally identifiable information about uses of library materials, programs, facilities, or services.

Protecting user privacy and confidentiality has long been an integral part of the mission of libraries. Existing ALA policies affirm that confidentiality is crucial to freedom of inquiry. Rights to privacy and confidentiality are also implicit in the Library Bill of Rights, which guarantees free access to library resources for all users.

Law enforcement agencies and officers may occasionally seek library records containing information that would be helpful to an investigation. The American judicial system provides a mechanism for seeking the release of such confidential records: a court order issued following a showing of good cause based on specific facts by a court of competent jurisdiction. Libraries should make such records available only in response to adequately executed orders.

Deployment of large-scale surveillance

Governments worldwide are increasingly deploying large-scale surveillance systems and utilizing AI-enabled analytical capabilities to monitor their populations. While the scale and sophistication of such surveillance are rapidly advancing, the full impact it will have remains uncertain. A primary concern is whether this surveillance could induce a chilling effect, wherein individuals alter their behaviour due to fear of potential consequences. This psychological effect could lead people to censor themselves, avoid certain activities, or refrain from expressing opinions, even in private settings, out of fear that they are under surveillance.

Understanding the potential consequences of such surveillance is essential. Suppose these activities interfere with how individuals develop their identities or compromise the functioning of democratic processes. In that case, the effects may not be immediately apparent but could be deeply damaging in the long term. These subtle shifts in behaviour may go unnoticed initially but can lead to long-lasting changes that affect individual rights and the public sphere.

Currently, the chilling effects of surveillance are not well understood, and too little attention goes to the potentiality of their far-reaching societal impacts. To address this gap, empirical research conducted in Zimbabwe and Uganda has shed light on how state surveillance has directly influenced behaviour, particularly with regard to the exercise of fundamental rights. In both countries, individuals do not have unbridled freedom to express their opinions or engage in public demonstrations due to concerns about government monitoring. This research highlights the tangible risks to core rights, including freedom of expression and the right to assemble peacefully, both of which are essential to personal development and democratic functioning.

The research also reveals common patterns and recurring themes related to the broader consequences of surveillance, allowing for a deeper understanding of how these effects manifest in different contexts. By moving beyond individual anecdotes and hypothetical situations, these insights provide a clearer picture of the potential social and psychological impacts of large-scale surveillance. The findings can help inform more thoughtful and balanced decision-making in the ongoing debates surrounding digital surveillance practices and their societal implications.

Landmark Supreme Court judgment on the right to privacy

On August 24, 2017, the Supreme Court of India issued a rare, unanimous nine-judge decision holding that the Constitution of India protects the right to privacy. The case is all the more noteworthy because the Court reversed its prior decisions, holding that the country's Constitution did not protect the right to privacy. It arose out of the government's creation of a national database of biometric and demographic information for every Indian. Rejecting the government's arguments, the Court found that the right to privacy applies across the gamut of "fundamental" rights, including equality, dignity (Article 14), speech, expression (Article 19), life, and liberty (Article 21). The six separate and concurring judgments in Justice K.S. Puttaswamy (Ret'd) and Anr v. Union of India and Ors are trailblazing for their commitment to privacy as a fundamental freedom and for the judges' use of foreign law across jurisdictions and spanning centuries.

This part addresses the ethics of placing large groups of people under mass surveillance to ascertain who, amongst them, is planning to take part in rights violations at the behest or on behalf of foreign actors. It reviews contemporary mass surveillance practices as described by Edward Snowden and mounts the best possible case in their favour. Of all the objections levelled against mass surveillance, two stand out: the claim that it violates the right to privacy and the claim that it is parasitic and entrenches unfair inequalities. The chapter argues that the privacy objection is not as decisive as it seems and that the fairness objection, though contingent on extant practices, is compelling. In the world as it is, it concludes, mass surveillance is morally wrong. The right to privacy in India is a fundamental right protected under Article 21 of the Constitution, as well as the Directive Principles of State Policy and the expression "personal liberty" under Article 21. The Supreme Court of India unanimously ruled that the right to privacy is a fundamental right and is "intrinsic to life and personal liberty". The Supreme Court also established that the right to privacy is related to other constitutional freedoms, such as equality, free speech, and religion.

The right to privacy in the Constitution of India is protected by Article 21, which states that no one should be the victim of arbitrary or unlawful interference with their privacy, family, home, or correspondence. It also states that everyone has the right to the protection of the law against such interference or attacks.

The first case in India to extensively discuss the right to privacy was the State of Madhya Pradesh case in 1975. In this case, a three-judge bench of the Supreme Court challenged the constitutionality of police surveillance of criminals on the list of "history sheeters". Another example of the right to privacy in action is the case of telephone tapping, where a division bench held that telephone tapping is an invasion of privacy.

As a concept, privacy has been debated consistently concerning its role in an individual's sphere since antiquity. The inception of international instruments such as the Universal Declaration of Human Rights and the International Covenant on Civil and Political Rights, along with institutions such as the United Nations, the Inter-American Commission on Human Rights, and the Council of Europe, have codified the global concern of privacy, global concern. However, despite the inception of these institutions, several states have refused to codify and respect privacy as a fundamental right guaranteed to an individual. Thus, the need arises to highlight the development of a right to privacy as a customary right with the help of widespread state practice around the world. The most recent country to address the question of what status privacy holds in the legislative framework of that state is India. Here, each citizen gets a unique identifying number based on biometric and demographic information. Known as the 'Aadhaar' scheme, this is giving rise to grave concerns about bodily integrity, informational self-determination, and decisional freedom. Indeed, a nine-judge Constitution Bench has just unanimously affirmed that the right to privacy is a fundamental right under the Constitution of India (Justice K S Puttaswamy (Retd.), and Anr v Union of India and Ors (2017)

This article traces the evolution of the right to privacy in India, starting with an exploration of its conception in the Constituent Assembly Debates of the longest Constitution in the world. It attempts to ascertain the intent behind the exclusion of the right to privacy as a fundamental right from the Constitution. It analyses the contemporary position developed by the inconsistent jurisprudence of the Courts in India. Finally, by scrutinizing the practices of states from around the world, it argues that the right to privacy, and in particular data privacy, can be considered a binding principle of customary international law.

Right to privacy

The right to privacy does not find a place as a specific provision under the Indian Constitution. However, the Courts have evolved this right from Article 21 and several other provisions, including Directive Principles of State Policy.

At the time of drafting the Indian Constitution, there were limited examples of codification of the right to privacy. Everyday law, for instance, did not clearly articulate the privacy doctrine. The European Convention on's Rights, which contains one of the most powerful articulations of the right to privacy, was not in force at the time. However, the United States of America used a patchwork of laws to protect privacy in diverse contexts, and the principles from this law almost made their way into the Indian Constitution in the form of an amendment based on the U.S. Fourth Amendment.

The Constituent Assembly did not take the right to privacy whilst crafting the Fundamental Rights. This might have been because of the relative scarcity of material on the right to privacy at the time. An amendment to insert the right against unreasonable searches almost evoked consent from the House but ended up being dropped. This resulted in some initial reluctance on the part of the Supreme Court to read this right into the Constitution. However, the Supreme Court of India eventually read the right to privacy into fundamental rights and has been tracing it through the different cases that implicate this right.

Kazi's right to privacy

Initially, the House found two varying forms of privacy, but both got lost with very little debate. One of these had to do with safeguards against unreasonable search, and the other protected the confidentiality of correspondence. Kazi Syed Karimuddin moved the amendment to With almost 1 billion people connected to the Internet, India has pioneered one of the world's most extensive digitization drives, capturing citizens' personal information through its Aadhaar ID system and building out a comprehensive network of digital infrastructure known as the India Stack. However, it lacks a law governing the sharing of data by companies, government agencies, and others. Human rights groups said this left information open to misuse, and businesses complained that it made their position vulnerable.

India has suffered several high-profile breaches in recent years, most recently in June when researchers said sensitive data had leaked from government-linked vaccination databases. The government denied there had been a breach. The data protection law has been years in the making, gathering momentum after the Supreme Court ruled in 2017 that Indians had a fundamental right to privacy. Multiple versions of the bill were floated and subsequently revised after backlash from business groups, civil society advocates, and opposition politicians.

The latest draft was ultimately adopted with minimal resistance, passing the upper House by a voice vote after opposition politicians — who wanted the bill sent to committee for further review — walked out of the chamber. The latest version addressed some business concerns, including loosening restrictions on companies' ability to transfer data overseas.

The law also mandates the creation of a government-controlled data protection board responsible for tracking compliance. However, the law remains a source of concern to civil society activists, who say exemptions for the government from data protections amount to a greenlight for state surveillance.

One provision allows the government to bypass aspects of the bill on broad grounds relating to the "sovereignty and integrity of India, security of the state, friendly relations with foreign states, maintenance of public order. The government is one of the largest collectors of personal information in the world. They're now through this legislation giving themselves carte blanche, said Salman Waris, managing partner at Delhi-based law firm TechLegis. "It's saying this act is only going to apply to private companies and individuals, which defeats the purpose of the act itself."

He said: "This is a significant amendment. You will be pleased to find that this finds a place as Article 4 in the American Constitution, and in the Irish Constitution, there are clauses (2) and (5) which are similar. In the German Constitution, Articles 114 and 115 are on the same lines. In the book of Dr Ambedkar—Minorities and States—on page 11, item No. 10, a similar provision has been made. What is the situation in India today? Arrests take place without warrants and searches without justification. Lawless laws are governing us, and there is no remedy for redress of grievances on account of unauthorized arrests and searches."

Dr Ambedkar pointed out that this clause was already in the Criminal Procedure Code and was, therefore, a part of Indian law, but also acknowledged that it might be desirable in the interests of personal liberty to 'place these provisions beyond the reach of the legislature'. Despite Ambedkar's support, the members disapproved of the amendment.

However, Karimuddin's amendment in the Constituent Assembly re-emerged through the process of judicial engineering in Kharak Singh v. State of U.P where the Court discussed the relationship between surveillance and personal liberty and found that unauthorized intrusion into a person's home would interfere with her right to individual freedom. The Court recognized "the right of the people to be secure in their persons, houses, papers, and effects" and declared that their right against unreasonable searches and seizures was not to be violated.

Along with Kharak, this marks the beginning of the judiciary=reading parts of the Karimuddin amendment into the Constitution. The Supreme Court acknowledged in the Gobind case25 that the right to privacy is likely to be built through a process of case-by-case development. This case also made it very clear that when the State implicate wherever the fundamental right to privacy, a law infringing this right must satisfy the compelling state interest test.

What was implicit in the privacy cases after Kharak Singh was stated explicitly in Italy in Collector v. Canara Bank 28, where the Supreme Court said quite clearly that the right to privacy 'deals with persons not places', and reiterated this position more recently in Directorate of Revenue v. Mohd. Nisar Holia.29 The doctrine has therefore expanded beyond the Kharak Singh30 majority judgment to the broader interpretation advocated by Justice Subba Rao in his dissent. Canara Bank also made it clear that inroads into the right to privacy for surveillance must be for permissible reasons and according to just, fair, and reasonable procedure. 3 ' State action in violation of this procedure is open to a constitutional challenge. Most specific to communication surveillance are the safeguards resulting from People's Union for Civil Liberties (PUCL) v. Union of India3 2. In this case, the Indian Supreme Court declared that "Somebody can hold a telephone conversation in the privacy of one's home or office without interference as 'right to privacy'. Telephone conversation is an important facet of a man's private life". The Court ruled that telephone tapping would violate Article 21 of the Indian Constitution unless permitted by the procedure established by law. It would also violate the right to freedom of speech and expression under Article 19 unless it came within the restrictions allowed by Article 19 (2). 34 Further, the Supreme Court clarified that even where the law clearly defines the situations in which interception may take place, this law must have procedural backing to ensure that the exercise of power is just and reasonable.[35] The lack of adequate procedural safeguards can mean that the substantive law violates Articles 19 and 21 of the Indian Constitution.

The dilemma of absolute privacy

After a very promising narrative that recognized the role played by procedural safeguards in protecting citizens' right to privacy, the Supreme Court regrettably accepted Kapil Sibal's argument that it could not impose prior judicial scrutiny in the absence of a statutory provision supporting such scrutiny. Had the Court declared the power to intercept communication under the Telegraph Act constitutionally untenable, this may have resulted in the introduction of robust safeguards. However, the Court opted instead to craft interim procedural safeguards for the interception of communication under the Telegraph Act. These safeguards consisted mainly of proper record-keeping and internal executive over-sight by senior officers such as the home secretary, the cabinet secretary, the law secretary, and the telecommunications secretary.[36] They are opaque and rely solely on members of the executive to review surveillance requests, leaving little for third party scrutiny, or challenge by affected parties (who may never find out that they were under surveillance).

This highly inadequate and flawed process in the Telegraph Act and the Information Technology Act was a result of which the Supreme Court of our communication interception jurisprudence has focused on targeted surveillance for years. Rapid evolution in technology has, however, enabled surveillance, which is different from targeted surveillance and its identification of particular individuals or organizations for monitoring. Mass surveillance operates very differently from targeted surveillance: states have bulk access to communication content and related information. They can mine all communication data for specific keywords or other information that might result in the Verses from Dharmashastras.

Dharmashastras has set forth various laws on privacy in the Indian subcontinent. During that time, the King was obliged to endorse Dharma and respect the citizens' privacy. 8Be it the Upanishads, or the Vedic culture, be it the Ramayana or Mahabharata or Manu Smriti, they have all considered privacy to be an essential aspect of an individual's life. A review of these scriptures demonstrates the existence of rules that would respect the privacy of an individual in ancient Indian society. In his Arthashastra9 Kautilya, Kautilya wrote that in his Arthashastra written around 321-296 B.C., he prescribed a detailed procedure ensuring the right to privacy, even ed civil liberty, which is indispensable to the freedom and dignity of an individual. From the ancient history of India, as we gradually moved further, we will find that by the nineteenth and twentieth centuries, the so-called privacy was the inviolability of the House of Property. The Constitution of India Bill 1895 is one of the earliest documents that stated that every citizen has inviolable asylum in his House. Then, with time, there was the Commonwealth of India Bill 1925, which protected unwanted interference to one's dwelling without due. The Nehru Report of 1928 echoed similar rights. As we moved towards modern times, especially the time when India became independent, we approached the time for the framing of the Constitution for an independent India.

In December 1946, the Constituent Assembly constituted various committees whose main work was to provide reports to the Drafting Committee, which would, in turn, formulate a draft of the Constitution. It was at the committee stage that a sub-committee group tried to advocate for the right to privacy as a part of the fundamental rights. During the meetings of the various sub-committees, distinguished members like K.M. Munshi, Harman Singh, and Dr Ambedkar vigorously promoted the inclusion of the right to privacy as one of their fundamental rights. The sentiments were echoed in Ambedkar's draft, which advocated for what was called 'the right of the people to be secure in their persons, House, papers and effects against unreasonable searches and seizures shall not be violated and no warrants shall issue but upon probable cause, supported by oath or affirmation.

However, from the very beginning, there were substantial differences of opinion related to the right to privacy, such as members like B.N Rau A. K Ayyar and M.K. Panikkar had a solid objection to the right to privacy to be raised to the status of a Fundamental Right. In fact, the ballad's ballads Krishnaswami Ayyar and B. N. Rau were members of the Constituent Assembly. The comments of both these members show their resentment towards the right to privacy. A. K. Ayyar was of the opinion that granting the right to privacy and secrecy in correspondence would be disastrous: it would elevate every private/ civil communication to that of State papers. This would adversely affect civil litigation, where documents form an essential part of the evidence. B.N. Rau was primarily concerned with the interference of the right to privacy with the investigative powers of the police authorities.14 Later, Rau and Ayyar were successful in persuading the Advisory Committee to leave out provisions relating to the right to privacy. So, the final report of the Advisory Committee did not feature anything related to the right to privacy.

On April 30, 1947, one of the members of the Constituent Assembly, Somnath Lahiri, presented a proposal to make the right to privacy of correspondence a fundamental right, 'the privacy of correspondence shall be inviolable and may be infringed only in cases provided by law........ 'However, this proposal failed to get a positive response in the assembly."

Promises and illusions of data protection in Indian law

India is the world's most populous democracy (estimated population of 1.2 billion), with a multi-party bi-cameral parliamentary system at the national level. The Indian economy, previously very state-dominant, has developed an energetic private sector in the last two decades. It has the world's twelfth-largest economy and is at present the second-fastest growing major economy, as well as being one of the world's most prominent destinations for the international outsourcing of processing of personal information ('business process outsourcing') through telecommunications call centres, transcription of medical consultation notes, and in many other areas.

We cannot understand the data protection laws of a country in isolation from the surveillance systems operating within the country. Indian governments have long had the power to intercept messages 'on the occurrence of any public emergency, or in the interests of public safety' if it was satisfied with some issues. However, this is constrained by 1996 Supreme Court guidelines as to who could tap phones and under what circumstances. More recent 'anti-terrorism' laws faced criticism because they 'gave law enforcement sweeping powers to arrest suspected terrorists, intercept communications and curtail free expression',

However, they do include audit mechanisms involving judicial review and parliamentary oversight. The Indian courts are active in placing limitations on searches without warrants. Amendments in 2008 to the Information Technology Act 2000, discussed below, include provisions for extensive data surveillance. The Credit Information Companies (Regulation) Act 2005 is a blueprint for a comprehensive credit surveillance system.

In summary, the Indian state is not yet involved in pervasive personal surveillance of its population; the rule of law is administered by an activist (if sometimes slow-moving) judiciary that is sensitive to issues of civil liberties, including privacy. India is a frequent target of terrorist attacks, so there is a constant temptation to extend every form of surveillance. India's private sector has not yet embraced systemic data surveillance techniques for commercial purposes. Indian law is, therefore, at a crossroads in the development of data protection and privacy law. While there has been considerable legislative activity and case law concerning data protection in recent years, an overview of Indian data protection and privacy law reveals numerous significant hurdles before the country had the status of an international standard legal framework. Many of the protections are not yet in effect, either, because essential regulations are still missing. To that extent, some of India's data protection structures are illusory or can, at best, be promising future improvements.

Convinced of its necessity, he said that the Criminal Procedure Code offered adequate safeguards, but it needed to be respected. He argued that similar principles inserted in the Constitution may meet a similar fate. In a speech riddled with inconsistencies, he made the very curious argument that the liberties granted to the people before independence would be unsustainable after independence and that fettering the parliament's discretion with the procedure in the context of law and order would be wrong. The surveillance of communication was a product of the amendment of Somnath Lahiri. This included a clause protecting the privacy of correspondence within the fundamental right of liberty (which later became Article 19) in the Constitution. The House resolved to take up the Lahiriproposal towards the end of the discussion on the fundamental rights instead of in the context of the right to liberty. It appears, however, that the proposal was never seriously considered or even put up for vote.

Disappointing records of Constituent Assembly

The records of the Constituent Assembly debates are, therefore, disappointing. The iPhone is seeking powerful reasoning to explain the omission of the right to privacy. Some members made a robust case for the inclusion of this right on more than one occasion, but for reasons that are not entirely clear, their arguments have not elicited any convincing responses.

B. The Supreme Court of India Traces Out Citizens' Rights Against Illegal SurveillanceWhile the Constitution and the choices made about the Fundamental Rights were still fresh in public memory in 1954, the apex court refused to read the right to privacy eight into the Indian Constitution. This was in A.P. Sharma v. Satish Chandra, where the Supreme Court declared that it could not import the right to privacy analogous to the U.S. Fourth Amendment into a different fundamental right given that the constitution makers had not thought to recognize this right toprivacy.19However, the apex court gradually moved away from this position, to acknowledging that other rights and liberties guaranteed in the Constitution would be seriously affected in the absence of protection of the right to privacy. This process began in Kharak Singh v. State of U.P.20, where the Court discussed the relationship between surveillance and personal liberty and found that unauthorized intrusion into a person's home would interfere with her right to individual freedom. The right to privacy around the house and unauthorized intrusions into homes were an interference with the right to personal liberty. The Court recognized "the right of the people to be secure in their persons, houses, papers, and effects" and declared that their right against unreasonable searches and seizures was not to be violated. However, this right does not extend to the shadowing of citizens outside their homes. In a dissenting opinion that exhibited extraordinary foresight, JusticSubba Rao maintained that broad surveillance powers put innocent citizens at risk and that the right to privacy is an integral part of personal liberty. Subba Rao recognized that when a lady is shadowed from behind, her movements are constrained, and she can't have free movement. Although he did not use the phrase, in effect, he took into account what is now known as the 'chilling effect' of law. The right to privacy, as defined by the Supreme Court so far, now extends beyond government intrusion into private homes. In Gobind v. State of A.P.23, the Supreme Court said that the Constitution makers 'must be deemed to have conferred upon the individual as again the government a sphere where he should be allowed to let alone'.

International safeguards for surveillance

The international safeguards recommended for targeted surveillance assume some prior suspicion of the target of surveillance. The clarity about the objective and the target makes it easier to 'objectively assess the necessity and proportionality of the contemplated surveillance, weighing the degree of the proposed intrusion against its anticipated value to a particular investigation'. These safeguards for targeted surveillance emerge from International Human Rights legal norms that require that there must be clear justification whenever there is any interference with the right to privacy, such that there is a proportionality analysis that ensures that there is a compelling justification for any severe interference with protected human rights.40 The European Court of Human Rights has had to consider this question of mass surveillance in Liberty v. United Kingdom. This was a case that resulted after the Ministry of Defence in the United Kingdom operated a powerful facility that simultaneously intercepted a vast number of telephone channels carrying facsimile, email, telephone, and data communication. The only safeguards in place were internal, consisting of broad warrants that covered several classes of communication, certification by the Secretary of State of broad classes of information extracted with no discusses of specific targets, or3 Mass surveillance is described as "generalized suspicion" that as yet unidentified members of a group may be of interest, as opposed to personalized surveillance which deals with identified individuals who have triggered suspicion or concern.

The Court found these safeguards inadequate, mainly since the warrants and certification have extensive terms. It found that there should be a clear articulation of the scope or manner of exercise of the state's interceptive power, and there was no publicly accessible and clearly defined procedure for the selection, examination, storage, sharing, and destruction of intercepted material. However, the Court found that the United Kingdom's process contravened the privacy protection offered under the European Convention on Human Rights. It did not clarify the specifics of what might be an acceptable set of safeguards in the context of mass surveillance. Drawing upon its past jurisprudence, the European Court insisted on reasonable procedural safeguards. It stated quite clearly that there are significant risks of arbitrariness in executive power if applied in secrecy and that the law should be sufficiently clear to give citizens an adequate indication of the circumstances in which interception might take place. Additionally, the extent of discretion conferred and the manner of its exercise must be clear enough to protect individuals from arbitrary interference. This question is likely to be examined in more detail by the Court in the near future: London-based organizations Big Brother Watch, Open Rights Group, English PEN, and Constanze Kurz have brought the U.K. government before the ECHR for the mass surveillance of data conducted by British spy agencies.

The United Nations is also veering towards framing applicable norms - it has recently passed a resolution 42 calling upon states to review their procedures, practices, and legislation with respect to communication surveillance, including mass surveillance, to uphold privacy rights. The U.N. Special High Commissioner for Human Rights Navi Pillay, in her report titled 'The right to privacy in the digital age', has emphasized the importance of safeguards to protect rights during mass surveillance and has pointed out that internal procedural safeguards without independent external monitoring are inadequate for the protection of rights. 43 This report declares that we can achieve adequate protection of the law if all the branches of government, as well as an independent oversight agency, are built into the procedural safeguards. 44 It also lists among these safeguards that known and accessible remedies are made available to those whose privacy is compromised. These remedies must be effective, and must42 U.N. General Assembly, Resolution on Right to Privacy in the Digital Age, six 9th session, include a thorough and impartial investigation, the capacity to end the ongoing violation and must even offer criminal prosecution as a remedy for gross abuses.

Safeguards in India

Our safeguards in India apply only to targeted surveillance and require written requests for a periodical review of telephone tapping or intervention. India has no requirements for transparency, whether in the form of disclosing the quantum of interception taking place each year or in the form of subsequent notification to people whose communication was under interception. It does not even have external oversight in the form of an independent regulatory body or the judiciary to ensure that no abuse of surveillance systems takes place. Given these structural flaws, the Gujarat illegal surveillance controversy is unsurprising. The complete lack of accountability for the misuse of the surveillance framework in that context bodes ill for how surveillance is likely to be used in India. In this context, mass surveillance and the Central Monitoring System (CMS) raise real concerns about the extensive misuse of power by the state. News reports in India indicate this is a move towards intercepting all communication over the Internet and scanning it for keywords like 'attack', 'bomb', 'blast', and 'kill'. This system scrutinises tweets, status updates, emails, chat transcripts, and even voice traffic over the Internet (including from platforms like Skype and Google Talk). In the context of phone call surveillance, CMS is even more opaque than targeted surveillance since the state can intercept communication directly without making requests to private telecommunication service providers. This means that there is one less layer of scrutiny through which abuse of power can reach the public. There is no one to ask whether the requisite paperwork is in place or to notice a dramatic increase in interception requests. Unfettered mass surveillance does not augur well for democracy. Understanding why this is so can be difficult owing to the nature of privacy alarms arising from mass surveillance. Different kinds of privacy harms may result from surveillance, like the disruption of valuable activity and the chilling of socially beneficial behaviour like free speech.4 Among these is the creation of power imbalances like (excess executive power) that damage the social structure. 48 These different harms tend to be acknowledged in a piecemeal fashion depending on context. For example, in Kharak Singh, the problem was the right to privacy in the digital age, a Report of the Office of the United Nations High Commissioner for Human forr disruption of the target's activities as well as one of chilling socially beneficial behaviour. However, only Justice Subba Rao was willing to acknowledge that the matter was also a privacy problem. This acknowledgement of the chilling effect on speech as a privacy problem is, however, unambiguous in PUCL case 50. Privacy harms in the form of power imbalances that damage the social structure are the most difficult to identify clearly. Their impact remains invisible for a large part. Solove points out that one of the problems with the identification of such harms is that privacy violations are often framed as injuries to individuals and weighed against security interests (seen as societal interests). This is a misleading characterization, as the protection of privacy is necessary to ensure that abuse of power and inhibition of democratic participation.., both of which are societal interests, are regulated. The acknowledgement of the right to privacy as a societal interest offers a more helpful way to frame the surveillance debate. It clarifies the need to focus on oversight and accountability mechanisms, bearing in mind the impact of unrestrained surveillance on the health of our democracy.

These arguments need to be articulated more forcefully in the context of mass surveillance in India. There are currently minimal safeguards to protect the right to privacy in the face of mass surveillance or even targeted surveillance in India. While the argument for surveillance is justified in the interests of national security and public order interests, this does not protect the absence of safeguards that might defend human rights and the balance of power in our democracy. The U.N. Special High Commissioner for Human Rights has outlined essential components of a legal framework that protects privacy rights in the face of mass surveillance. 3 She has done so clearly, offering examples of what works and what does not, such that it is apparent that the Indian privacy safeguards fall short of her best practices guidelines.

There is no excuse for a democracy like India, which has articulated its commitment to human rights, not to put these privacy safeguards in place. However, since the safeguards essentially check the wielding of executive power, it seems unlikely that the executive will voluntarily put them in place without external pressure. One hopes that the Supreme Court of India recognizes the damage that unrestrained mass surveillance will wreak on our democracy and that it takes its jurisprudence forward by several steps unimpeded by its initial reluctance to create robust safeguards in the PUCL telephone tapping case.

4. KAZI KARIMUDDIN'S APPROACH TO HUMAN PRIVACY

Our personal space is de ar to us all. We live our lives in full public view on social media - posting photos of the food we just ate or even expressing intimate feelings for our loved ones - but there are still things we would instead not share with the world. Indeed, it is privacy that sets man apart from the animals who must stick together in the wild for their safety. But humanity was not born private. Our primitive ancestors, too, lived in large groups, every member of which knew all there was to know about the others. Privacy is a fundamental right that protects human dignity and autonomy and is a foundation for many other human rights. In the modern world, privacy is a topic of international debate, with many issues surrounding its legal protections. Here are some things to consider about privacy in the contemporary world: Privacy evolved as man developed technologies to wall himself off, even as he remained part of the society at large. But just as some technologies enhanced privacy, others - such as the printing press or the portable camera - chipped away at it. Every time this happened, a man opposed the technology at first but eventually made peace with it to benefit from the apparent good it could do.

Today, people often talk about "responsible" AI use, but what do they really mean? Generally speaking, being responsible means being aware of the consequences of our actions and making sure they don't cause harm or put anyone in danger. But there's a lot we don't know about AI. It's very hard to say, for example, what the long-term consequences will be of developing machines that can think, create and make decisions on our behalf. It will impact human jobs and lives in ways that no one can be certain about yet.

One of the potential dangers is an infringement on privacy, which is a fundamental human right. AI systems can now recognize us by our faces when we're in public and are routinely used to process highly sensitive information such as health and financial data.

Privacy has become more than a regulatory checkbox; it's now a powerful driver of consumer behaviour. Privacy is central to customer trust and loyalty. Privacy has grown from a compliance matter to a customer requirement," highlighting the critical role data transparency plays in shaping consumer perceptions. As artificial intelligence (AI) applications expand, people are becoming increasingly conscious of the engagement of their data with brands that prioritize ethical data use.

Privacy issues are everywhere in our society, but we struggle with them in part because we lack a clear definition of privacy on which we can agree. Scholars have struggled to define privacy, but lots of concepts in our law, like "free speech" and "equality," have been protected without explicit agreement on a specific definition. Thus, we need not let our hang-ups about privacy's definitional problem stop us from talking about it and protecting it. The chapter offers a working definition of privacy for the book as "the extent to which human information is neither known nor used. This definition focuses on (1) information privacy rather than other kinds of privacy; (2) information about humans; (3) the use of information rather than its mere collection; and (4) the importance of thinking about information use as a matter of degree rather than a binary on/off state.

The right to privacy became an international human right before it was a nationally well-established fundamental right. When created in the years after World War II, state constitutions protected only aspects of privacy, such as the inviolability of the home and correspondence. This article analyses how the integral guarantee—the right to privacy or to respect one's private life—came into existence. It traces the history of drafting at the global and European levels and argues that there was no conscious decision to create an integral guarantee.

The right to be left alone and to keep certain matters secluded from public view forms part of Article 8 of the European Convention on Human Rights and the Human Rights Act 1998. The right includes the privacy of communications (telephone calls, correspondence, etc.); privacy of the home and office; environmental protection (including freedom from excessive noise: Hatton v UK the protection of physical integrity; protection from unjustified prosecution and conviction of those engaged in consensual nonviolent sexual activities; and protection from being photographed and described in circumstances where the individual has a reasonable expectation of privacy). This right is qualified. Public authorities have a limited but positive duty to protect privacy from interference by third parties.

The right to privacy refers to the legal framework that provides legal protection to individuals and their data. Internationally, the right to privacy forms part of Article 12 of the United Nations Declarations of Human Rights (UDHR) 1948 and Article 17 of the International Convention on Civil and Political Rights (ICCPR) 1966. The right to privacy legally protects an individual against 'arbitrary interference. India is committed to ICCPR and UDHR.

The right to privacy made its first appearance in the Constituent Assembly Debates when Kazi Syed Karimuddin, a member of the Constituent Assembly and Rajya Sabha in independent India, moved clause (4) under Article 14.

On December 3, 1948, KS Karimuddin proposed protection against unreasonable searches of houses, papers and persons. He argued against such searches because laws like the 'Goonda Act' or 'Public Safety Act' gave excessive power to the executive. These acts offered no legal representation and required no warrant for arrest.

His argument stemmed from his concern for the Muslim minority groups who had faced the wrath of unfounded suspicion earlier. Additionally, as part of the 'States and Minorities Report', Dr B.R. Amedkar, KM Munshi and Harman Singh strongly voiced the need to include privacy as a fundamental right. Plus, Somnath Lahiri, a member of the Constituent Assembly from West Bengal, favoured protecting citizens' right to privacy. Lahiri had also objected to the curtailment of freedom even during grave emergencies.

In his book, 'Privacy 3.0: Unlocking Our Data-Driven Future', Rahul Matthan states how many Constituent Assembly members were against making privacy a fundamental right, including BN Rau and Alladi Krishnaswamy Ayyar. He writes, "One of the more vocal critics was Alladi Krishnaswamy Ayyar, who voiced his vehement dissent in his comments on the draft."

Matthan continues to expound on BN Rau's reservation, including the right to privacy. According to him (BN Rau), such a right could place impediments in the way of law enforcement, particularly given the fact that India was a large country where the administration of criminal justice was bound to be difficult… His principal objection to the inclusion of privacy as a fundamental right seemed to stem from a concern that allowing for such a right would make the administration of justice in a country as large as India difficult."

We are at a similar crossroads today with data technologies. Aadhaar is one example of the many ways in which we have begun to use data in everything we do. While it has made it far easier to avail of services from the government and private enterprises than ever before, some rightly worry about people's private data `being ill-used and, worse, without consent. But this anxiety is no different from that which we felt during the teething troubles of every previous technology we adopted. What we really need is a new framework that unlocks the full potential of a data-driven future while still safeguarding what we hold most dear - our privacy. In this pioneering work, technology lawyer Rahul Matthan traces the changing notions of privacy from the earliest times to its evolution through landmark cases in the UK, the US and India. In the process, he re-imagines the way we should be thinking about privacy today if we are to take full advantage of modern data technologies, cautioning against getting so obsessed with their potential harms that we design our laws to prevent us from benefiting from them at all.

Kazi Syed Karimuddin had given references to Article 4 of the American constitution, Clauses (2) and (5) of the Irish Constitution, and Articles 114 and 115 of the German Constitution, which provided similar kinds of rights to their citizens in order to support his proposal. But, this proposed amendment has not garnered any support. So, the Indian Constitution failed to recognize the right to privacy as a part of the fundamental rights conferred to the citizens of India. The challenges and concerns before the Supreme Court had agitated the clairvoyant minds of some of the founding fathers of the constitutions, even though digitization was inconceivable in those days.

But over some time, none other than the Supreme Court of India has played an essential role in addressing several cases that have dealt with the right to privacy in some form or the other and which has helped the right to confidentiality attain its rightful position as a part of Right to Life and Liberty under Article21.

The first attempt to protect the privacy of an individual against unreasonable state interference was in the Constituent Assembly when Kazi moved an amendment to protect individuals from unjustified search and seizures along the lines of the American and Irish Constitutions. Human civilization has always believed that there is something primal about the need for privacy, secrecy, and personal space. This has, in the world of some judicial authorities, taken to mean "the right to be let alone"— that is, the right to privacy. They believe "privacy is the beginning of all freedom". Every one of us seems to ensure that our privacy remains a sacred space. However, jurisprudence has still not been able to harness this legal concept into a clear beacon for law enforcement authorities.

A significant reason is that the whole idea of privacy is highly nebulous, and it seems very difficult to pin it down to a definable idea. But assuming our right to privacy is guaranteed, how do we know what the boundaries are that make private space exclusive and confer an absolute and unfettered right?

The digital era upends many traditional privacy safeguards. Nations now have unprecedented capacity to spy on global communication, and yet they typically acknowledge no legal restrictions on their right to surveil non-citizens outside their borders. People now have minor protection against spying by foreign countries, and the realities of incidental collection and inter-governmental cooperation can put their private communications in the hands of their governments as well. Privacy advocates recognize the need to plug this loophole, and there is growing support for doing so by a multilateral agreement that would establish internationally applicable safeguards. The present article concludes that such an agreement, far from strengthening global privacy protection, would almost certainly weaken it. Even among Western democracies, the search for transnational common ground and institutional learning nations all nations free to go their way. The paper discusses the political and economic dynamics that render needed reforms more likely through US domestic law than through international agreements and the reasons for optimism that such laws would benefit not only Americans but also the world at large.

Pre-independence history of the right to privacy in India

Human civilization has always believed that there is something primal about the need for privacy, secrecy, and personal space. This has, in the world of some judicial authorities, taken to mean "the right to be let alone"— that is, the right to privacy. They believe "privacy is the beginning of all freedom".Every one of us seems to ensure that our privacy must be a sacred space. However, jurisprudence has still not been able to harness this legal concept into a clear beacon for law enforcement authorities.

The Founding Fathers and the Constitutional struggle over Centralized Power realized that the documents were inadequate for the task of unifying a diverse group of newly independent colonies. A debate thus ensued between the Federalist side, led by Alexander Hamilton and James Madison, and the Anti-Federalists, led by Thomas Jefferson and Patrick Henry, over exactly how much power and authority to give Congress and the other central branch of the new government. Hamilton et al. argued that a strong central government would be essential to the nation's survival and prosperity. At the same time, his opponents insisted that most of the nation's power should rest within the state and local governments. By 1787, there was a sort of compromise that resulted in our Constitution and its first set of amendments, the Bill of Rights. The Founders were justifiably proud of their historic achievement. Still, unfortunately, that stubborn tension between federal and state power would eventually push the nation into the Civil War, and even today, it remains a divisive point of contention.

The announcement of the United States Supreme Court in 1965 that a right to privacy existed and that it predated the Bill of Rights launched a historical and legal quest to sound the origins and extent of the right that has continued to the present day.' Legal scholars quickly grasped hold of the new star in the constitutional firmament, producing countless books and articles examining the caselaw pedigree and the potential scope of this right to privacy. Historians, however, have, for the most part, shied away from tracing the origins of the right to privacy, perhaps hoping to avoid the ignominy of practising "law-office history."' Instead, some historians have engaged in subtle searches for markers of confidentiality such as an emphasis on family, three a notion of the home as an oasis, four or a minimal* Doctoral candidate, Department of History, Harvard University.

The digital challenge

One hundred thirty years ago, a young lawyer saw an amazing new gadget and had a revolutionary vision — technology can threaten our privacy. Recent inventions and business methods call attention to the next step for the protection of the person," wrote the lawyer Louis Brandeis, warning that laws needed to keep up with technology and new means of surveillance or Americans would lose their "right to be let alone.

Decades later, the right to privacy discussed in that 1890 law review article and Brandeis's opinions as a Supreme Court justice, especially in the context of new technology, would be cited as a foundational principle of the constitutional protections for many rights, including contraception, same-sex intimacy and abortion.

Now, the Supreme Court seems poised to rule that there is no constitutional protection for the right to abortion. Surveillance made possible by minimally-regulated digital technologies could help law enforcement or even vigilantes track down women who might seek abortions and medical providers who perform them in places where it would become criminalized. Women are urging one another to delete phone apps like period trackers that can indicate they are pregnant.

But frantic individual efforts to swat away digital intrusions will do too little. What's needed is a complete legal and political reckoning with the reckless manner in which digital technology has been allowed to invade our lives. The collection, use, and manipulation of electronic data require to be finally regulated and severely limited in the interest of human safety. Then, we can comfortably enjoy all the good that can come from these technologies alone.

Brandeis's concern about technology's threat to liberty was stoked by the introduction, two years before his article, of a Kodak camera that was small enough to carry, cheap enough to afford, worked at the press of a button, and came loaded for 100 shots. This new portability meant that intrusions that would once have been impractical were now easy.

The Constitution doesn't mention cameras wiretapping cellphones, electronic data, or artificial intelligence. However, it does talk about the protection of beliefs (First Amendment), the sanctity of the home (Third), the right against unreasonable searches of persons, houses, papers and effects (Fourth) and protection against self-incrimination (Fifth). Those were some of the pillars upon which Brandeis rested his argument that laws need to enforce our liberty against intrusion, even as technology morphed its shape. In 1928, as a Supreme Court justice, Brandeis dissented from the majority, which allowed the government to listen to suspects' telephone conversations without warrants. Brandeis pointed out that opening and reading a sealed envelope requires a warrant, so wiretapping should also require a warrant. In the latter half of the century, though, the court began to catch up with the need to protect privacy and regulate technology more broadly.

Privacy widened the scope and coverage for the hitherto deprived groups. In 1970, there was a regulation for the use of information on creditworthiness. The Privacy Act of 1974 established protections for personally identifiable information that was collected or held by federal agencies. The government tightened oversight for wiretaps in 1967 and then in 1977, requiring warrants for domestic wiretaps.

However, in the decades since then, there has been an explosion in the technological part of digital networks, and billions of people carry pocket computers that leave constant footprints. All this is the jurisdiction of a vast apparatus of surveillance, which could be under the surveillance of powerful computational techniques, along with images from cameras on streets, phones, and satellites. There was comfort in that this was aggregated bulk data — without names attached. Researchers have repeatedly shown that even in such data sets, it is often possible to pinpoint a person's identity — deanonymizing data — by triangulating information from different sources, like, say, matching location data on someone's commute from home to work or their purchases in stores. This also helps evade legal privacy protections that apply only to "personally identifiable information" — records explicitly containing identifiers like names or Social Security numbers.

Recently, Grindr, the world's most popular gay dating app, was selling data about its users. A priest resigned after the Catholic publication The Pillar deanonymized his data, identified him and then outed him by tracking his visits to gay bars and a bathhouse. Phone companies were detected selling their customers' real-time location data, and it reportedly ended up in the hands of bounty hunters and stalkers.

In 2014, BuzzFeed News reported that an Uber executive had admitted to tracking at least one journalist who had reported on the company. In 2012, the company also posted data analyses on its blog revealing possible one-night stands people were having in significant cities. In criticizing such practices in a piece I co-wrote at the time, I pointed out that such methods could also track visits to Planned Parenthood offices.

None of these options works well

For one thing, turning off settings in apps doesn't stop the phone or the cellphone company from continuing to collect location data. It's also not that reliable. I have turned off location tracking many times in reputable apps only to be surprised to notice later that it turned itself back on because I clicked on something unrelated that, the fine print might reveal, turns location tracking back on.

Using burner phones — which you use and discard — sounds cool but is difficult in practice. Matt Blaze, a leading expert on digital security and encryption, said that trying to maintain a burner phone required "using almost everything I know about communications systems and security," and he still wasn't sure he had evaded surveillance and identification entirely.

How about leaving your phone behind?

Let me say good luck.

Even if you don't carry a digital device and only use cash, commercially available biometric databases can carry out facial recognition at scale. Clearview AI says it has more than 10 billion images of people taken from social media and news articles that it sells to law enforcement and private entities. Given the ubiquity of cameras, it will soon be not easy to walk anywhere without being algorithmically recognized. Even a mask is no barrier. Algorithms can recognize people from other attributes as well. In China, the police have employed "gait recognition" — using artificial intelligence to identify people by the way they walk and by body features other than their faces.

The protections you think you have may not be as broad as you think. The confidentiality that federal health privacy law provides to conversations with a doctor doesn't always apply to prescriptions. In 2020, Consumer Reports exposed that GoodRX, a popular drug discount and coupons service, was selling information on what medications people were searching for or buying to Facebook, Google and other data marketing firms. GoodRx said it would stop, but there is no law against them or any pharmacy doing this.

That data becomes even more powerful when merged. A woman who regularly eats sushi and suddenly stops or stops taking Pepto-Bismol or starts taking vitamin B6 may be easily identified as someone following guidelines for pregnancy. If that woman doesn't give birth, she might find herself questioned by the police, who may think she had an abortion. (Already, in some places, women who seek medical help after miscarriages have reported questioning to this effect.)

In 2019, when Kashmir Hill — now a reporter at The New York Times — tried to cut Google out of her online life, she found it everywhere. Apps like Lyft and Uber, which relied on Google Maps, and Spotify, which relied on Google Cloud, wouldn't work. The Times loaded very slowly (trying to load for Google Analytics, Google Pay, Google News, Google ads and a Doubleclick, and then waiting for them to fail before proceeding). By the end of a week, her devices had tried to communicate with Google's servers more than 100,000 times. Hill tried this for other Big Five tech companies, too, and found them similarly hard to avoid.

There are many calls to boycott Facebook, but the reality is that it is much more complicated than many realize to avoid it entirely. First, a large number of civic and local activities, particularly for disadvantaged people, are available solely through Facebook. Some essential patient groups, for example, exist only on Facebook. I've even encountered situations where school districts sent updates on active shooter alerts on Facebook.

Facebook doesn't just collect data on its two billion users, and it also doesn't just collect it from what those people do while using its products. Billions of web pages (including those of The New York Times) and mobile apps contain code from the company — tracking pixels — that collect detailed data and communicate them back to Facebook. They try to match this to existing Facebook users but keep it even for nonusers, creating what's called "shadow profiles." Google's tracking, too, is all over the web and in many apps through its ubiquitous ad products. "Just don't use it" doesn't get people too far.

Now, let's get to the horrifying stuff.

About a decade ago, The Times reported about a father whose teenage daughter suddenly started getting promotional materials for baby items from Target. The angry dad went to a Target store and got an apology from the manager, only to learn after confronting his daughter that she was pregnant. Maybe it was something overt, like the girl purchasing a pregnancy test. However, increasingly, such predictions are made by analyzing big data sets with algorithms (often called "machine learning") that can arrive at conclusions about things that aren't explicitly in the data.

For example, algorithmic interpretations of Instagram posts can effectively predict a person's future depressive episodes — performing better than humans assessing identical posts. There were similar results for predicting future manic episodes and detecting suicidal ideation, among many other examples. Such predictive systems are already in widespread use, including for hiring, sales, political targeting, education, medicine and more.

Given the many changes pregnancy engenders even before women know about it, in everything from sleep patterns to diet to fatigue to mood changes, it's not surprising that an algorithm might detect which women were likely to be pregnant. (Such lists are already collected and traded). That's data that could be purchased by law enforcement agencies or activists intent on tracking possible abortions.

Many such algorithmic inferences are statistical, not necessarily individual, but they can narrow down the list of, well, suspects. How does it work? Even the researchers don't really know, calling it a black box. How could it be regulated? Since it's different, it would need new thinking. As of yet, few to no laws regulate most of these novel advances, even though they are as consequential to our Fourth Amendment rights as telephones and wiretaps.

Despite what my concerns might lead some to believe, I am not a technophobe. Like many others who study privacy and technology, I'm often an early adopter of tech, and I am enthusiastic about its many potential uses.

Many of our existing legal protections are effectively outdated. For example, law enforcement can obtain emails, pictures, or any data you store in the cloud without a warrant and without notifying you, so long as it is older than six months. This is because when the initial law on email privacy was drafted in 1986, online, or what we now call cloud storage, was costly. People downloaded or deleted their emails regularly. So, anything older than six months was considered abandoned. Almost three decades later, it simply means years of personal digital history — which didn't exist at the time of drafting the law — are up for grabs.

This doesn't mean we should snuff out digital technology or advances in algorithms. Even if it were possible, it wouldn't be desirable. The government should regulate these technologies so we can use them and enjoy their many positives without out-of-control surveillance. Congress and states should restrict or ban the collection of many types of data, especially those used solely for tracking, and limit the period of retention of data for necessary functions — like getting directions on the phone. Selling, trading and merging personal data should be restricted or outlawed. Law enforcement could obtain it subject to specific judicial oversight.

Researchers have been inventing privacy-preserving methods for analyzing data sets when merging them is in the public interest. Still, the underlying data is sensitive, such as when health officials are tracking a disease outbreak and want to integrate data from multiple hospitals. These techniques allow computation but make it hard, if not impossible, to identify individual records. Companies are unlikely to invest in such methods or use end-to-end encryption as appropriate to protect user data if they can continue doing whatever they want. Regulation could provide these advancements with good business opportunities and spur innovation.

People don't like things the way they are. When Apple changed the default option from "track me" to "do not track me" on its phones, few people chose to be traceable. Many who accept tracking don't realize how much privacy they're giving up and what this kind of data can reveal. Many location collectors get their data from ordinary apps — it could be weather, games, or anything else — that often bury that they will share the data with others in vague terms deep in their fine print.

The challenge of privacy hinders historians

Does the use of privacy as an analytic tool compromise the historian's ability to separate the term's modern connotations from its historical ones? Can early uses of the words"private" and "privacy" ever be understood as the speakers meant them, or has the Supreme Court's pronouncement that a right to privacy has existed all along lulled us into believing that the meaning of these words remained unchanged and that a stable notion of "privacy" has endured and been celebrated throughout American history? In short, the concept of privacy has not lent itself to easy historical application. Consequently, many historians seem to have abandoned privacy as both an analytical framework and a topic of analysis.

The report of the founding fathers

The Nehru Report (Motilal Nehru,1928), an outcome of the All Parties Conference, guaranteed a similar right. A few years before the beginning of formal constitution-making, a draft of the Indian Constitution (M.N. Roy, 1944), as endorsed by the Radical Democratic Party, for the first time, extended the right to privacy to include private correspondence. Four years later, another Draft Constitution (Socialist Party, 1948) granted protection against unlawful entry into one's dwelling except under the due process of law.

The Constituent Assembly constituted Principal Committees, with internal sub-committees, to prepare reports that would enable the Drafting Committee to develop a draft Constitution. Prominent among these was the Advisory Committee on Fundamental Rights. Members of this committee- including Dr Ambedkar, K.M. Munshi, and Harman Singh – staunchly advocated for the inclusion of a fundamental right to privacy.

The Czech Constitution inspired Harman Singh, and he stated in his report that 'Every dwelling shall be inviolable'. KM Munshi sought to make the right to the inviolability of one's home and the right to the secrecy of one's correspondence a fundamental right. In his States and Minorities Report, Dr BR Ambedkar advocated for 'the right of the people to be secure in their persons, houses, papers, and effects against unreasonable searches and seizures'.

The aborted Kazi Karimuddin effort to introduce privacy

There were two separate attempts later. On April 30, 1947, Somnath Lahiri proposed to make the right to privacy of correspondence a fundamental right. However, his proposal did not receive traction. A year later, Kazi Syed Karimuddin moved an amendment to include the right of the people to be secure in their persons, houses, papers, and effects against unreasonable searches and seizures in Article 20 (Draft Article 14) of the Constitution.

Ambedkar noted that it was a beneficial provision, though it was part of the Criminal Procedure Code. He observed that legislatures of the future may abrogate the provision. Hence, on account of their criticality to personal liberty, it was desirable to place them beyond the reach of the legislature.

The Vice-President of the Constituent Assembly attempted twice to put the Karimuddin text to vote. Although he declared the amendment as having been accepted both times, T.T. Krishnamachari objected, saying both times that the majority vote was for those who were not in favour of the amendment.

Privacy in the technological world

Digital advancement has brought immense benefits and conveniences. By having access to copious amounts of personal data that can be freely extracted, certain apps make the online world seem customized for us.

Those who want to recruit clients for their products can know how old we are, where we live, what our eating habits are, what books we like, or which brand of products we use.

There is so much individual data in public space that ill-intentioned entities can mine and harvest it for vicious objectives. It is now abundantly clear that our privacy is in a parlous state, and much of the stuff has already come into the public eye. There is a consistent warning that we should not manage even our insignificant details clumsily because sharing them carries invisible and unfathomable hazards.

The government now has many methods, besides tapping into your phone wire, to find out what you're up to. Most of us store more in the cloud than in lock boxes. It does not make sense to constrain the technological capacities of law enforcement just because technologyallows it to work more efficiently. However, those capacities can also lead to a society whose citizens have nowhere to hide, and the very idea of privacy becomes an oxymoron.

We can only re-emphasize, at the cost of an overstatement, that functional anonymity is as valuable in commerce as in speech. In its judgment in Justice K. S. Puttaswamy v. Union of India, the Supreme Court ended the constitutional limbo by recognizing privacy as the constitutional core of human dignity and the foundation of constitutional morality. It held that privacy is a natural right that inheres in all natural persons and is part of fundamental freedoms enshrined under Part III of the Indian Constitution.

The judgment came at a time when an invasive state, a domineering society, and intrusive businesses were regularly confronting individuals. The court emphasized privacy as a necessary condition for "seclusion", which in turn enables the exercise of freedoms like speech, expression, and association. The Supreme Court overruled verdicts given in the M.P. Sharma case in 1958, and the Kharak Singh case in 1961, both of which said that the Indian constitution does not have a right to privacy is.

The challenges and concerns before the Supreme Court had agitated the clairvoyant minds of some of the founding fathers of the constitutions, even though digitization was inconceivable in those days. Yet, the vast possibilities of the human mind and creativity were already becoming evident.

But more importantly, even after three years of the judgment in 'K.S. Puttaswamy', we hardly see rights-based handling of personal data. The judgment affected little change in the government's thinking or practice. It has continued to commission and execute mass surveillance programs.

The candidness of Supreme Court

The Supreme Court has been very candid in its observations on the pervasive scope of the Right to Privacy in the Puttaswamy case. The contention that the right to privacy should be subordinate to the economic needs of poverty did not favour the Supreme Court, which held for the first time that there is a fundamental right to privacy in India.

The response of Justice Chandrachud, who delivered the Plurality Opinion, is epochal: "The refrain that the poor need no civil and political rights and are concerned only with economic well-being has been utilized through history to wreak the most egregious violations of human rights.... The pursuit of happiness rests on autonomy and dignity. Both are essential attributes of privacy which makes no distinction between the birthmarks of individuals."

5. THE ANATOMY OF A CONSTITUTION

As the clock struck 11 am on December 9, 1946, the story of India's constitution-making goes, the Constituent Assembly convened for the first time in Constitution Hall, New Delhi, to begin the enormous task of framing a Constitution for the soon-to-be-independent India. After three years of debates, spread over 5,546 pages, the so-called founding fathers and mothers produced a constitution on a grand scale, unprecedented in terms of its territory, population size, and demographic complexity. At the time, the Constitution of India, adopted in the Constituent Assembly on November 26, 1949, was the foundational law of the land that provided the essential moorings for the basic structure and principles of governance. It also establishes a framework for an enlightened social contract that lays down the fundamental rights and duties of citizens. The contract also provides a charter for inclusive development on the principle that no one should be left behind and a framework for a rule of law-based

A constitution is a compilation of the rules and practices that determine the composition and functions of the organs of central and local government in a state and regulate the relationship between the individual and the state. Most states have a written constitution, one of the fundamental provisions of which is that it can itself be amended only in accordance with a special procedure. The constitution of the UK is largely unwritten. It consists partly of statutes, for the amendment of which by subsequent statutes no special procedure is required (see Act of Parliament), but also, to a very significant extent, of standard law rules and constitutional conventions. The Indian Constitution is one of the world's longest and most important political texts. Its birth, over six decades ago, signalled the arrival of the first paramount post-colonial constitution and the world's largest and arguably most daring democratic experiment. Apart from greater domestic focus on the Constitution and the institutional role of the Supreme Court within India's democratic framework, recent years have also witnessed enormous comparative interest in India's constitutional experiment.

The ideology of the Indian constitution

There has been a lot of discussion about the Constitution of India, but seldom have we tried to delve into its origin, which dates much before November 26, 1949, when it was formally adopted. The foundation of our Constitution was laid down on December 13, 1946, well before India even got its independence.

The Constituent Assembly had a meeting chaired by Dr Rajendra Prasad in the Constitution Hall in New Delhi. During this meeting, Jawaharlal Nehru tabled a resolution, which was known as the 'Objective Resolution'. This resolution intended to set up guidelines for the Constitution and give a direction to the way the country would progress. The most critical points of this Objective Resolution were:

- All power and authority of the Sovereign Independent India, its constituent parts and organs of government emerge from the people.
- Shall be guaranteed and secured to all the people of India justice, social, economic and political; equality of status, of opportunity, and before the law; freedom of thought, expression, belief, faith worship, vocation, association and action, subject to law and public morality
- Adequate safeguards shall be provided for minorities, backward and tribal areas, and depressed and other backward classes,

The Constituent Assembly accepted this Objective Resolution, and points mentioned in the resolution became the "Basic Principles of the Indian Constitution". Socialism, Secularism, Democracy, Justice, Liberty,

Equality and Fraternity are the foundations of the Constitution and not merely words in the preamble.

The Constitution has been amended more than 100 times, and these basic principles have remained intact. Whenever they interfered with the basic structure, the Supreme Court struck down such an amendment.

The framing of India's constitution was a critical event in the global history of both constitution-making and democracy. Conventionally, it is a founding moment. Its success against multiple odds was a result of a vision and consensus among the elite over what would become a pedagogical text for an 'ignorant' and undemocratic public. This focus among academics on political elites and an underlying assumption that constitutional details were beyond the public's imagination limited the scope of investigations primarily to the Constituent Assembly debates. By directing the inquiry away from these debates towards hitherto unstudied documents, this article offers a paradigm shift in the method of research and understanding of India's constitution-making. It explores the constitution as it emerged from beyond the Constituent Assembly through engagement with its making among diverse publics. In doing so, it shows that the Indian constitution was not simply founded and granted from above but came about through many more minor acts of assembly away from the Constitution Hall. It was the public who set normative expectations and tried to educate the members of the Constituent Assembly, and this was critical for the constitution's future reception and endurance. The Supreme Court sits at the apex of the integrated federal judiciary in India, comprising the High Courts in the states, district courts, and subordinate courts. In the hierarchy of this general judiciary dealing with all kinds of civil, criminal, and family law cases (excepting courts-martial or military courts dealing with members of the armed forces subject to military laws), only the High Courts and the Supreme Court are also constitutional courts empowered to adjudicate disputes arising out of the fundamental rights of citizens, Article 21 of the Constitution of India states that "No person shall be deprived of his life and personal liberty except according to the procedure established by law." A perusal of the Constituent Assembly Debates on Article 21 (Article 15 of the Draft Constitution) would show that the debate around the Article focused on "procedure established by law" irrespective of the substitution of the words "due process of law".

Architects of the Indian Constitution

The Constitution was the product of the efforts of several political leaders, judges, civil servants, and other drafters. I believe we do a disservice to them by forgetting or not acknowledging the role they played. The Indian Constitution has no one 'architect' but instead has many 'architects' who played a significant role in envisioning, drafting, and creating the document. I pay homage to some of them here.

First, we cannot forget the significant role played by Pandit Jawaharlal Nehru in our freedom struggle and the constitution-making process. In our current political climate, there are severe attempts to belittle Nehru's contribution to India, but one cannot change history. Nehru was responsible for setting the agenda of the Constituent Assembly. On 13 December 1946, he moved the Objectives Resolution, which laid down the guiding principles and objectives on which the Constitution was to be framed. The Preamble of our Constitution bears a resemblance to Nehru's Resolution. Nehru also chaired significant committees like the States Committee, Union Powers Committee and Union Constitution Committee, and hence, informed the content of the provisions they recommended. He also participated in key debates, and often, his position on an issue was the final word.

Second, Sardar Patel played an equal role in the constitution-making process. He chaired the Provincial Constitution Committee and the Advisory Committee (including Committees on Fundamental Rights and Minority Rights). Given his stature in Congress, he shaped the party's position on many contentious issues. T.T. Krishnamachari, a member of the Drafting Committee, called Nehru and Patel 'the real architects of the Constitution' in the Constituent Assembly. Similarly, President Rajendra Prasad, in his closing remarks, credited them for envisioning the 'fundamentals of the Constitution'. In fact, in addition to Nehru and Patel, Rajendra Prasad and Maulana Abul Kalam Azad played a significant role as well.

Third, Sir BN Rau, the Advisor to the Assembly. The first draft of the Constitution had actually prepared the draft that the Drafting Committee worked on and improved. However, Rau's role was not limited to mere drafting. He ensured that the debates in the Assembly were well-informed and reasoned. To that effect, he prepared a series of pamphlets titled 'Constitutional Precedents', which contained key features of the new Constitution for the use of the members of the Assembly. In the process of drafting the Constitution, Hence Rau was the apparent choice for deputation to other countries for further exploration. As a result, Rau met the Chief Justice of the United States Supreme Court, Former Chief Justice Hughes, Justice Frankfurter, Justice Thorsen (President of the Exchequer Court), Justice Learned Hand etc. In fact, Justice Frankfurter was so pleased after meeting Rau that he remarked to the then Secretary General of the Ministry of External Affairs, "If the President of U.S.A. were to ask me to recommend a Judge for our Supreme Court on the strength of his knowledge of the history and working of the American Constitution, B.N. Rau would be the first on my list."

Rau was the unsung hero who kept the Assembly running, but unfortunately, he never got his due amidst the stalwarts he was surrounded by. Another such name is Shri SN Mukherjee (Joint Secretary of the Drafting Committee), who Ambedkar himself called the Chief Draftsman of the Constitution. The Drafting Committee also consisted of Alladi Krishnaswamy Ayyar, N. Gopalaswamy Ayyangar, KM Munshi, TT Krishnamachari, N Madhav Rau and Mohammed

Sadullah, who, together as a team with Dr. Ambedkar as the Captain, produced the draft of the Constitution.

In the matter of direct e; election of the President, The difficulty with all those who advocated direct election of the President was their utter confusion as to the actual position of the President in the new Constitution or as to the true nature of the Constitution itself. Mahomed Isherif, who made the same plea, thought that "the President would be at the helm of affairs^and to whom so many powers would b4 given and so many responsibilities". Syed Kazi Karimuddin even advocated a non-parliamentary executive for the sake of having a strong President, "a man who will represent the entire nation on the all-India economic basis or all-India issues".^ K. T. Shah persisted with the demand of the popular election of the President when the DraftConstitution was being adopted in the Constituent Assembly. It is far from clear as to what K. T. Shah thought of the Indian President. He had moved an amendment seeking to describe the President as the Chief Executive and Head of the State. He wanted the President "to be the head of the Stale and representative of the people in their collective capacity and their sovereignty", "no mere gramophone of the Prime Minister"^functioning "only in an emergency";

The ideology of the Indian constitution

since it entered into force seventy years ago on January 26, 1950, the Indian Constitution has become one of the main reference points of comparative constitutional law scholars not only in Asia but also in the rest of the world. It has given rise to a vibrant constitutional culture which is unique in the regional context and in terms of impact and resilience resume-

bless the more stable constitutional democracies in the Indian Constitution, which is one of the world's longest and most important political texts. Its birth, over six decades ago, signalled the arrival of the first primary post-colonial constitution and the world's largest and arguably most daring democratic experiment. Apart from greater domestic focus on the Constitution and the institutional role of the Supreme Court within India's democratic framework, recent years have also witnessed enormous comparative interest in India's constitutional experiment.

The historical commitment to the idea of constitutionalism and how the framers understood India's constitutional project began with an overview of the concept of 'constitutional morality' as it relates to the Indian Constitution, along with the cosmopolitan character of Indian constitutionalism. It then considers some of the tensions that have characterised constitutional law in India, with particular emphasis on some of the sources of these tensions, such as the debate between centralisation and decentralisation. It also discusses the significant axes around which the normative and institutional imagination of the Indian Constitution is articulated and concludes by analysing the character of constitutional development in India and paying attention to the forces that have shaped its evolution.

Kazi's endeavour for privacy

Kazi Syed Karimuddin moved an amendment to include the right of the people to be secure in their persons, houses, papers, and effects against unreasonable searches and seizures in Article 20 (Draft Article 14) of the Constitution.

We can only re-emphasize, at the cost of an overstatement, that functional anonymity is as valuable in commerce as in speech. The next attempt at recognizing privacy came from Pandit Thakur Das Bhargava. He moved an amendment to add a new article after Article 15, which said: 'No person shall be subjected to unnecessary restraints or unreasonable search of person or property'.

To record the words of B.N Rau, the Constitutional Advisor to the Constituent Assembly, "The courts, operated by an irremovable judiciary not so sensitive to public needs in the social or economic sphere as the representatives of a periodically elected legislature, will, in effect, have a veto on legislation exercisable at any time and at the instance of any litigant."Ambedkar put forward the conflict in the Constituent Assembly in a simple manner, one that gave the drafting committee a choice between two alternatives. The first, where the Legislature was trusted with the power of making laws which did not abrogate the fundamental rights of an individual and would have to stand the test of constitutionality alone by the Judiciary, and the second, where the Judiciary was not only empowered to question a law as being beyond the scope of authority of the Legislature but also whether it was good law. There is no doubt that the framers of the Constitution chose the latter option, where the court was empowered to assess whether the law was good.

The various dilemmas in constitution-making

Constitution-making in deeply divided societies—where the transaction cost of securing consensus over key decisions is exceptionally high—poses a dilemma. On the one hand, the usual aspiration to create an enduring constitution demands a broad consensus over its contents. On the other hand, its very potential endurance signals to groups that believe they have lost out in the constitutional negotiation that their loss might be permanent, encouraging intransigence.. This literature treats constitution-making as an elite-driven process of interest-bargaining, where the minority group seeks political insurance in the form of power-sharing arrangements, decisional vetoes, or legal disabilities on majoritarian decision-making. Ethnocultural minorities are not, however, the only groups threatened by liberal democratic constitutions.

While liberal constitutions tend to provide the widest latitude to future governments of different ideological make-ups, certain ideological groups— especially those whose political agendas sit uncomfortably with the liberal commitment to individual human rights—also have reasons to withhold consent. These groups typically care about religious or economic ideologies (religious establishment, state socialism, etc.), which often concern the very identity of the State itself. The distinction between ideological and ethnocultural groups is, admittedly, not entirely neat, but it is nonetheless a helpful heuristic. In this article, I will show that (i) the accommodational needs of ideological dissenters are different from those of ethnocultural minorities and (ii) one of the ways to secure their consent for a broadly liberal democratic constitution while also keeping their ideological opponents on board is the contained and instrumentalized one expressive accommodation of their ideological agenda in the form of constitutional "directive principles."

The Constitution of India provides numerous rights to its citizens, some of which talk about the rights of minorities. The founding father of the Constitution tried to satisfy the hopes, aspirations and desires of the minority by safeguarding their educational rights of the minority.

The preamble of the Constitution itself talks about the purpose of framing the Constitution and its secure justice- social, economic, and political- providing liberty of thought and worship and equality in status to secure the unity and integrity of India. Due to this reason, the framers of the Indian Constitution incorporated various provisions in the Constitution, such as fundamental rights, as well as other places of the Constitution.

The rights of minorities are well defined under the Constitution of India, but who constitutes a minority is not defined anywhere under the Constitution. As the Supreme Court of India is working as a final Interpreter of the Constitution under this power, the Court has provided its views on defining the term minorities and the rights of minorities as well.

According to Mahatma Gandhi, "The claim of a country to civilization depends on the treatment it extends to the minorities". The Constitution maker was aware of that, so it provided adequate provisions for safeguarding the status of minorities.

The Constitution of India provides 6 Fundamental Rights to its citizens and some rights to non-citizens as well—some of them talk about minorities' rights.

The founders of the Constitution tried to satisfy the hopes, aspirations, and land desires of the minority by safeguarding their educational rights. At the fifth session of

the Constituent Assembly of India, The Chairman (TheHonorable Dr Rajendra Prasad) [1] assured the minorities that:

"To all the minorities in India, we give the assurance that they will receive fair and just treatment, and there will be no discrimination against them. The religion, their culture, and their language are safe, and they will enjoy all the rights and privileges of citizenship. They will be expected, in turn, to render loyalty to the country in which they live and its constitution. To all, we give the assurance that we will endeavour to end poverty and squalor and companions, hunger and disease, to abolish distinction and exploitation and to ensure the decent condition of living".

Definition of Minorities

The rights of minorities are well defined under the Constitution of India, but who constitutes a minority is not defined anywhere under the Constitution. As the Supreme Court of India is working as a final Interpreter of the Constitution under this power

1 C.A. Deb, Vol 5, P-2

The court held that if a community is less than 50% in a particular region, it is to be considered a "minority". So, according to that, Christians, Muslims and Anglo Indians would be minorities in Kerela. However, the problem arises: a community may be minor in a particular area but not in other places. This issue was further discussed in the TMA Pai Foundation case [3], and clarified that minorities for Article 30 could not have different meanings depending upon who was legislating the minority status, i.e. Union or State.

In Bal Patil v Union of India [4], it was held that the identification of a community as a minority has to be done on a state basis and not an Indian basis. It was observed that the word minority had not been defined in Articles 29 & 30 of the Constitution. Still, from the Preamble and Art.25 to 30, it is clear that it refers to an identifiable group of people who require protection from likely deprivation of their religious, cultural, and educational rights by the community, which are in the majority.

The U.N Sub -Commission on Prevention of Discrimination Minorities has defined minority as the:

1. The term "minority" includes only those non–document groups of the population which possess and wish to preserve stable ethnic, religious or linguistic traditions and characteristics markedly different from those of the rest of the population;
2. Such minorities should adequately include the number of persons sufficient by themselves to preserve such traditions or characteristics and
3. Such minorities should be loyal to the state of which they are nationals.

In the case of Maneka Gandhi v Union of India [Justice Bhagvati said- these Fundamental rights represent the essential value cherished by the citizens of India since the Vedic times. Fundamental rights protect the dignity of individuals. These rights are regarded as basic because they are essential to the individual to live a life with full dignity. The object behind the inclusion of Part III is to establish a "Government of Law or Law and not of Man.

- Article 14 of the Indian Constitution: The state shall not deny, to any person, equality before law or equal protection of law within the territory of India. The concept of equality does not mean absolute equality. It is a concept that provides the absence of any special privilege by reason of birth, creed, etc., in favour of individuals.

- Article 15 (1) directs the State not to discriminate against citizens on grounds only of religion, race, caste, sex, and place of birth or any of them.§ Article 15 (2) prohibits citizens as well as the State from making such discrimination with regard to access to shops, hotels and all the places of public entertainment, public resorts, wells, tanks, roads, etc. It is to be noted that while clause (1) prohibits discrimination by the States, clause (2) prohibits both States as well as individuals.

The Constitution of India, adopted in the Constituent Assembly on November 26, 1949, is the foundational law of the land that provides the essential moorings for the basic structure and principles of governance. It also establishes a framework for an enlightened social contract that lays down the fundamental rights and duties of citizens. The contract also provides a charter for inclusive development on the principle that no one should be left behind and a framework for a rule of law-based polity whose scaffoldings are the principles of equity and fairness. The founding fathers and the founding mothers of our Constitution bequeathed to us an extraordinary document — an embodiment of the hopes, dreams, and aspirations of a nation at the dawn of independence from foreign rule. The 75th anniversary of our Constitution is a fitting occasion to recognize the role played by countless Indians, who considered it their right and moral duty to engage with the Constituent Assembly and present their dreams and opinions about the future of the nation and the form and substance of its governance model through petitions and representations. The Constitution that we revere and hold sacred is as much a product of this engagement of the familiar people as the learned debates in the Central Hall of Samvidhan Sadan. The words of BR Ambedkar placed the importance and essence of this sacred document in perspective when he remarked that "The Constitution is not a mere lawyer's document; it is a vehicle of life, reflecting the spirit of the age."

The framers of the Indian Constitution, in their profound wisdom, crafted a monumental document with 395 Articles, 22 Parts, and eight Schedules. This intricate framework sought to provide clarity on governance and accountability while accommodating the cultural, linguistic, and regional diversity of the nation.

Yet, even the most meticulously designed document could not foresee every eventuality. Anticipating the need for adaptability, the framers deliberately left room for flexibility and interpretation, allowing the Constitution to evolve with changing times.

However, this inherent dynamism also carries risks. As Professor Upendra Baxi insightfully observes, "Constitutional silences are made to speak in the name of the people," underscoring these unarticulated gaps filled with interpretations that may diverge from the democratic ethos. Ambedkar, the principal architect of the Constitution, poignantly warned, "However good a Constitution may be, if those who are implementing it are not good, it will prove to be bad. However bad a Constitution may be, if those implementing it are good, it will prove to be good." This enduring truth serves as a reminder that the strength of any constitution lies not just in its text but in the integrity and intent of those who wield its provisions. The challenge lies in ensuring that the spaces left for evolution to strengthen democracy, not to undermine it.

Pocket vetoes

One of the most pressing examples of constitutional silence in recent times is evident in the functioning of state governors under Article 200. This article grants governors the authority to grant or withhold assent to bills passed by the state legislatures, return them for reconsideration, or reserve them for the president's consideration. The provision is a testament to the intricate checks and balances built into the Constitution.

However, it does not specify a timeline within which governors must act on these bills. This lack of a timeframe has led to a troubling practice of indefinite delays, or what has come to be known as 'pocket vetoes'.

Governors, often appointed by the ruling party at the centre, have increasingly used this silence as a tool to obstruct state governments led by opposition parties. Tamil Nadu, Kerala, and West Bengal are among the states that have faced significant delays in securing gubernatorial assent for critical legislation. The Tamil Nadu Prohibition of Online Gambling Bill is a case in point. Despite being rooted in public demand and addressing pressing social issues, the bill was subjected to prolonged delays, undermining the legislative process and the will of the electorate.

These delays raise fundamental questions about federalism, democracy, and accountability. India's federal structure envisions a delicate balance between the Union government and the states. The indefinite withholding of assent by governors disturbs this equilibrium, reducing elected state governments to subordinate entities. This practice directly undermines the principle of representative democracy, where laws passed by legislatures are presumed to reflect the collective will of the people.

The judiciary has intervened to address these constitutional silences on several occasions. In Purushothaman Nambudiri v. State of Kerala and Shamsher Singh vs State of Punjab cases, the Supreme Court upheld the discretionary powers of governors under Article 200. Still, it emphasized that India operates under a Cabinet system of government. Governors, therefore, must act on the advice of the council of ministers, serving as constitutional figureheads rather than independent authorities.

More recently, in a case involving the Punjab governor, the Supreme Court offered a progressive interpretation, asserting that governors "cannot be at liberty to keep bills pending indefinitely." By reading "as soon as possible" into the provisions of Article 200, the court sought to curb the misuse of this constitutional silence. The judgment also emphasized the role of governors as constitutional statesmen tasked with upholding the Constitution rather than obstructing governance.

Ambiguous terms are a potential tool for interference

Article 201, which deals with bills reserved for the president's consideration, suffers from a similar lack of specificity. While state legislatures are bound to respond to bills returned by the president within six months, the Constitution imposes no such timeline on the president. This asymmetry effectively grants the Union government the power to stall legislation indefinitely.

As the clock struck 11 am on December 9, 1946, the story of India's constitution-making goes, the Constituent Assembly convened for the first time in Constitution Hall, New Delhi, to begin the enormous task of framing a Constitution for the soon-to-be-independent India. After three years of debates, spread over 5,546 pages, the so-called founding fathers and mothers produced a constitution on a grand scale, unprecedented in terms of its territory, population size, and demographic complexity. At the time, the Constitution of India, adopted in the Constituent Assembly on November 26, 1949, is the foundational law of the land that provides the essential moorings for the basic structure and principles of governance. It also establishes a framework for an enlightened social contract that lays down the fundamental rights and duties of citizens. The contract also provides a charter for inclusive development on the principle that no one should be left behind and a framework for a rule of law-based

While liberal constitutions tend to provide the widest latitude to future governments of different ideological make-ups, certain ideological groups— especially those whose political agendas sit uncomfortably with the liberal commitment to individual human rights—also have reasons to withhold consent. These groups typically care about religious or economic ideologies (religious establishment, state socialism, etc.), which often concern the very identity of the State itself. The distinction between ideological and ethnocultural groups is, admittedly, not entirely neat, but it is nonetheless a helpful heuristic. In this article, I will show that (i) the accommodational needs of ideological dissenters are different from those of ethnocultural minorities and (ii) one of the ways to secure their consent for a broadly liberal democratic constitution while also keeping their ideological opponents on board is the contained and instrumentalized one expressive accommodation of their ideological agenda in the form of constitutional "directive principles."

The issue of ambiguity extends further to Article 356, which empowers the President to impose President's Rule in a state on the recommendation of the governor or "otherwise." The term "otherwise" has been a source of controversy, allowing for discretionary and, at times, arbitrary decisions. During the politically turbulent decades of the 1970s and 1980s, This provision invoked often to dissolve opposition-ruled state governments, often on tenuous grounds. While judicial scrutiny has curtailed the misuse of Article 356 in recent years, the ambiguity surrounding the term "otherwise" remains a potential tool for political interference.

Such practices reveal the darker implications of constitutional silences and enable executive overreach. Moreover, these silences erode public trust in democratic institutions. When an elected government's decisions are blocked or delayed without justification, it creates a perception of governance paralysis and fuels disillusionment among citizens.

Definition of Minorities

The rights of minorities are well defined under the Constitution of India, but who constitutes a minority is not defined anywhere under the Constitution. As the Supreme Court of India is working as a final Interpreter of the Constitution under this power

1 C.A. Deb, Vol 5, P-2

The court held that if a community is less than 50% in a particular region, it be considered a "minority". So, according to that, Christians, Muslims, and Anglo Indians would be minorities in Kerela. However, the problem arises: a community may be minor in a particular area but not in other places. This issue was further discussed in the TMA Pai Foundation case, where it was clarified that minorities for Article 30 could not have different meanings depending upon who was legislating their minority status, i.e. Union or State.

In Bal Patil v Union of India, the identification of a community as a minority is to be on a state basis and not an Indian basis. The word minority has not to be defined in Articles 29 & 30 of the constitution. Still, from the Preamble and Art.25 to 30, it is clear that it refers to an identifiable group of people who require protection from likely deprivation of their religious, cultural, and educational rights by the community, which is the majority.

The U.N Commission on Prevention of Discrimination Minorities has defined minority as under:

1. The term "minority" includes only those non–document groups of the population that possess and wish to preserve stable ethnic, religious, or linguistic traditions and characteristics markedly different from those of the rest of the population;
2. Such minorities should adequately include the number of persons sufficient by themselves to preserve such traditions or characteristics and
3. Such minorities should be loyal to the state of which they are nationals.

In the case of Maneka Gandhi v Union of India - Justice Bhagvati Said- these Fundamental rights represent the essential value cherished by the citizens of India since the Vedic times. Fundamental rights aim to protect the dignity of individuals. These rights are regarded as fundamental because they are essential to the individual to live a life with full dignity. The object behind the inclusion of Part III is to establish a "Government of Law and not of Man. Article 14 of the Indian Constitution: The state shall not deny any person equality before the law or equal protection of the law within the territory of India. The concept of equality does not mean absolute equality. It is a concept that provides

the absence of any special privilege because of birth, creed, etc, in favour of individuals. Article 15 directs the State not to discriminate against a citizen on the grounds only of religion, race, caste, sex, and place of birth or any of them. Article 15 prohibits citizens as well as the State from making such discrimination with regard to access to shops, hotels, all places of public entertainment, public resorts, wells, tanks, roads, etc. In contrast, the clause prohibits discrimination by the States. The clause prohibits both the State and individuals. The object of Art 15 is to eradicate the abuse of HinSocial Syste Article 15 enables the State to make special provisions for the protection of the interests of the Socially Educationally backward classes of citizens.

The Evolution of the Indian Constitution

The Constituent Assembly sat for the first time on 9th December 1946. Over the next 2 years and 11 months, the Assembly sat for a total of 167 days to frame the Indian Constitution. The final session of the Constituent Assembly took place on 24th January 1950. The Indian Constitution is unique in both spirit and content. Notwithstanding the fact that several features of the Constitution are from other constitutions of the world, it is really a unique piece of work. The original Constitution has been considerably by various amendments, such as the 7th, 42nd, 44th, 73rd, and 74th Amendments.

The literature on constitutional breakdown in India is now widespread, but the precise nature of the breakdown remains understudied.

This presentation will focus on the breakdown by thinking about the nature of the Indian state and the way in which its rise is closely linked to its capacity to modulate itself according to different preferences. Crucial to this understanding is appreciating the longer-run anomalies that have shaped the construction of state power in India. A turn to the nature of state power helps us grasp the distinct nature of the present constitutional transformation in India. There may be lessons regarding democratic strain in other polities.

Essential amendments of the Constitution of India

The Indian Constitution is not rigid. It can be amended by the Parliament following a few rules. The Constitution of India has changed. Some of the significant amendments to the Indian Constitution are:

1. 42nd Amendment
2. 44th Amendment

The 42nd Amendment is also known as the "Mini Constitution" because it made several sweeping changes to the Constitution. This was during the Emergency in 1976. In 1973, the Supreme Court ruled in the Kesavananda Bharati case that the constituent power of the Parliament under Article 368 does not empower it to alter the basic structure of the Constitution.

Constitution of India – Preamble

The first Constitution to start with a preamble was the American Constitution. The Indian Constitution also begins with one. The Preamble is basically the introduction or preface to the Constitution. It sums up the essence of the Constitution. N A Palkhivala, a constitutional expert, referred to the Preamble as the 'Identity card of the Constitution.

The Preamble rets on Pandit Nehru's Objective Resolution, which he moved and secured the approval of the Constituent Assembly.

The Preamble was amended in 1976 by the 42nd Amendment, which added the words 'socialist', 'secular' and 'integrity' to it.

Ingredients of the Preamble

The Preamble has four components:

1. Source of authority of the Constitution: it mentions that the Constitution derives its power from the people of India.
2. Nature of the Indian State: it says India is a sovereign, socialist, secular, democratic and republican State.
3. Objectives of the Constitution: It gives the objectives of justice, liberty, equality, and fraternity.
4. Constitution date of adoption: 26th November 1949

Why is the Constitution of India called Bag of Borrowing?

The Constitution has many borrowed features. The country's founders were wise enough to borrow good features from different nations and mould a constitution that best suits India. The influences from other constitutions are listed below.

The chief features of the Indian Constitution,

Federal System with Unitary Bias

The Constitution establishes a federal government system in India. All the expected features of a federal state, such as two government levels, division of power, supremacy and rigidity of the Constitution, written Constitution and bicameralism, are present. But, the Constitution also contains many features of a unitary form of government such as single citizenship, intense Centre, single Constitution, flexibility of Constitution, all-India services, integrated judiciary, appointment of state governor by the Centre, emergency provisions, and so on. In addition, the term 'federation' is not mentioned in the Constitution. Article 1 says India is a 'Union of States', implying –

1. The Indian Federation was not the result of an agreement between the states.
2. States do not have the right to secede from the federation.

Parliamentary Form of Government

The parliamentary form, borrowed from the British system, is based on the principle of cooperation and coordination between the legislative and executive. This form of government is alternatively known as the Westminster model of government. It is also called responsible government and cabinet government. According to the Constitution, not only the Centre but also the parliamentary form is followed even in the states.

In India, the features of the parliamentary form of government are as follows:

1. Nominal and real executives
2. Rule of the majority party
3. Collective responsibility of the executive to the legislature
4. Membership of the ministers in the legislature
5. The leadership of the prime minister or the chief minister
6. Dissolution of the Lower House

There are some fundamental differences between the Indian and the British models, even though both follow the parliamentary form of government. The Indian Parliament is not a sovereign body; the British Parliament is. Also, the Indian State has an elected head (since it is a republic), while the British head is hereditary (since Britain is a constitutional monarchy).

Parliament: Structural and Functional Dimensions

1. According to Article 79, there is a Parliament and 2 Houses or chambers – the House of the People (Lok Sabha) and the Council of States (Rajya Sabha).

2. The President is the head of the executive branch and a constituent part of the legislature. He performs many functions for the Parliament.
3. However, the President cannot sit in or take part in the discussions in the houses.
4. The President summons and prorogues the houses whenever required.
5. He is also a vital part of the process of legislation in India, as he has to give his assent to every bill passed before it can become law.
6. He has the power to dissolve the Lok Sabha.
7. At the start of the first session after each general election to the Lok Sabha and at the commencement of the first session each year, the President addresses both chambers, which is known as the unique address.
8. Article 123 also gives the President the power to promulgate ordinances.

6. THE CONSTITUTION ON MINORITY RIGHTS

Minorities form an essential fabric of the cultural diversity of India, which is a multi-religious and multi-lingual country. While innumerable references to minorities exist, there is no generally accepted definition of the term "minority" in international legal instruments. The word "minority" is also not defined in the Indian Constitution but has been divided into religious and linguistic minorities. During the colonial period, minorities were referred to as 'depressed classes' and measured based on religion, untouchability and tribes. Still, after the Independence of India, the partition of British India played a crucial role in shaping the discourse on the majority-minority and the new criteria to describe minorities was based on numerical status and cultural identity. The framers of the Constitution of India were acquainted with the complex character of the problems of minorities.

Throughout the history of international law, examples of protective treaties concluded for the benefit of minority groups, often on the basis of some bond of religion, nationality, or culture between the protecting power and the protected minority. The most notable example was the inter-governmental system of the League of Nations. In the aftermath of the First World War, the new and greatly enlarged states of Central and Eastern Europe were under compulsion either to sign minority protection treaties or to guarantee various rights for their minority groups. The rights of minorities included not only the right to equality under the law but also specific cultural, educational and language rights. The League of Nations' scheme provided for the protection of certain minorities in certain States but did not recognise any general rights of minorities.

Absent treaty obligations and no duty to protect the distinctive identities of minority groups existed for states in international law.

India's law system is a legal pluralism that governs different religious communities by their laws. These laws cover issues such as marriage, divorce, maintenance, adoption, 00€inheritance, guardianship, and succession. €Each religious community in India has its law, including Hindu law, Muslim law, Christian law, Parsi law, and Jewish law. Personal laws in India were primarily enacted for Hindu and Muslim subjects. The British were concerned about opposition from community leaders and did not interfere much in this domestic sphere.

Minority rights and practices

The mainstream discourse on minority rights embodies a series of normative biases and assumptions which ignore the colonial underpinning of some of the core concepts, such as the definition of minority and the notion of minority protection. In this paper, I argue that contemporary minority rights discourse needs to engage closely with relations of power and subaltern agency to 'decolonise' conventional thinking within the discipline. I unpack this decolonising agenda and map out what such an agenda would entail by critically analysing five key areas of relevance: reconceptualising the minority to expose 'otherness' embedded in the concept; scrutinising the reification of the state as a prerequisite for decolonising minority rights discourse; mainstreaming subaltern resistance; reevaluating a priori assumptions about the need for legal interventions; and finally, taking seriously the political economy of neo-colonial violence. Thus, the paper offers a framework for systematically thinking about decolonial promises of minority rights discourse. Why has American democracy come so close to a breaking point while other Western democracies appear more stable? In this sobering study, Levitsky and Ziblatt blame the United States' eighteenth-century constitutional order for its modern democratic woes. Those who have refrained from embracing this order thwart the will of an expanding multicultural majority in favour of a shrinking rural white minority. The drafters of the U.S. Constitution worried that the significant threat to democracy was "the tyranny of the majority," so they devised necessary counter-majoritarian instruments, such as an independent judiciary and the Bill of Rights.

Many of these constitutional innovations are essential for the preservation of democracy, but others are more worrisome. The electoral college system allows the candidate who receives fewer votes to win the presidency. The U.S. Senate overrepresents less populated states, and the filibuster requires a supermajority of 60 votes to pass legislation. The result is that majorities often cannot gain power, and if they do, they find it hard to govern. Levitsky and Ziblatt show that this paralyzing majoritarian rule makes the United States unique among its peer democracies. Germany and the United Kingdom have reformed their upper chambers to make them more representative of the population. Other democracies, with constitutions modelled on the United States, have abolished indirect voting and the lifetime tenure of judges.

Kazi Karimuddin's fight for minority rights

Kazi had anticipated the upcoming communal frenzy in sensitive Muslim regions in the aftermath of the Partition. He didn't remain a silent spectator, and the body introduced seers legislates in the Constituent Assembly that protect vulnerable sections of Muslims. The law against such search and seizure of individuals without due o=procwess is his architecture. It is a different matter that despite these laws, the ground realities have remained unfulfilled, and Muslims continue to remain insecure. Given that there are thousands of civil rights lawsuits each year, it might seem counterintuitive that the sheer unavailability of affordable lawyers is a significant barrier.

In most cases, these ordinary citizens became offenders on concocted grounds and could not afford a lawyer to defend their innocence. They couldn't protect themselves against unfair legal devices. A narrow-minded adherence to a particular sect (political, ethnic, or religious) often leads to conflict with those of different sects or possessing different beliefs. Sectarian conflicts are usually breeding grounds for acts of terrorism and the formation of terrorist groups.

Communalism has been an essential theme in Indian politics since the 1880s. During the first three decades after independence, even after the Partition of the subcontinent into India and Pakistan in 1947, no political force gained substantial power in the name of Hinduism. Since the mid-1980s, there has been a resurgence of a belligerent and new kind of Hindu nationalism in India's public life and its political institutions. In the main, the Hindu nationalist movement has defined itself in opposition to Islam and Muslims. Hindu revivalists have promoted a claim that the Muslim minority in India threatens Hindus and have sought to establish India as a primarily Hindu nation (*rashtra*) based on a notion of Hindu ethos, values and religion. The ideology and politics of *Hindutva* – the quality of being a Hindu – were accompanied by a rapid increase in large-scale communal (Hindu–Muslim) riots in the 1980s and 1990s. Significant communal violence spread throughout India in 1990 following the destruction of the Babri Masjid mosque at Ayodhya in 1992

Sectarian violence, common in India, impacts Muslims disproportionately. While often instrumentalized for political gains, communal violence and other forms of communal targeting draw on and exacerbate a climate of entrenched discrimination against India's religious minorities with far-reaching social, economic, cultural and political dimensions. Such violence has impunity and, in certain instances, direct complicity from state actors, ranging from inciting violence through hate speech to refusing to investigate communal incidents after they have occurred properly. This includes a significant number of state officials affiliated with the ruling BJP. Agents often ask outright if families are Muslim; landlords are reluctant to rent to them.

Kazi pointed out the rise of Hindu nationalism and the presence of organizations like the Rashtriya Swayamsevak Sangh (RSS). He underscored the historical failure of the first-past-the-post system to provide adequate representation to minorities, citing the example of South and West Ireland's lack of parliamentary representation from 1855 to 1911. Karimuddin claimed that proportional representation was profoundly democratic, and it brought people closer to "near equality" by not wasting anyone's vote. India's Muslim population, particularly the poorest sections, experience some of the most acute social marginalization of any community. This situation, reflected in their access to education, health and employment, is also driven by the limited enforcement of minority rights protections in India and the persistence of discriminatory provisions in the country's domestic law.

India's long argumentative tradition and tolerance of heterodoxy, going back thousands of years, have greatly helped democracy flourish with such ease. This would be remarkable enough for any underdeveloped country. Still, it was a much more challenging task in a land with many significant languages, each with a long and proud history, and rich and old India is passing through a dark era of sectarianism. One hopes that the worst will soon be over. We will emerge to a new prosperous dawn. For instance, the exclusion of Muslims (as well as Christians) from the officially recognized scheduled castes has meant that even the most impoverished of Indian Muslims have not been able to benefit from those affirmative action programmes in place. The limited and poorly funded minority rights structures in place in India at present have also come under increasing threat since the Bharatiya Janata Party (BJP) took power in 2014. Key institutions such as the Ministry of Minority Affairs and the National Commission of Minorities are now under threat. In some states, budgets for minority issues have suffered,

While significant differences exist between Hindus and Muslims in their religious, cultural and social outlook, in many cases, the religious divide may be only a contributing factor to intercommunal discord.

The leading causes of dissension and divisiveness are equally likely to be poverty, lack of access to resources, unemployment, illiteracy, and so on. Hindu extremist groups such as the Shiv Sena and the Rashtriya Swayamsevak Sangha (RSS) consider Muslims to be disloyal to the Indian State. On the other hand, Muslim extremist groups preach a militant Islam that argues for a separate way of life for Muslims.

There are occasions in the proceedings of the debate in the Constituent Assembly where Kazi Syedi Karimuddin made pertinent interventions. The first was in the discussion of Dradft Article 7.66.13, in which Kazi Syed Karimuddin argued that we have seen in 1947 and at the beginning of 1948 that hundreds of thousands of people were arrested and houses were searched merely on suspicion. The morale of the Muslim minority community was undermined, and they were treated just like criminals in their own country. He gave one significant instance. Whenever they went to an aerodrome to go to Delhi, their belongings were searched without any reason, without any cause, and without any warning. We will now give another instance. When there was police action in Hyderabad, every Muslim was arrested without any justification in the adjoining provinces as if those Muslims were really traitors. People who had nothing whatever to do with Hyderabad were arrested under the pretence of protective custody. If they were taken only under protective custody, why were their women and children who were outside not taken under this protective custody?

Several studies have found restrictions on minority faith-based communities to be related to the onset of violent religious hostilities. Absent from this work, though, is a consideration of the fact that minority religious discrimination can take different forms and, consequently, may encourage violence in various ways. This paper seeks to fill this void by examining other forms of minority religious restrictions and their relationship to religious violence. Specifically, we analyze the comparative strength of three basic types of religious discrimination—restrictions on minority religious *practices*, restrictions on minority religious *institutions*, and restrictions on *conversion and proselytizing*—on violence carried out by both religious majority groups and religious minority groups. Interestingly, our analysis shows all three forms of restrictions encourage violence from religious majorities but not from minorities.

Debates concerning integration and accommodation are a familiar feature of the domestic political life of many countries. However, these debates increasingly have an international dimension as well. Global organizations can strongly influence the way state–minority relations are framed and resolved, endorsing some models of accommodation while discouraging others. For those who have decided, these are not simple questions to answer. Many international organizations have struggled with this issue for the past fifteen years without any clear resolution, and their current policies and practices are full of ambiguitics and inconsistencies. The goal of this paper is to bring out some of these complexities, focusing mainly on how the rights of Indigenous peoples have enlarged at the United Nations and the way in which the rights of national minorities have received attention within European organizations. Very different assumptions and principles underlie the two cases. Each raises its own moral and political dilemmas.

Indian democracy, which was once considered remarkable in scale and duration, has been weakened by the rise of xenophobic nationalism and threats to religious minorities. Although these trends were evident in the past, they have dramatically increased amidst the growth of Hindu nationalism. The Bharatiya Janata Party (BJP), which came to power in 2014, has promoted or tolerated attacks on women, Dalits, Christians, and Muslims by members of its party, government, and civil society organizations. The BJP government has also centralized state power and curtailed civil rights and liberties. Clearly, the protection of democracy and religious freedoms are closely intertwined. India has proposed a Uniform Civil Code, which would apply personal laws equally to all citizens, regardless of religion. The Indian Constitution's Article 44 expects the state to use common law and directive principles for all citizens when formulating national policies.

Mutual consciousness should have grown if minorities were guaranteed liberty, equality, fraternity and justice. The House adopted a balancing approach to bring equality to society. The cultural and educational rights of the minorities became part of the Constitution of India to fulfil the demands of the Karachi Session and Cabinet Mission Plan of pre-partition India. It envisaged the preservation of religious and cultural minorities. The Constituent Assembly had a consensus to provide certain rights to religious and linguistic minorities in the Constitution of India. Still, it failed to provide political representation as a separate electoral and reservation in government employment on the basis of fulfilment of social backwardness criteria. Many Committees set up from time to time on minorities' issues have discussed the pathetic and miserable conditions of minorities on educational and social fronts candidly. Riots against religious minorities occurred from time to time, and the dominance of the Hindi language over regional languages reflected the vulnerability of minority rights to uphold their rights of linguistic and cultural identity in India. Post-independence, minorities in India got certain rights to preserve their linguistic and cultural identity. However, despite all the provisions in the Constitution and the right intentions of the Government, the situation of minorities is still deplorable. This paper presents the historical aspects of minorities' rights from the colonial period to the present times in India. It sheds light on some of the divergences with regard to the minorities in India. The paper also highlights the need to protect fundamental human rights and freedoms without any discrimination against minorities in existing circumstances and a requirement of positive support from the State in the preservation of their distinctive characteristics or partial or complete autonomy.

Secularisn, democracy, Equality and justice

The concepts of secularism, democracy, equality and justice, and national unity and development defined this legitimate vocabulary. Second, there was the assumption that the constitution-makers subscribed to a single notion of secularism or democracy, and different conceptions of these political ideals were at play in arguments about minority rights in the Constituent Assembly. Third, against dominant understandings of Indian political discourse, this Article emphasizes that different kinds of liberal norms were a crucial part of the legitimating vocabulary on minority safeguards.

Our knowledge of an important and neglected development in India's constitutional history, the withdrawal of political safeguards for religious minorities during the making of the Indian Constitution, is furthered by an analysis of the legitimating vocabulary on minority rights in the Constituent Assembly debates. The rights of minority groups in liberal democracies have been at the centre of the intellectual and political debates of the last decade. In India, one of the oldest and most extensive regimes of minority preference exists within the framework of a polity formally committed to liberal democratic norms. The Constituent Assembly debates mark a crucial turning point in the history of state policies of minority preference in India. Since the late nineteenth century, colonial states, as well as some princely states, extended special provisions for a vast array of groups designated as minorities or `backward'. During the deliberations of the Constituent Assembly, the framework of state policies that suited the interests of minorities changed. Under the Indian Constitution of 1950, preferential provisions in legislatures and government employment were restricted mainly to the Scheduled Castes and `backward' tribes. This paper focuses on the arguments about minority rights in the Indian Constituent Assembly. It examines the concepts and norms invoked in the arguments advanced for and against minority rights in these debates. During my analysis, I first show that arguments about different kinds of minority provisions, advanced from diverse political and ideological positions, employed a shared legitimating vocabulary. The concepts of secularism, democracy, equality and justice, and national unity and development defined this. The colonial State first introduced group representation provisions in central legislatures in the Morley-Minto Reforms of 1909, which granted separate electorates to Muslims. The Government of India Act of 1919 extended separate electorates to Sikhs, Indian Christians and Europeans. In the Government of India Act of 1935, a total of thirteen communal and functional groups got exceptional representation, and political ideals were at play in arguments about minority rights in the Constituent Assembly. Further, conceptions of secularism, democracy, and national unity were mutually interdependent, drawing upon each other for their connotations and normative force. Third, against dominant understandings of Indian political discourse, this paper shows that different kinds of liberal norms were a crucial part of the legitimating vocabulary on minority safeguards. Arguments about minority rights in the Constituent Assembly debates, while undoubtedly inflected by indigenous cultural and historical idioms, were underpinned by conventional liberal values such as those of religious freedom, equal individual rights and equality of opportunity. Finally, I argue that our understanding of an essential and forgotten political outcome, the withdrawal of political safeguards for religious minorities during the making of the Indian Constitution, is furthered by an analysis of the legitimating vocabulary on minority rights in the Constituent Assembly debates.

Debates concerning integration and accommodation are a familiar feature of the domestic political life of many countries. However, these debates increasingly have an international dimension as well. Global organizations can strongly influence the way State–minority relations are framed and resolved, endorsing some models of accommodation while discouraging others. c for these types of groups and in which contexts. These are not simple questions. Many global organizations have struggled with this issue for the past fifteen years without any clear resolution, and their current policies and practices are full of ambiguities and inconsistencies. The goal of this paper is to bring out some of these complexities, focusing mainly on how the rights of Indigenous peoples got their due at the United Nations and the way in which the rights of national minorities have been dialogued within European organizations. very different assumptions and principles underlie the two cases. Each raises its own moral and political dilemmas.

The Supreme Court has consistently maintained that minorities have no right to maladminister their institutions and that the Government can come up with reasonable regulations to insist on proper safeguards against maladministration, to maintain fair standards of teaching, and to ensure "excellence of the institutions." in St. Xavier (1974), the top court explicitly observed that "under the guise of *the* exclusive right of management, minorities cannot decline to follow the general pattern.

Ambedkar dreamt of a society based on modern liberal ideals of 'Liberty, Equality and Fraternity' throughout his life. To translate his dream into a reality, he strove harder to put 'Depressed Classes' under the 'Minority' category. While arguing in favour of his argument, he put forth the socio-economic status of Dalits before the Southborough Committee in 1919. After a long struggle, he was able to achieve constitutional safeguards for Dalits.

Ambedkar had roped all the principles into India's Constitution in the post-independence period to peaceful social revolution. However, after Independence, the protection of Dalits came under the Scheduled Castes category. Nonetheless, his epistemological origin and engagement with the minority as an 'idea' and creating favourable space within the democratic political structure has been still relevant. This Article has engaged with Ambedkar's idea of minorities and their political and economic welfare in a communal majoritarian polity.

The concept of minority rights

Ambedkar was a strong advocate for minority rights and made several notable statements on the subject:

- **Minority rights are absolute**

Ambedkar said that minority rights are absolute.

- **Social discrimination is the test of a minority.**

Ambedkar said that social discrimination is the best way to determine if a social group is a minority, not religious separation.

- **Minority rights in a parliamentary democracy**

Ambedkar said that in a parliamentary democracy, minorities should not be. He advised leaders to develop the art of persuasion and public speaking.

- **Democracy is incompatible with isolation.**

Ambedkar said that democracy is incompatible with isolation and exclusiveness.

- **Indian Nationalism and the divine right of the majority**

Ambedkar said that Indian nationalism has developed a doctrine of the divine right of the majority to rule over the minorities. He said that any claim by the minority to share power is interpreted as communalism, while the majority monopolizing power is called nationalism.

- **People should decide how society should be organised**

Ambedkar said that people should choose how society should be organised and that the Constitution should not take away this liberty.

To protect the minority from majoritarianism, Ambedkar suggested specific provisions mentioned in a memorandum to the Constituent Assembly on behalf of the All-India Scheduled Caste Federation. Ambedkar argued for protection against the communal executive, social/official tyranny and social boycott.

Contemporary Scenario

In the contemporary period, Indian politics has not aligned with Muslim issues. There are two dimensions to the debate—negative and positive. The rise of the Bharatiya Janata Party (BJP) into parliamentary politics and the establishment of social and political hegemonic dominance over every institution has impacted the Muslim issue. Right-wing social and political mobilizations are rooted in Muslims' history, present and future. The negative image of Muslims presented as an existential threat to Hindus seems to be an apparent modus operandi.

On the other hand, some individuals and organizations invoked secularism, the rights of minorities, sectarian violence, and institutions' failure to deliver to raise a concern of dwindling space for Muslims in Indian democracy. Going through the various Commissions' reports on Minority status, the latter group argued about the protection of Muslims through extraordinary measures. However, the former group termed it as a 'pseudo-secular' approach and 'appeasement'. The debate is still not settled. Nevertheless, consensus on Minority issues is ever elusive in Indian democracy and, since 2014, has tilted heavily toward the right-wing interpretation.

The amendment proposed by Kazi Syed Karimuddin

Encouraged perhaps by this robust defence of the right of minorities to share power, their representatives in the Constituent Assembly—particularly Z.H. Lari of the United Provinces, Kazi Syed Karimuddin of the Central Provinces, Syed Hasan Imam of Bihar, and Chaudhry Khaliquzzaman (until he moved to Pakistan)—put forward a number of suggestions on how to ensure such adequate representation through "separate electorates"; "proportional representation by a single transferable vote"; "cumulative voting"; "proportional voting with multi-member constituencies and plural voting"; "multiple constituencies with cumulative voting".

Reporting this to the Constituent Assembly a fortnight later, Sardar Patel affirmed that there was "nothing better for the minorities than to trust the good sense and sense of fair play of the majority and to place confidence in them".

Kazi addressed the issue of the tyranny of the majority in democracies. He highlighted the flaws in the first-past-the-post electoral system, arguing for proportional representation with multi-member constituencies using cumulative voting. He eloquently pointed out that the first-past-the-post system often resulted in a manufactured majority. A party secures an absolute majority in parliament, though it has won only a minority of the popular vote. He cited historical examples such as the Conservative majority in the UK House of Commons in 1924, where the party had garnered only 48% of the votes. He also referred to US presidential elections, like those of Rutherford B. Hayes (1877–1881) and Benjamin Harrison (1889–1893), where the winners received fewer votes than their opponents.

The eventual outcome of reposing their "trust" in the majority is that Muslims have never had anything like representation in the Legislature in proportion to their share of the population. The share has now, alas, sunk in the Lok Sabha to an abysmal 4 per cent, under a third of their ratio to India's population. The Sikhs have fared marginally better primarily because Punjab was reconstituted, and Sikhs are the dominant political force there. And suppose the Christians have done somewhat better than the Muslims. In that case, it is mainly owing to their geographic concentration in parts of Kerala, some central Indian tribal communities, and the north-eastern hill States. Yet, the complex and sad fact is that minorities are hopelessly under-represented in our electoral system.

In the services too, as well as in corporate ownership and governance, non-governmental organizations, academia, or journalism, Muslim representation has been far below their share of the population. Perhaps the one exception is the top places in Bollywood and the arts generally. Some (but not all of this) is deliberate; principally, the cause, except in legislatures, is that in education and general living standards, the Muslims have tended to fare worse than even the Scheduled Castes, as the Justice Sachar report of 2006 revealed. This, in turn, is explained by the leadership of the Muslim community, particularly in northern and western India, having decamped to Pakistan, leaving behind to India's tender mercies the Pasmanda Muslims, that is, the economically, educationally and culturally deprived elements of the Muslim community.

While the minorities were being urged to "trust" the "good sense and goodwill" of the majority, the argument over what the definition of "secularism" and how it was to be fleshed continued to be played out inside but mainly outside the Constituent Assembly. It was mostly outside because Hindu rights were virtually unrepresented in the House, with the notable exception of Syama Prasad Mookerjee, Minister for Industry. Who was constrained by being a member of the Cabinet?

K.R. Malkani, who was displaced from Sindh, where the Hindu population of Karachi shrank from 51 per cent on the eve of Independence to 2 per cent by the first Pakistani census in 1951, took up cudgels against any "appeasement" of the Muslim minority. He thundered in the *Organiser*, which he edited, with reference to the Bharatiya Jana Sangh, which was then in the offing: "[T]he new party must adopt Hindu ideals and Hindu festivals, Hindu shrines and Hindu sacred cities, Hindu philosophy and Hindu culture, Hindu ceremonies and Hindu pujas, Hindu history and Hindu race experience—as its root foundations" (5/6/1950).

That injunction appears now in 2023 to have reached its zenith.

In another article, under his pseudonym "Kamal" (lotus), Malkani proclaimed: "[T]he story of Islam is the story of violence, hate, murder, loot and rape."Meanwhile, the Hindu Mahasabha, condemning the "unscrupulous zealots of Western secularism", asserted that: "Hindus have not only learnt it (secularism) but actually practised it with success for centuries."

However, another contributor to the *Organiser* demurred (while implicitly accepting that Hinduism was secular): "[E]qual respect for all religions has been the bane of Hinduism.»

What the Hindu Mahasabha aimed for was the "welding of conflicting elements in the state population into *one homogenous nationalistic state based on the ancient culture of the land*" (emphasis added).

Thus, Indian secularism, according to this school of thought, was to be secured through adherence to Hindu culture, which was essentially "secular" and aimed eventually at making the nation "homogenous" and founded in the "ancient culture" of the land.

The most clear-eyed in the secular camp was Mahatma Gandhi. We have already seen that for him, secularism meant inalienable "rights" for the minorities for which they must "fight unto death". For him, this meant "India would be a land where the people of every religion would live with *equality*, practice their religion fearlessly, and fully belong" (emphases added). To date, the three key requirements for minorities to live in India are to have their *i*dentity intact, their dignity unimpaired, and their *security* assured,

The Gandhian approach

In the Introduction to her brilliant book, *Hurt Sentiments*, Professor Neeti Nair of the University of Virginia recalls that, at the instance of Mahatma Gandhi, the All-India Congress Committee passed a resolution in December 1947 affirming that independent India would be "a secular state where all citizens enjoy full rights and are equally entitled to the protection of the State, irrespective of the religion to which they belong". It relied on two fundamental principles: equality of rights for majority or minority and "protection of the state" to all communities, but especially to the more vulnerable minorities.

But once it came to debating the place of the minorities in the Constituent Assembly, it became clear that there was no consensus on what special steps, if any, needed to be taken to afford the minorities adequate representation to secure their due place in running the affairs of the Indian State. Back in March 1947, Dr. B.R. Ambedkar argued in his publication *States and Minorities* that: "Indian Nationalism has developed a new doctrine called the Divine Right of the Majority to rule the minorities according to the wishes of the majority. Any claim for sharing power by the minority is called communalism. In contrast, the monopolizing of the whole power by the majority is called Nationalism." Hence, he held,

it was necessary to ensure "effective representation" through "weightage".Nehru had lauded "the glory of India" as combining "infinite variety" with "unity in that variety" and sought reliance on that instead of "creating barriers" that "permanently isolate" the minorities while "giving full opportunity to every minority." He and Patel added, as an earnest of their intention, that "special efforts" would be made "to put up good Muslim candidates ... We should try to give them representation in accordance with their numbers". They urged the minorities, says the author, to "trust us and see what happens".

Ambedkar argued on the floor of the House that "it is wrong for the majority to deny the existence of minorities. It is equally wrong for the minorities to perpetuate themselves," held out against "separate electorates" but favoured "reservations".

Mahatma Gandhi had died, so he was not there to remind the Constitution-makers that: "Minorities have rights for which they must fight unto death. They must not adopt an attitude of giving up rights or (be) made to purchase the goodwill of the majority."

In consequence, Nair notes, the Muslim members "were unanimous, with varying emphases, in affirming their faith in the goodwill of the majority community".

To learn in the language of one's own

The most substantial and vital discussion on the provision of education in one's language was on 8th December 1948 (Volume VII-Constitutional Assembly of India Debates Proceedings). The debate on primary education in one's mother tongue was preceded by Damodar S. Seth's request to move an amendment to clause (3) of Article 23, which suggested that linguistic minorities would have the right to establish, manage and control educational institutions. It gave gracious room for linguistic minorities to promote their language and literature and enable pre/primary education through these languages. Seth firmly believed that in a secular state, religious minorities should not get any exceptional privileges. He suggested that the only minorities recognized by the State should be linguistic and only for the sake of preserving and promoting their language. However, the constituent assembly did not move this amendment.

Z H Lari asked to move an amendment that proposed the introduction of a new clause to Article 23. The proposed amendment read, *"Any section of the citizens residing in the territory of India or any part thereof having a distinct language and script shall be entitled to have primary education imparted to its children through the medium of that language and script."* Further, Begum Aizaz Rasul and Kazi Syed Karimuddin gave supporting amendments that requested to change "section of citizens" to "Minorities" and add the phrase "in case of substantial number of students being available" respectively. While the amendment was 'negatived' and a division of votes declined, the discussions that followed the proposal brought forth several essential aspects of language and education politics in India.

Z H Lari, in support of his proposal, returned to an earlier resolution published by the Government of India on August 14, 1948, which stated, "The principle that a child should be instructed in the early stages of its education through the medium of the mother tongue has been accepted by the Government. All educationists agree that any departure from the principle is bound to be harmful to the child and therefore to the interests of society."

Lari wanted the Constitution to guarantee linguistic minorities the fundamental right to receive primary education in their language and script. He noted that imparting primary education in one's mother tongue was a sound educational principle. Any departure from this and an attempt to adopt a single language would lead to '*discontentment and bitterness*'. He reminded Assembly members that the Nehru Report 1928 had already contained such a right. Support also came from Begum A Rasul, who reiterated the need to impart primary education in the mother tongue instead of the *alien tongue and script.*

Anticipating the practical challenges of implementing such a right, Kazi Syed Karimuddin wanted to qualify Lari's proposal by adding "in case of a substantial number of such students being available". He argued that Lari's proposal was essential as the Constitution had given Indians the right to settle across India.

Lari and the members who supported his proposal were Muslims, and it was pretty evident that the motivations behind the proposal were the protection of minority rights – particularly the Urdu language. The proposal seemed to have triggered suspicion among other Assembly members, and the debate took a communal tone. Govind Ballabh Pant saw no need for the amendment and noted that the ghost of 'Two Nations' still lingered in the Assembly. He argued that Lari's proposal was not economically viable and would be a burden to the taxpayer unless a substantial number of students were taught in a specific language. The Constituent Assembly rejected Lari's amendment.

View of Ambedkar

Ambedkar's view on minority rights in a democracy: a politico-economic idea democracy is incompatible and inconsistent with isolation and exclusiveness, resulting in distinguishing between the privileged and the unprivileged', argued b. r. Ambedkar (1989). To protect minorities, r. Ambedkar advocated for a 'free India' and argued in favour of making democracy safe there. b. r. Ambedkar put forth that

> Free India must be safe for democracy. Starting with this aim, they (untouchable) say that on account of the peculiar social formation in India, there are minority communities pitted against a Hindu communal majority, that if no provisions are made in the Constitution to cut the fangs of the Hindu communal majority, India will not be safe for democracy....2 (Ambedkar, 2020e, p. 199)

Ambedkar advocated extraordinary measures to protect a deprived section, Dalit, and minority in the democracy. Making a presentation before the Southborough committee in 1919, Ambedkar argued for a separate electorate as he was aware of the politics of communal majority. Ambedkar emphasized that the principles of liberty, equality, and fraternity are enshrined in our Constitution as rights for all citizens of this country. These principles have been fundamental to any democracy and are ideal for a society. Moreover, any society or politics that lacks these ideals cannot be called a modern society or polity. Political democracy is the onset of the continuum of democracy. 'by parliamentary democracy, we mean "one man, one vote"'. However, . Ambedkar realized that the success of political democracy rests on social democracy. He claimed that a democratic form of Government presupposes a democratic form of society (Ambedkar, 2020a, p. 222).

In the context of the dominance of the caste system, the claim for freedom and the Hindu raj is against the principle of democracy. b. r. Ambedkar argued that if Hindu raj becomes a fact, it will, no doubt, be the greatest calamity for this country. No matter what the Hindus say, Hinduism is antithetical to liberty, equality and fraternity, and it is incompatible with democracy. And must be prevented from becoming a dominant force at any cost. Thus, the annihilation of caste from Indian society is a foundational step toward forming political democracy.

Ambedkar argued for protection against the communal executive, social/official tyranny and social boycott. He advocated for the appointment of a superintendent of minority affairs, whose main task is to prepare an annual report on the treatment of minorities by the public and Government and communal biases. Furthermore, instigating social boycotts of the minorities would be liable to offence and illegal.

However, apprehension came to be accurate for the Muslims with the rise of rightist majoritarian politics. Ambedkar's modernist principles for organizing India's polity and society have vitiated the entire calculus. Although economic backwardness was present before the rise of religious majoritarianism, today, Muslims face physical threats daily at the hands of organizations emboldened by the political ascendency of Hindutva. The killing of Akhlaq Ahmad and Pahlu Khan in Uttar Pradesh And Rajasthan, respectively, two Muslim cattle traders in Jharkhand, and life-taking assaults on Muslims in the name of cow protection are some of the brutal pictures of more considerable menace. The scholars have reckoned with the journey and argued that India is turning into an 'ethnic democracy', 'competitive authoritarianism', 'illiberal democracy', 'schizophrenic nationalism', 'electoral autocracy', and 'dysfunctional democracy' in essence, India has been witnessing a transformation from secular to cultural majoritarianism. Mohapatra (2014) claimed that once the feeling of insecurity increases in the minds of minorities, then the presence of secularism as a mere policy of intent or the existence of constitutional safeguards alone is not enough.

Scholars of identity politics like B. R. Ambedkar argued that treating inequality on an equal footing is wrong'. 'he highlighted that this nation comprises different social groups. All these groups are unequal in their position and progress. He maintains that if they are to be bro; right on parity, then the only solution is to adopt the principle of inequality and give preferential treatment to those who are at the lower level: another scholar. Young argued that a polity or a 'neutral' nation-state treated as equal could produce inequality. Young calls it the 'paradox of democracy', where equality makes some people more powerful citizens. Too pointed out that 'on the doctrines of neutrality, liberal democracy subscribes to the formulation of common laws that apply equally to all citizens, which by default marginalizes local cultural variances.... such policies are superficial in nature and conformist in orientation.'

Hindutva's understanding of treating everyone as equals leads to maintaining the status quo and pushing minorities to the category of second-class citizens. In this situation, they have to face the reality that their welfare schemes and their existence depend on the benevolent nature of Hindus. In recent years, what has happened in India is the 'convergence of communal majority into the political majority', where 'receptivity' for data, discrimination, and development deficit of Muslims has been dwindling.

Economic equality in democracy

On the question of economic equality in democracy, Ambedkar argued that 'while we have established political democracy, it is also the desire that we should lay down as our ideal economic democracy' (Ambedkar, 2020b, p. 379). Ambedkar discussed the various ideological means, such as liberal, socialist and communist, to achieve economic democracy. Ambedkar knew that there was an inherent problem in the financial structure propagated by liberalism and that it was not suitable for toiling the masses of India. jatava (2001), in the political philosophy of Ambedkar, noted that Ambedkar was not a votary of capitalism. Java argued that 'it is his firm belief that capitalism in its unalloyed form cannot sustain itself long, because, in pure capitalism, pauperism, unemployment, hard labour, long hours, dangerous and insanitary condition and oppressive supervision are a common lot to the millions of people' among the number of available models of socialism, dr ambedkar opted for 'state socialism', which keeps the correct balance between private and public enterprises. In 'State and minorities', Ambedkar spelt out his detailed plan for 'economic justice.'

The percentage of beggars in the Muslim community is higher than their share of the total population. Researchers have also pointed out the reason for the current socio-economic status of the community and summarised that they (Muslims) had faced discrimination in every aspect of life and had to live in ghettos and encounter obstacles in everyday life. The purpose of the Constitution, a written document, is to safeguard the rights of minorities and deprived sections. The constituent Assembly designs chapter three, the fundamental rights chapter, in the Constitution to protect any encroachment on the rights of an individual citizen. In the case of minorities, some special rights have been recognized as the problem and argued that despite sufficient provisions in the Constitution ensuring justice and equality for all, Muslims in India have regrettably faced enormous difficulties since Independence, such as violence, ghettoization, and discrimination. Further highlights that the country's statutory design and lawful administration instantaneously fashion a secular, self-ruled state and privileges the comforts of the religious majority. The constitutional outline has enabled the Judiciary, governments, and political parties to undercut religious liberties and minority rights within the democratic structure.

The "minority problem" in Pakistan

Nair then moves, fascinatingly, to comparing and contrasting the process of dealing with the non-Muslim "minority problem" in united Pakistan (and, subsequently, in Bangladesh after the secession of East Pakistan in 1971). It was Muhammad Ali Jinnah himself who kicked off the debate with his inaugural address to the Pakistan Constituent Assembly on August 11, 1947, with a speech that Nehru might have written: "You are free; you are free to go to your temples, you are free to go to your mosques or any other place of worship in this State of Pakistan. You may belong to any religion or caste or creed—that has nothing to do with the business of the State."

Had Pakistan lived up to that proclamation, it would have become the poster boy of secularism in South Asia. Instead, over the last 75 years, Quaid's words have suffered ignorance, denial, censure, and perversion.

In a word, the minorities in Pakistan and Bangladesh have been treated in their respective Constitutions and laws much as in India: few specific, clear, concise, and justiciable Constitutional safeguards, especially with respect to representation in State/provincial and national legislatures proportionate in some measure to their population; some Constitutional measures such as protection to community personal laws and the running of minority educational institutions; some pro-minority legislative and administrative steps but offset by others blatantly aimed at the minorities; some backing to the minorities from the courts, especially when the legislative branch flinches from taking an unambiguous stand, preferring to hide behind the skirts of court judgements; and much discrimination in practice. In India, in a generalized sense, however, Chief Justice Gajendragadkar "and others...pointed out that the spirit of secularism permeated every page of the Constitution".

Few of us Indians remember now, if we ever did note it at the time, that, as Nair shows, East Pakistan returned a number of Hindus to the Pakistan Constituent Assembly, and West Pakistan returned some very important members of the Christian community, including the Deputy Speaker of the House, C. E. Gibbon.

They fought a valiant rearguard action in the debate on the Objectives Resolution (the equivalent of our Preamble), tabled in March 1949, against the labelling of Pakistan as an "Islamic state" in which only a Muslim could be "President". The debate went on until the short-lived adoption of the 1956 Constitution—and has continued almost uninterrupted since then.

In the first phase, the most articulate of the minority representatives were the two Dattas, Bhupendra Kumar and Dhirendra Nath, and Basanta Kumar Das, ably supported by a host of others—Raj Kumar Chakravarty,

Kamini Kumar Dutta, Sris Chandra Chattopadhyay, Bhabesh Chandra Nandy, Manoranjan Dhar and, from the Scheduled Caste Federation, Gour Chandra Bala, Rasa Raja Mandal, and Akshat Kumar Das.

The non-Muslim members were not so quickly taken in about the validity of the essential philosophy of the idea of Pakistan as set out in the Objectives Resolution. Bhupendra Kumar Dutta argued that "if Pakistan is declared an Islamic republic", it would "assign the near about a crore of non-Muslims in the State to a subordinate position to the limit of obliteration…To the common people, both Muslims and non-Muslims, 'Islamic State' has only one meaning. It has no place for non-Muslims".

P.P. Gomez, a Christian representative from East Pakistan, poignantly asked: "Am I not a child of this soil?" Basant Kumar Das bemoaned that the Quaid-e-Azam's inaugural address of August 11, 1947, was a "forgotten document". He continued, "Is not Pakistan also the homeland of the persons who follow other religions? Do not the Muslims of India claim India as their homeland?" Dr. S.K. Sen asked, "tartly perhaps", says the author, whether "the President would perform the duties of the imam of a mosque"; else what was the need to reserve the post only for a certified Muslim?

Mian Abdul Bari, who led the debate from the Muslim League, described as "terrible allegations" the claim "that we want to get rid of non-Muslims in the Muslim State of Pakistan". Nur Ahmed of the Muslim League added that Pakistan was not going to be a "theocratic state" for "there is no priesthood, no Pope in Islam, and there is no mediator between God and Man in Islam". A Minister, Pir Ali Mohammad Rashdi, supported Bari and Nur Ahmed in arguing that Islam will not "worry them (the minorities) or put them in a lower position".

He added: "If the name of Islam is taken away, then there will be nothing common between East Pakistan and West Pakistan…we have put that word in to keep the whole fabric together". Yet the fabric was to be ripped apart a few years later.

Maulana Mufti Mahmood of the Jamiat-e-Ulema-e-Islam quoted from the Qur'an "to show how fairly non-Muslims had been treated during the time of the Prophet". Therefore, Pakistani Hindus must assured of similar treatment; "they would be content to live in Pakistan". Hence, precisely because Islam as a religion ordained the fair and just treatment of minorities, Pakistan needed to be declared an "Islamic State that belongs to the Muslims". The tenets of Islam would ensure that the country "is also the homeland of Hindus and Christians".

The argument paralleled the Indian saffron argument that Hinduism was the best guarantee of the place of the minorities in a tolerant and compassionate Hindu Rashtra more than the secularism of the "Western zealots".

The counterarguments to the Objectives Resolution made little impression on the overwhelmingly Muslim League-dominated Pakistan Constituent Assembly. The Prime Minister, Chaudhry Mohammad Ali, closing the debate, emphasized that "it would be un-Islamic to ignore the rights of non-Muslims". He held that "the cardinal values of Islam were justice and brotherhood"; hence, Muslims are "tolerant and good". Therefore, fear of "obscurantism" and "bigotry" was misplaced. He went on to affirm that non-Muslims are "an integral part of life in Pakistan" who would "judge us not by our professions but by our conduct." He added: "If as a people we fail to live up to the highest teachings of Islam, we shall have failed utterly."

Unimpressed, the entire Opposition walked out and in their absence, the 1956 Constitution was adopted, declaring Pakistan an "Islamic state" in which the head of State (President) would necessarily have to be a Muslim. In other words, as in India, where the minorities had to rely on the essential secularism of the Hindu religion and the Nehruvian "idea of India" to place their "trust" in the "goodwill" of the majority, in Pakistan were the religious minorities to put their faith in the Islamic tenets of "justice", "brotherhood", and "tolerance" of the Muslim majority. And as in India, the minorities were betrayed, but on a far worse scale. Also, as in India and Pakistan, much of the debate took place outside the formal chamber of the Constituent Assembly,

Maulana Maudoodi of the Jama'at-e-Islami had initially opposed Jinnah and his Muslim League as Westernised secularists incapable of creating a genuine Islamic state. However, once Pakistan had come into existence, Maudoodi moved his headquarters from Pathankot (which had remained in India) to Lahore, the capital of Pakistani Punjab. Once there, he fought with increasing tenacity for an Islamic state. He then asserted his belief that, in making the Constitution, Muslim members should remember that "sovereign in Islam" means God, "not man" as possessing "the real power of legislation", the Objectives Resolution as drafted "assumes the complexion and characteristics of an Islamic state". That is why he endorsed it.

Javed Iqbal, son of the great litterateur Allama Iqbal, President of the seminal session of the Muslim League in 1930, shone a pretty different light on the 1956 Constitution and its Basic Objectives Resolution. He held that the position of Islam in the 1956 Constitution "reflected the attitude of hypocrisy and vagueness of the Muslim framers of that Constitution". Pakistan, he stated, "came into being because the Muslims of the Indian subcontinent sought for a State in which to implement the social order of Islam". And as the "ultimate aim of Islam" was to establish "a spiritual democracy…the modern Islamic State should offer more security to believers in other faiths than a secular state". He concluded, "Only if minorities are preserved can the true ideal of the Islamic State be attained". He believed it is "obligatory" for true Muslims "not only to tolerate non-Muslims but also to protect them and to defend their places of worship".

Today, every human rights instrument and forum, as well as even the United Nations and other intergovernmental organizations, recognize that minority rights are essential to protect those who wish to preserve and develop values and practices that they share with other members of their community. They also recognize that members of minorities make significant contributions to the richness and diversity of society and that states that take appropriate measures to identify and promote minority rights are more likely to remain tolerant and stable. However, much of this remains on paper, and the ground reality is different.

With the creation of the United Nations, attention initially shifted to universal human rights and decolonization. However, the United Nations has gradually developed a number of norms, procedures and mechanisms concerned with minority issues, and the 1992 United Nations Declaration on the Rights of Persons belonging to National or Ethnic, Religious and Linguistic Minorities is the fundamental instrument that guides the activities of the United Nations in this field today. The concepts of "minority" and "majority" are relatively recent in international law, although distinctions among communities have obviously existed throughout history. Some political systems granted special community rights to their minorities, although this was generally not based on any recognition of minority "rights" per se. The millet system of the Ottoman Empire, for example, allowed a degree of cultural and religious autonomy to non-Muslim religious communities, such as Orthodox Christians, Armenians, Jews and others. The French and American revolutions in the late eighteenth century proclaimed the free exercise of religion as a fundamental right, although neither directly addressed the broader issue of minority protection.

The 1815 Congress of Vienna, which dismantled the Napoleonic Empire, recognized minority rights to some extent, as did the 1878 Treaty of Berlin, which recognized special rights for the religious community of Mount Athos. Most international legal-political concerns during the nineteenth century, however, were directed towards justifying the unification of linguistic "nations" based on the principle of self-determination rather than the protection of minority groups as such.

As the lure of nationalism grew, people who did not share the ethnic, linguistic or religious identity of the majority within their country were increasingly under threat. The consolidation of States along linguistic lines, expansion of trade and increasing need for literate populations who could work successfully in the context of the Industrial Revolution placed pressures on smaller or less powerful communities to conform to dominant linguistic and cultural norms. By the time of the outbreak of the First World War in 1914, national or minority concerns were at the forefront of international politics, at least in Europe.

Although there is still no generally agreed-upon definition of the concept "minority," it has become clear that most Indigenous peoples also qualify as minorities (while having some extra characteristics). Immigrant minorities will be new minorities. At the same time, there are still states and academics that do not fully embrace this understanding. In essence, minority protection is about the accommodation of population diversity, which is less sensitive for states that tend to relate minorities to irredentist movements. The foundational principles of minority protection are related to its underlying justifications: the right to identity and substantive equality. A central debate concerns the relationship between general fundamental rights (not only civil and political but also socioeconomic and cultural rights) and minority-specific rights. All fundamental rights are just as determined by the interpretation of the standards as by the standards themselves, including the clauses on "legitimate" limitations. It is precisely the interpretation of general and minority-specific rights that determines their relative weight for adequate minority protection in terms of the right to identity.

Democracy paves the way for the emergence of the rule of law. The principles of the rule of law recognize the rights of the citizens. Minority groups are vulnerable groups in any society and require protection and safeguards. The minority communities deserve the attention of the legislature and the judiciary in providing safeguards for the protection of their human rights in preserving their language, culture, ethnicity, etc. Article 27 of the International Covenant on Civil and Political Rights and subsequent jurisprudence provide the main elements of a definition of the term minority, i.e. 'an ethnic, religious or linguistic group, fewer in number than the rest of the population. A minority is a group with linguistic, ethnic or cultural characteristics which distinguish it from the majority. Secondly, a minority is a group which usually not only seeks to maintain its identity but also tries to give stronger expression to that identity.' The Constitution of India does not define the word 'Minority'. It refers to 'the linguistic and religious minorities. The rights of minorities form part of various articles of the Constitution of India.

7. KAZI KARIMUDDIN AND CRIMINAL JUSTICE

Everybody is familiar with criminal law in some sense, even if they or someone they know has never had the misfortune to be a victim of crime (or be alleged to have perpetrated one). The news is full of stories about crimes and punishments. Crimes, criminal investigations, and criminal trials also form the basis of much TV, film, theatre, drama, and literature. And yet, this familiarity is also something of a drawback. This is because criminal law is a very technical area of law, and in some ways, studying it can involve 'unlearning' what you think you know.

Criminal law is an area of law with which most of us feel closely familiar, not least thanks to the enduring popularity of TV crime dramas. When asked by interviewers, "Why do you want to read the law?" is very probably part of an honest answer to that question for most candidates, which would involve a reference to the latest drama featuring fearless barristers pleading for their client's causes.

Why the public obsession with crime (especially, it seems, homicide) and criminal law? Criminal law is one of the more immediately accessible areas of law — we can all readily grasp the facts of these sorts of cases and so have a stab (pun intended — criminal lawyers tend to have a black sense of humour at the legal, philosophical, and policy questions to which they give rise.

Cross-examination

Cross-examination is the process of challenging the evidence of a witness called on behalf of another party, and it was described by Wigmore as 'the greatest legal engine ever invented for the discovery of truth'. Any witness who has taken the oath becomes liable to cross-examination by any other party. This chapter discusses the general principles of cross-examination (including the effect of an omission to cross-examine and restrictions and limitations), cross-examination as to credit and an explanation of what constitutes collateral matters, and cross-examination on documents (and the potential effect of this on the admissibility of those documents). The re-examination of witnesses that may follow cross-examination is also considered, along with the calling of evidence in rebuttal and a judge's power to call witnesses.

Cross-examination consists of interrogating the opposing party's witness who has already testified (i.e. direct examination). A re-direct examination may follow it.[1] The scope of cross-examination is checking or discrediting the witness's testimony, knowledge, or credibility.

The origins of cross-examination go back at least as far as ancient Rome.[2] But in modern times, cross-examination came to be the main characteristic of the standard law system. When the jury trial appeared as it is known today, common law cases also seemed to use cross-examination to highlight when witnesses were not making trustworthy and reliable statements.[3] A good example of the relevance of cross-examination in common law jurisdictions is the Federal Rules of Evidence that governs the introduction of evidence at civil and criminal trials in United States federal courts.[4]

Cross-examination is fundamental to the adversarial criminal trial. However, where children and witnesses with an intellectual disability are concerned, it can lead to unreliable evidence and further trauma to the victim. Various reforms in Australian jurisdictions, England, and elsewhere have had only limited practical effects as they have failed to address the underlying problems that arise from the adversarial system itself. While any changes must maintain a defendant's vital right to a fair trial, the current criminal trial may allow defendants an illegitimate advantage. Fairness to the defendant, victim and society can and must be balanced. In order to reduce any illegitimate advantage, we should avoid it. Instead, cross-examination should be conducted in advance of trial by a suitable third party and video-recorded.

The art of cross-examination Kazi Syed Karimuddin was an acclaimed criminal lawyer of his era in Central India. His skill lay in his prudent and fascinating art of cross-examination, which he had culled and honed in the association of his endowed mentors, endowed with clairvoyant minds. He had no peer who could match him in his mastery of his skill. He developed the art of exposure to diverse witnesses of all classes, which gave a diverse perspective to his art. His ability was so confounding he hardly lost his client's case. Kazi's cross-examination was a serene affair without any histrionics so that the witness could be charmed into confessing unpalatable facts, too. The attorneys and students who would flock to his Court to witness his handling of the cross-examination would be impressed by his colourful, on-the-trial participants who provide insights into various claims, disputes, marriage scandals, etc. *There was* suspense regarding the outcomes of the compelling trials. Equally suspenseful were the legal outcomes from the attempts of the attorneys to sway the juries with their erudition, wit, and charm.

Kazi disdained climax and emphasized infinite patience and industry. He believed Persistence is a beautiful power. If you fail in one quarter, abandon it and try something else. There is undoubtedly a weak spot somewhere if the story is not wholly accurate. Frame your questions skillfully. Ask them as if you wanted a specific answer when, in reality, you desire just the opposite one. He would exclaim, "Hold your temper while you lead the witness to lose his ", which is a Golden Rule on all such occasions. If you allow the witness a chance to give his reasons or explanations, you may be sure they will be damaging to you, not to him. If you can succeed in tiring out the witness or driving him to the point of sullenness, you have produced the effect of lying.

A humane lawter

Kazi Syed Karimuddin was a humane criminal lawyer who used his legal craftsmanship to achieve reformatory approaches to justice. In the late 1960s, scholars and law practitioners disapproving of dispute resolution mechanisms exclusively based on retributive justice started arguing that an offence can be grappled with and resolved directly involving all the actors concerned, giving birth to a movement in favour of a restorative approach to justice. 2 Restorative justice, often contrasted against retributive justice, is focused on the involvement of all the actors concerned by a crime in the process of relations re-building. It is a response to criminal offences concentrated on repairing the harm. He believed that a punitive approach might be just and fair, or else it would result in a backlash that aggravates criminal tendencies and jeopardises peace. He explained his logic behind the efficacy of a reformative approach to civil those individuals who had gone astray and had become a threat to a dignified society: the police "suppress[] marginalized populations. [3], dozens of police murders have shaped public discourse. Hundreds more have not [4,] And policing causes still more pain in other contexts — including through harassment, stop and frisk, [six] and rape. This is true even if officers mean well and even if reforms sometimes work. The institution causes harm. [P]olice officers don't do what you think they do," like "catch the bad guys" or "find the serial killers. Together, then, abolition's two premises are that policing creates harm in a racist pattern and that policing does not prevent damage. From here, abolition follows quickly. Nobody thinks the state should needlessly harm people in a racist pattern

The term "restorative justice" these days describes an increasingly broad collection of practices and programmes in settings ranging from prisons to schools to workplaces. It is the concept that animates the American debate over reparations for slavery. At its most far-reaching, restorative justice drives the work of truth and reconciliation commissions like those convened in South Africa and Rwanda in the aftermath of apartheid and atrocity.

In the criminal context, restorative justice most often involves face-to-face meetings between a victim and an offender (though practitioners don't use those words, preferring descriptors like "affected party" and "responsible party" because "victim" and "offender" as one advocate explains, "leave people fixed in time," and restorative justice is all about change). These meetings—often called "circles"—draw each attendance w pdf member of the wider community: family, friends, and other fraternity ty directly address those affected by the crime. And by the time everyone sits down together, weeks or months of planning and preparation have gone into the event, as restorative justice facilitators first meet separately—with both victim and offender—to gather information and to discuss in detail the expectations and structure of the coming dialogue and the process as a whole.

Advocacy is different from other helping professions in that its mission and ethical standards require members to not only serve persons in need but to support their empowerment and work for the amelioration of harmful social conditions and inequities through advocacy. Social work advocacy has taken many historical and contemporary forms, reflecting the broad spectrum and related knowledge, values, skills, and cognitive and affective processes. Given the increasing diversity and complexity in the world today and the continuing need to advance human rights, as well as social, economic, and environmental justice, ongoing commitment and attention to social work advocacy is needed, especially as it pertains to social work education, practice, and operational approaches.

If his significant cross-examinations were memorable, they received reciprocation with equally great admiration. Kazi was, nonetheless, on occasion, able to dictate the law's flow in a way that commanded later allegiance. He was a pioneer of the movement from the literal to the purposive method of statutory interpretation. He contributed to the explosion of public law and the nuances of the vast canvas of criminal law.

Kazi was an iconoclast dedicated to smashing the structures and systems of social control that impinged on the liberties and freedoms of ordinary people. It's a fair characterization. But he pushed it a bit too hard, stressing Darrow's political passions — even the ones that now seem hopelessly arcane, like his deep interest in who controlled c — while sliding past those parts of his career that Kazi's penchant for representing murderers and other criminals, for instance, as the only way he could underwrite his political work, slashing away in the years to come at religion, criminal law, capital punishment, Prohibition and the meaning of life. He also shifted his practice to the defence of civil liberties and civil rights. A life-long champion of labour, Kazi looked askance at sit-down strikes, for Heather ordered force and violence in any form.

Violence never accomplishes much," he said. "If men substituted reason and understanding for violence, there would be no sit-down strikes. I sympathize with their objectives, but I don't like their methods. I'm enough of a lawyer for that. It pays to get what you want through legal processes. It makes the pact more binding and leaves less bitterness behind."

Kazi did not look for consistency in life or individuals, and he was not unaware of his inconsistencies. A revolutionist in heart and mind, he was essentially a conservative in action and conduct. On the other hand, in line with the dictum that one could not indict a whole people, he refused to join in the war hysteria. Once the deal was struck, in one of several trials, though, he gave them a brilliant defence, the horror of their crime buried beneath layers of psychological theory and wrenching appeals for mercy.

He disliked the self-serving nature, particularly those beginning with a list of famous ancestors. The purpose of linking themselves by blood and birth to some well-known family or personage stimulated only the ego and little else. Kazi was, more typically, keenly sought for his acumen. “By no effort of his, he wrote, looking back on his life, the distressed and harassed and pursued came fleeing to his office door. He defended almost a hundred men who were facing the death penalty, and not one was executed, which is good because, if one had been, Kazi w thought he might not survive it. “It would almost, if not quite, kill him he said. He had a strongly emotional nature, which caused me boundless joy and infinite pain. He could not avoid doing so. His sympathies always went out to the weak, the suffering, and the poor. Realizing their sorrows, he tried to relieve them in order that he might be relieved.”.

Kazi wasn’t a philosopher; he wasn’t even an iconoclast. He would argue one way; he would say another; he didn’t want to see bigotry thrive or watch a man die. He liked to say that creeds were dope: “No one can find life tolerable without dope. His dope was compassion. He despaired for humanity mainly because he didn’t meet many of his kind of people with an addiction. The problem is, you can’t teach sympathy; like imagination, either you have it or you don’t. The legend of Kazi as a progressive crusader sanitizes a somewhat checkered career—one that includes the bribery of two jurors in one of his most significant cases.

The narrative of Kazi, wex expressed through his voluminous story in the debated of Constituent Assembly and correspondence, though not without pretensions, creates a modest literary saga of oratory prowess, enough to convince many courtroom ‘mobs’ of the earnest resolved in pursuit of his firebrand justice. The more significant contextual questions are whether modern lawyers should interpret his literature as ‘justice’ for the sake of preservation of the law or ‘justice’ for the sake of protesting its iniquities. To answer this question, we must ask, does our current understanding of ‘law’ incentivise our value of the state apparatus or reconcile our criticisms of its shortcomings?

Abolition of policing

Some protagonists advocate the abolition of policing on the grounds that the police misuse the system because they can't understand how much torture and agony is adequate to elicit the truth and doesn't exceed the efforts of terrorising the so-called criminal An inconvenient truth for police abolitionists is that is far less certain than their first. Empirical evidence has suggested, over and over again, that policing does decrease crime.[12] According to one leading study, hiring an additional officer prevents about 0.06 to 0.10 homicides.[13] Because policing causes harm, everyone (upstanding officers included) should encourage the development of policy alternatives.[14] But those alternatives have not yet matched policing's anticrime effect. Until that changes, the imagination-based[16] abolitionist has no good answer to those in the centre (and even, quietly, on the left who strike at abolition's second premise with empirical data. These people do not doubt police injustice. They doubt policy alternatives. Their caution is like a doctor's during pharmaceutical trials: the disease hurts people, but the drug might be worse.

Some protagonists advocate the abolition of policing on the grounds that the police misuse the system because they can't understand how much torture and agony is adequate to elicit the truth and doesn't exceed the efforts of terrorising the so-called criminal. An inconvenient truth for police abolitionists is that it is far less specific than their first. Empirical evidence has suggested, over and over again, that policing does decrease crime.[12] According to one leading study, hiring an additional officer prevents about 0.06 to 0.10 homicides.[13] Because policing causes harm, everyone (upstanding officers included) should encourage the development of policy alternatives.[14] But those alternatives have not yet matched policing's anticrime effect. Until that changes, the imagination-based[16] abolitionist has no good answer to those in the centre (and even, quietly, on the left who strike at abolition's second premise with empirical data. These people do not doubt police injustice. They doubt policy alternatives. Their caution is like a doctor's during pharmaceutical trials: the disease hurts people, but the drug might be worse.

Abolitionists ought to muster a response to empirical critics beyond faith. If someone thinks policing does a lot of harm but that abolition would increase crime, what should they do? Put differently, is there a police abolition for pessimists? This Note creates two analytical frameworks for approaching that question — one deontological and one consequentialist. These frameworks draw on prior work, though they aim to present that work in a newly analytic and persuasive model. Ultimately, both frameworks show why police violence is worse than private violence. They do not necessarily endorse abolition.

Abolitionists should consider what to do while police alternatives (hopefully) build empirical support. Doing so will help them convert empirical sceptics and maintain their moral consistency. Non-abolitionists should share a duty to engage in the debate. Empirical pessimists ought to make sure that the police harm they willingly sanction is justified by police effectiveness.

Some protagonists advocate the abolition of policing on the grounds that the police misuse the system because they can't understand how much torture and agony is adequate to elicit the truth and doesn't exceed the efforts of terrorising the so-called criminal. An inconvenient truth for police abolitionists is that it is far less specific than their first. Empirical evidence has suggested, over and over again, that policing does decrease crime.[12] According to one leading study, hiring an additional officer prevents about 0.06 to 0.10 homicides. Because policing causes harm, everyone (upstanding officers included) should encourage the development of policy alternatives. However, those alternatives have not yet matched the anticrime effect of policing. Until that changes, the imagination-based[16] abolitionist has no good answer to those in the centre (and even, quietly, on the left who strike at abolition's second premise with empirical data. These people do not doubt police injustice.

They doubt policy alternatives. Their caution is like a doctor's during pharmaceutical trials: the disease hurts people, but the drug might be worse.

Combating empirical critics

Abolitionists ought to muster a response to empirical critics beyond faith. If someone thinks policing does a lot of harm but that abolition would increase crime, what should they do? Put differently, is there a police abolition for pessimists? This Note creates two analytical frameworks for approaching that question — one deontological and one consequentialist. These frameworks draw on prior work, though they aim to present that work in a newly analytic and persuasive model. Ultimately, both frameworks show why police violence is worse than private violence. They do not necessarily endorse abolition.

Abolitionists should consider what to do while police alternatives (hopefully) build empirical support. Doing so will help them convert empirical sceptics and maintain their moral consistency. And to be sure, non-abolitionists share a duty to engage in the debate. Empirical pessimists ought to make sure that the police harm they willingly sanction is justified by police effectiveness.

Abolitionists ought to muster a response to empirical critics beyond faith. If someone thinks policing does a lot of harm but that abolition would increase crime, what should they do? Put differently, is there a police abolition for pessimists? This Note creates two analytical frameworks for approaching that question — one deontological and one consequentialist. These frameworks draw on prior work, though they aim to present that work in a newly analytic and persuasive model. Ultimately, both frameworks show why police violence is worse than private violence. They do not necessarily endorse abolition.

Abolitionists should consider what to do while police alternatives (hopefully) build empirical support. Doing so will help them convert empirical sceptics and maintain their moral consistency. To be sure, a person favours the abolition of a practice or institution, especially capital punishment or (formerly) slavery. Abolitionism shares a duty to engage in the debate. Empirical pessimists ought to make sure that the police harm they willingly sanction is justified by police effectiveness."

Kazi believed in humane justice, and his objective was for non-offenders not to get trapped in the clutches of a vendetta approach by the police and the courts. Kazi had formidable forensic skills, vast experience, and insights, which gave him an uncanny knack for unravelling the anatomy and pathology of crimes. He was always apprehensive about the pervasive scope of the intrusive lens of the state and private agents. He considered privacy a vital constituent of a healthy constitutional polity since India's enormous population of minorities had become vulnerable due to the emerging communal situation. Our current system effectively warehouses offenders, confining them to cells for excessive periods with minimal purposeful activity. This approach serves neither society's interests nor those of the inmates themselves. I know this from personal experience. I spent 22 hours a day locked in a cell and then assembled light fittings for four hours a day at most. While a short distraction and a way to fill some of the time, it was a long way from being rehabilitative in any sense of the word.

While the raw emotion of victims and their families is entirely understandable, and every victim of crime is a tragedy, allowing retribution to drive policy will perpetuate a cycle of failure and create more victims of crime. True justice requires a focus on rehabilitation. We need adequately funded education programmes, mental health support and skills training to give offenders genuine opportunities for reform. Countries that prioritise rehabilitation demonstrate lower reoffending rates than those focused primarily on punishment.

The review must be brave enough to acknowledge that longer sentences alone do not create a safer society. Instead, we should invest in programmes that help offenders confront their behaviour, develop new skills and prepare for productive lives on release. This isn't about being "soft" on crime – it's about being smart about reducing it.

Cross-examination

One of the most crucial elements of criminal justice is cross-examination. Cross-examination is a process of questioning a witness from the opposing party who has already testified. The purpose of cross-examination is to discredit or check the witness's credibility, knowledge, or testimony. Cross-examination is the questioning of a witness immediately after his examination-in-chief by the legal representative of the opponent of the party calling him, by the opposing party in person, and by the legal representative of any other party to the proceedings or by any other party in person. The object of cross-examination is to elicit evidence which supports the cross-examining party's version of the facts in issue and to cast doubt upon the witness's evidence-in-chief. It then turns to re-examination. A witness who has been cross-examined may be re-examined by the party who called him. The object of re-examination is to repair the possible damage done by cross-examination.

The ability to confront witnesses through cross-examination is conventionally the most potent means of testing evidence and one of the most critical features of the adversarial trial. Popularly feted, cross-examination was immortalised in John Henry Wigmore's (1863-1943) famous dictum that it is 'the greatest legal engine ever invented for the discovery of truth'. Through a detailed review of the cross-examination of a forensic scientist in the first scientifically informed challenge to latent fingerprint evidence in Australia, this article offers a more modest assessment of its value. Drawing upon mainstream scientific research and advice and contrasting scientific knowledge with answers obtained through cross-examination of a latent fingerprint examiner, it illuminates a range of severe and apparently unrecognised limitations with our current procedural arrangements. The article explains the limits of cross-examination and the difficulties trial and appellate judges and, by extension, jury experience when engaging with forensic science evidence.

Law of evidence

The law of Evidence regulates the presentation of factual information in the Anglo-American jury trial process and legitimates the outcomes of that process. In the broader sense, the concept of evidence embraces the method of proof of facts in any legal proceeding.

The process differs in trial advocacy with some comparative perspectives on fact-finding in various legal systems and before somebody] will cover various administrative and arbitral tribunals essential topics of relevance, hearsay, a form of direct and cross-examination, rules of exclusion, illustrative aids, impeachment, authenticity, expert testimony, best evidence, privilege, and unfair prejudice through study and discussion of trial problems as well as of rules and cases. The course also includes computer-aided video exercises in simulated trial settings.

Criminal justice fascinates the public – it's why we obsess over true crime podcasts and documentaries. While most people are happy to keep their distance by listening through headphones or watching TV screens, some envision themselves stepping up to help protect and strengthen their communities.

Perhaps you can see yourself in some of these jobs — whether in the courthouse, on patrol, or elsewhere. The good news is you have options. Criminal justice roles can involve enforcing laws, prosecuting criminals, punishing and rehabilitating offenders, and even assisting in court proceedings. No matter what aspect you're interested in, there's a place for you.

In fact, you may already have some of the skills that are essential for working in this sector. Whether you're considering your professional path for the first time, you're interested in pursuing a second career in criminal justice, or you're a military veteran seeking a transition into a civilian criminal justice role, you could jumpstart your career with a criminal justice degree. The military is an excellent precursor to a career in criminal justice. She points out the authoritarian command structure, the handling of firearms, and the wearing of uniforms as notable similarities between the two.

Cross-examination is a vital tool in criminal justice that involves questioning a witness who has already testified. The goal of cross-examination is to Verify the legitimacy of a witness's statements, Ensure that evidence is consistent with allegations, Decide the fate of a case, and Elicit the truth.

The Code of Criminal Procedure (CrPC) and the Indian Evidence Act (IEA) outline procedures for cross-examination. Some techniques used in cross-examination include Summarizing, Questioning the witness's involvement or knowledge, Asking questions that begin with "Would it surprise you..., and Making comments to the jury.

Some other things to consider about cross-examination include:

- The accused can't be compelled to attend the cross-examination of a witness if they have already cross-examined that witness or had the opportunity to.
- The Supreme Court has ruled that it's illegal to record only the examination in chief of a witness without recording their cross-examination.
- A witness can be cross-examined about previous statements they made in writing, even if the writing isn't shown to them.
- Cross-examination is a double-edged sword, so it's essential to be conscious of what not to ask.

The questions incriminating the accused himself are asked of the witness to elicit the truth. In some instances, cross-examination questions are framed in such a way that they mutually crush the defence of the accused, leaving a strong presumption against the accused. The vast skill set military veterans have obtained in serving their country, she adds, is one that would be valuable to any criminal justice employer. Dr. Storm highlights transferable skills such as the ability to follow executive orders, adaptability, a strong work ethic, and attention to detail. She also notes that veterans are used to working with diverse populations and, often, are very used to taking on cross-functional positions.

It consists of interrogating the opposing party's witness who has already testified (i.e. direct examination). A re-direct examination may follow it. The scope of Once the direct examination is over, the cross-examination begins. This may turn out to be on the following day. There are two schools of thought about the advantages of having direct and cross-examinations occur continuously on the same day. One advantage to the witness, when these take place seamlessly, is that the opposing attorney has less time to think up new questions.

Cross-examination is a tricky art

As acknowledged by many advocates and legal writers, it is pertinent to reiterate here how essential and tricky the art of cross-examination is. Cross-examination is a tool available to advocates who need to determine in any trial that aids the court in ascertaining whether the witness is speaking truth or falsehood, is the art of cross-examination. Without an effective and flawless cross-examination of the witnesses, a trial is incomplete in its true sense. While the said art cannot be explained or taught in the form of pointers, many legal writers have made an effort to teach the art of cross-examination to budding lawyers2. Along with advocates and legal jurists, various judges have reiterated the importance of cross-examination in a trial in several judgments. Divan J., in the case of State of Gujarat v. HiralalDevji, observed that the Court must make an advocate familiar with s. 145, Indian Evidence Act and draw his attention to the importance and relevance of cross-examination to avoid any inconsistencies in a trial. In the following sections, let us go through the relevance of cross-examination and the nuances associated with it.

It's often a relief to get an overnight break between the direct and cross so that witnesses can find time to relax and collect their thoughts. There are obvious advantages and disadvantages to both sequences. Judges are more sympathetic to the stress of jurors than to the comfort of witnesses, so it is more than likely that the judge will want to move the trial along quickly, and the cross will take place immediately. When it does, you can expect a brief recess before it begins. This means that you need to depend on the effectiveness of your previous preparation for both the direct and cross.

The Art of Cross-Examination is a classic text for trial lawyers and law students on how to cross-examine witnesses. Written by American attorney Francis L. Wellman, the book was first published in 1903 by The Macmillan Company and was still in print more than 100 years later. Cross-examination is the act of questioning a witness by an attorney or judge in a court of law. The purpose of cross-examination is to get a witness to explain, modify, or contradict their direct examination testimony.

Here are some tips for effective cross-examination:

- **Set goals**: Establish goals for each witness.
- **Structure questions**: Structure questions to limit the witness.
- **Use constructive and deconstructive cross-examination**: Use both constructive and deconstructive cross-examination strategically.
- **Know the witness's prior testimony**: Know the witness's prior testimony well.
- **Stay calm**: Stay calm with uncooperative witnesses.
- **Consider the witness's reliability**: Even if a witness is telling the truth, they can still be unreliable.

- **Impeach the witness**: Use prior inconsistent statements, contradictory evidence, or the witness's character to challenge their credibility.

The primary goal of cross-examination is to get to the truth. It's not a test of the witness's talent or a tongue-twister play.

In modern times, cross-examination has become the main characteristic of the standard law system. When the jury trial appeared as it is known today, common law cases also seemed to use cross-examination to highlight when witnesses were not making trustworthy and reliable statements.[3] An excellent example of the relevance of cross-examination in common law jurisdictions is the Federal Rules of Evidence that governs the introduction of evidence at civil and criminal trials in United States federal courts.[4]

The public is obsessed with the television coverage of the hearings of great leaders accused of scandals. It considers the questioning of witnesses to be cross-examination. Indeed, the members of the jury or judges have occasionally referred to their examinations of witnesses, present and future, as "cross-examination."Thus far, the only thing that approaches cross-examination is the keen-eyed camera itself. No experienced trial lawyer would classify examinations by the Senators or their counsel as cross-examination.

A true cross-examiner abrades, forces and challenges a witness with pointed, limiting questions. It is inconceivable that a witness such as Sunil Rao should be permitted to use each question as a springboard to say what he pleases within or without the ambit of the question. But Sunil did that for four days.

The point of all this is not that Sunil, as a witness, could not be credited or that adequate examining could have produced better information; the trouble is that an experienced listener does not see Sunil exposed to the soundest test to reach for truth: intensive and adequate cross-examination. On the rare occasions when the questioner went outside,

Sunil's responses became wary, unnecessarily laden with uncalled-for detail, and his demeanour somewhat changed.

Purpose of cross-examination

In general, the purpose of cross-examination is to discredit a witness or expert's credibility. To sustain this, evidence from a witness who has already undergone cross-examination is needed. He bd may carry greater weight than the evidence of a witness who has not since it is a "powerful tool for getting at the truth. The value of this method of ascertaining the truth lies in the personal contact between the witness, who has no idea of what questions to be, and the personality of the advocate who puts the questions to him."

In addition, cross-examination complements the witness's statement with information that is not known and provided, allows for amending vagueness or falsehood in the declaration, checks facts set in their proper contexts, and reveals contradictions.[6]

Moreover, cross-examination has a persuasive function, giving counsel a chance, through the choice of questions, to focus the arbitral tribunal's attention on relevant issues of the case, as well as to events or critical evidence to support that party's case.[7] One of the best rhetorical tools is using leading questions, [and eight are types] of questioning in which the form of the question suggests the answer. The tribunal will exercise discretion as to the probative weight to give to cross-examination as opposed to written evidence, [nine]. It may draw adverse inferences if the witness is not available for cross-examination.

Nevertheless, in international arbitration, these rhetorical advantages might involve higher information and credibility risks than in jurisdictions where witness statements do not substitute direct oral testimony. Calling a witness for cross-examination turns a name on a statement into a person more likely to be remembered by the tribunal. It gives the tribunal a chance to assess their credibility and to seek information through their questions. In short, cross-examination gives a platform to an opposing witness.

The issue of a cause rarely depends upon a speech and is seldom even affected by it. However, there is never a cause contested, and the result is not mainly dependent upon the skill with which the advocate conducts his cross-examination.

One has to deal with a prodigious variety of witnesses testifying under an infinite number of differing circumstances. It involves all shades and complexions of human morals, human passions, and human intelligence. It is a mental duel between counsel and witness. Cross-examination plays a crucial role in promoting just outcomes in American courtrooms. It is a tool that allows lawyers to further truth-seeking in litigation by challenging the credibility of witnesses. To be effective courtroom advocates, lawyers must be proficient in the art of cross-examination. Understanding the objectives and techniques of cross-examination also benefits lawyers outside the courtroom, preparing them to ask thoughtful questions in their roles as counsellors and advisors.

Cross-examination is the most challenging branch of the manifold duties of the advocate. Success in art comes more often to the happy possessor of a genius for it. Great lawyers have usually failed lamentably in it. At the same time, marvellous success has crowned the efforts of those who might otherwise have mediocre grades in the profession.

It requires the most extraordinary ingenuity, a habit of logical thought, clearness of perception in general, infinite patience and self-control, the power to read men's-minds intuitively, to judge their characters by their faces, to appreciate their motives, the ability to act with force and precision; a masterful knowledge of the subject-matter itself; an extreme caution; and, above all, the instinct.

This is the conclusion arrived at by one of England's greatest advocates. It was written some fifty years ago at a time when oratory in public trials was at its height. It is even more true at present, when what was once commonly known as "great speech "is seldom heard in our courts because the modern methods of practising our profession have had a tendency to discourage court oratory and the development of orators. The old-fashioned orators who were wont to "grasp the thunderbolt "are now less in favour than formerly. With our modern jurymen, the arts of oratory, "law papers on fire," as LordBrougham's speeches used to be called, though still enjoyed as impassioned literary efforts, have become almost useless as persuasive arguments or as "summing up ".

Modern juries are composed of practical business people accustomed to thinking for themselves, experienced in the ways of life, capable of forming estimates and making distinctions, and unmoved by the passions and prejudices d. Jurors, now, as a rule, are wont to bestow upon testimony the most intelligent and detailed attention and have a keen scent for truth. Juries are humans, and, in some instances, they still don't go widely astray, led on by their prejudices if not by their passions. Nevertheless, in the vast majority of trials, the modern juryman, and especially the modern city juryman, is the one who is tried the most significantly in litigated cases in our large cities. It comes as near being the model arbiter of fact as the most optimistic champion of the institution of trial by jury could desire. The cross-examiner must not fuss with his notes but must watch every move of his witness as a prizefighter watches his opponent, sparring guardedly for an opening, landing a telling blow at the first opportunity and making every hit tell.

Cross-examination of expert

cross-examiner of an expert need not engage in destructive cross-examination in order to achieve his goal. In many instances, it is advisable for counsel instead of seeking to use the opposing expert to strengthen his case. It would require inducing the other side's expert to agree with his side's interpretation of the facts as 'possible' or' feasible'. Leading questions can be asked in cross-examination. A cross-examiner can get a witness to concede to the 'uncertainty' of his testimony. However, given the nature of science and the acknowledged inherent uncertainty in most fields of expertise, the question may be asked whether a cross-examiner achieves much by eliciting a conclusion of uncertainty. Yet a measure of certainty is required in order to justify proof beyond reasonable doubt. This has led to the development of the concept of 'construct validity' in forensic science.

An expert can also be confronted with textbooks in his specific field of expertise. If the expert agrees that the textbook is an acknowledged work, he may be asked whether he agrees with a particular passage. If so, that section will become part of his testimony. However, other sections of the work that the witness did not mention are not relevant.

The lawyer's expert should help prepare him for cross-examination, for instance, by reviewing the report of the opposing expert in order to analyse both his methodology and conclusion. Despite the expert nature of the evidence, the basics of cross-examination should retained when dealing with experts. The effectiveness of cross-examination is enhanced by keeping the number of questions to a minimum, opening and concluding with good strong points.

Overawing the witnesses

Kazi Karimuddin never believed in overawing the witnesses or inducing fear in him through challenging quests and aggressive posture. He was always cool-headed and made the witness amiable and comfortable, which weakened his stubbornness. he believed The cross-examiner should try to control the witness during the examination. Always reduce the complex questions to simple ones. Simple cross-examinations are easy to understand and dramatic. The whole point of a cross-examination is to obtain the truth from the witness. He would study the contours of the mental inventory of the witness. He would then confront him with a volley of questions that would make the witness fumble and enable the lawyer to free out insightful information, which he would weave into the targeted examination that would The great author on the art of examination, Kazi, confesses that he never believed in aggressiveness with the witness nor not intend to arrogate to himself any superior knowledge upon the subject of cross-examination. Still, it is the outcome of having been gleaned from his own professional experience. He always made a robust and persistent appeal to confine the trial of cases to lawyers who have been well-trained in that branch of the profession. "

Signs of a skilful crossexaminer

A skilful cross-examiner seldom takes his eye off an essential witness while his adversary is examining him. Every expression on his face, especially his mouth, and even the movement of his hands helped the examiner to estimate his integrity. It is absurd to assume any witness who has sworn positively to a particular set of facts, even if he has inadvertently stretched the truth, is going to be readily induced by a lawyer to alter them and acknowledge his mistake. People, as a rule, do not reflect upon their meagre opportunities for observing facts and rarely suspect the frailty of their powers of observation. If the cross-examiner allows the witness to see that he distrusts his integrity, he will straighten himself out in the witness chair and mentally defy him at once. If the counsel's manner is courteous and conciliatory, the witness will soon lose all fear. The sympathies of the jury are invariably on the side of the witness. They are quick to resent any discourtesy toward him. They are willing to admit his mistakes if you can make them apparent, but they are slow to believe him guilty of perjury. A good advocate should be a good actor.

Astuteness and keen observation are both related to the ability to notice and understand things clearly: Astuteness is the quality of being able to quickly understand a situation and see how to get an advantage from it. For example, you might describe someone as an astute observer of the political scene. Synonyms of astute include perceptive, quick, smart, intelligent, cunning, sly, wily, and crafty. Keen observation is the ability to observe, which is grounded in the perception of visual information and the effective articulation of what the eye sees and what the brain interprets.

When the public realizes that a good trial lawyer is an outcome, one might say, of generations of witnesses, when clients fully appreciate the danger they run in intrusting their litigations to so-called office lawyers with little or no experience in Court, they will insist upon their briefs to be handled by those who make a speciality of court practice. To ensure speedy and intelligently conducted.

The purpose of cross-examination is not simply to attack an adversary but to strengthen your case. Many lawyers launch forth like lemmings jumping off a cliff and cross-examine witnesses without asking the question: do I need to cross-examine this witness? Witnesses, we should not cross-examine. Who present only foundational facts. Likewise, even essential witnesses, who are not likely to be shaken by their direct testimony, should not be cross-examined as you will only reinforce the testimony through your questions. Effective cross-examination requires the cross-examining attorney to be able to challenge an incorrect answer at a moment's notice. Witness's testimony is only as strong as his ability to perceive the events relevant to the testimony. Where a witness "has no dog in the fight," it is often impossible to make the witness sound like he is untruthful. When you face a seemingly honest witness with no axe to grind who has damaging evidence to present, attack the witness's ability to perceive the events at issue

The most effective attack on a witness is an attack on the witness's truthfulness

Often, the most effective attack on a witness is an attack on the witness's truthfulness. Where a witness is a proven liar, even the jury disregards the witness's entire testimony. Jurors are very unforgiving of witnesses they find not to be truthful – especially in the case of party witnesses. Where you can show a party is lying, you may prevail on the case even if other elements of the case are weak. Witness preparation is any communication between a lawyer and a prospective witness-client or non-client, friendly or hostile, that improves the substance or presentation of testimony at a trial or other hearing. Witness preparation enables lawyers to present witnesses who are thoroughly familiar with the subject matter of their testimony and who say what they know in a clear, coherent manner. 2 American litigators regularly use witness preparation-

Mr. Wellman's book is not, as its title might lead many people to suppose, written solely for lawyers. It has no place with the great company of dreary and dignified tomes of sheepskin that fill the bookshelves in attorneys' offices. The cross-examiner must not fuss with his notes but must watch every move of his witness as a prizefighter watches his opponent, sparring guardedly for an opening, landing a telling blow at the first opportunity and making every hit tell.

In most common law jurisdictions, cross-examination is on customary oath. The trial process, civil or criminal, is an interrogative exercise done under oath or affirmation of a witness called by the opposing party. It will or should only be resorted to if a witness gives evidence contrary to the interest of the cross-examiner's client. Unnecessary cross-examination is not only wasteful of court time but can sometimes produce disastrous results. Cross-examination is usually preceded by examination in chief and is followed by re-examination. Leading questions are allowed in cross-examination but usually not in examination in chief nor re-examination. In many jurisdictions, there are rules of the Court regulating the procedure to be followed during cross-examination, mainly where there are multiple cross-examiners. There are also professional conduct rules dealing with cross-examination, which, if breached, may have severe consequences for the practitioner.

Establish your goals for each witness

Not every witness needs cross-examination. When cross-examining a witness will add nothing to your client's case (or perhaps might even hurt it), you should probably avoid it. However, when cross-examination could help your client's case, it's critical to establish your goals before you begin.

- Do you want the witness to confirm essential facts?
- Is your goal confirming the theory of your client's case?
- Is your goal damaging the witness's credibility?

Knowing where you want to go with a witness will dictate the cross-examination road you take. You will then pave this road with strategic, leading questions based on your thorough review of the witness's prior testimony in depositions and at trial, as well as relevant admissible evidence.

Structure your questions to box witnesses

A tenet of cross-examination is that you should only ask questions you know the answers to. When you do, you can control a witness and force them to testify to facts beneficial to your client's case. But how you ask your questions is the key to getting the answers you are looking for.

Each question you ask during your cross-examination should be a leading question, such as "It was raining that evening, correct?" Leading questions nudge witnesses in the direction you want them to go while also limiting their ability to explain their answers.

Each question you ask should focus on one fact. When it does, it will necessarily be succinct. Concise questions are tricky for witnesses to dodge while also staying credible in the eyes of jurors.

Finally, it would help if you were cross-examining witnesses about facts, not opinions. Opinions are pliant and differ from person to person. Facts are not and do not. For example, you should not ask a witness if they thought an item was "heavy." Instead, you should ask questions that show the witness *knew* it was heavy, such as, "For safety reasons, you required your coworkers to move the machine with a forklift, correct?"

Strategically use constructive & deconstructive cross-examination

There are two types of cross-examination. You would use *constructive* cross-examination to build your client's theory of the case and *deconstructive* cross-examination to damage a witness's credibility. Each requires a different approach.

Constructive cross-examination

When constructively cross-examining a witness, you are attempting to draw out helpful testimony from an adverse witness. The cross-examination should feel like a conversation and not an attack. When you establish a helpful fact through constructive cross-examination, the jury is likely to give it significant weight in its deliberations because it came from an adverse witness instead of one of your witnesses. When you can confirm a fact that is helpful to your client's case through constructive cross-examination, you should.

Deconstructive cross-examination

When deconstructively cross-examining a witness, you are attempting to control an adverse witness and damage their credibility. This is the type of cross-examination jurors are used to seeing in movies and on television. That means they'll expect you to start strong and finish with a bang by constantly challenging the witness and boxing them in (using the above structure for questions). If you fail to do so, *you* may lose credibility. Deconstructive cross-examinations are most effective when they call into question facts integral to your opponent's theory of the case.

There may be some instances where you will want to both constructively and deconstructively cross-examine a witness. If you do both, be sure to do the former before the latter. If not, jurors may not view the witness's confirmation of facts favourable to your client's case as credible.

Know witnesses' prior testimony inside & out

No matter your goal for each witness or how you plan on accomplishing it, to elicit the testimony you seek, you must know each witness's prior testimony and relevant admissible evidence regarding the witness, like the back of your hand.

Of course, in deciding to cross-examine a witness, you will have already reviewed that witness's deposition testimony, trial testimony and relevant, admissible evidence to find every opportunity to bolster your client's case or damage the witness's credibility. But you will need more than a cursory knowledge of that testimony or evidence -- you can use tools like Public Records to help.

If, during their cross-examination, a witness answers a question that conflicts with what you expected their answer on their prior testimony or evidence, you will need to reassert control and hold the witness to their prior testimony or evidence. The only way to do that is to know (and equip yourself at trial with) all the times when that witness has previously testified to, or where admissible evidence supports, the testimony you are now attempting to elicit from that witness. Otherwise, you will be unable to pin the witness down.

Keep your cool with uncooperative witnesses

No matter how strategically you prepare for and execute a cross-examination, chances are that at some point, the witness is not going to give you a simple "yes" or "no" answer and will begin to challenge you. When they do so, you must keep your cool. Otherwise, you will likely lose credibility.

As a witness becomes less cooperative, stay calm and professional. Maintain eye contact. Politely interrupt their evasive answers and remind them of your question and that they should answer with only "Yes" or "No." Use subtle body language clues such as holding your hand up to the witness to stop them or shaking your head from side to side so as to say "No." If the witness is still not cooperating, politely ask the judge to instruct the witness to answer the question.

Rise to the occasion

The stakes are high with cross-examinations. The testimony you elicit from a witness can make or break your client's case. But with the proper preparation, strategy, and execution, you can conduct effective cross-examinations that positively advance your client's cases.

A key aspect of preparation and building a winning strategy is using tools that set you up for success. It's essential to be able to research your witness before entering the courtroom -- and not all tools equip you to win equally. Public Records, offered through LexisNexis, uses SmartLinx technology to pull information from over 86 billion available nationwide records and compile it into a digestible report. If you'd like to learn more about Public Records, contact us or click below to visit the product page to learn the nature and origin of public record information. The public records and commercially available data sources used in reports may contain errors.

The crux of cross-examination

In cross-examination, the other party's representative will ask you questions based on your witness statement. The cross-examination aims to discredit you as a witness, to undermine or neutralize your evidence, or to get you to change it. This is no cause for alarm as most advocates are pretty average and not of the standard you will have seen on and in films. Contrary to the impression from fiction in movies and T.V., T.V. cross-examination is rarely aggressive.

Advocates do not ask questions because they want to know your answers. A good advocate already knows how he wants you to answer, and he will attempt to control your answer so that it comes out in a way that supports his case. The golden rule for advocates is that usually, they should never ask a question they don't know the answer to. If an advocate doesn't know what a witness is likely to say, there is a danger that the witness will say something the advocate doesn't like. For this reason, the better advocates are unlikely to ask you to comment in a general way on the evidence or for your opinion. They don't want to know, and they don't want the panel to hear your views either. When you get an opportunity, and it seems appropriate, exercise your right to free speech. Your role isn't to give the advocate just what the advocate wants. Your responsibility is to tell the truth.

The advocate is trying to get you to say things in front of the panel which in some way support their argument. At the same time, they will not want you to say anything that damages their case. You often see examples on TV or in films of advocates saying to witnesses that they wish for a "yes" or "no" answer. That is usually because a simple "yes" or "no" will give the limited view that they seek to present without explaining the larger reality. As we know, reality is often far more complex.

We should not try to appear evasive or unwilling to give a straight answer, but we should not trap them to provide an inaccurate or misrepresentative answer. Indeed, do not allow yourself to say something that isn't entirely true or of which you are not sure. If what you have to say is not accurate, say so.

There is no shortcut or royal road to proficiency in the art of advocacy and cross-examination. It is experience alone that brings success. On the other hand. "whose art and graceful qualities of mind entitle him to the foremost rank among American advocates in cross-examination" never aroused the opposition of a witness by attacking him. He disarmed his man by the quiet and courteous manner in which he pursued his cross-examination.

The distinction between general practitioners and specialists is already established in the medical profession and approved by the public.

Who would think nowadays of submitting himself to a severe operation at the hands of his family physician instead of calling in an experienced surgeon to handle the knife? Yet, the family physician may have once been competent to play the role of surgeon, and doubtless, he has had, years ago, his quota of hospital experience. But he so infrequently enters the domain of surgery that he shrinks from undertaking it, except for the underrepresented.

There is a marked distinction between discrediting the testimony and discrediting the witness. It is essentially a matter of instinct on the part of the examiner. A skilful cross-examiner seldom takes his eye from an essential witness while his adversary is examining him. Every expression on his face, especially his mouth, and even the movement of his hands helped the examiner to estimate his integrity.

If the cross-examiner allows the witness to see that he distrusts his integrity, he will straighten himself out in the witness chair and mentally defy him at once. If the counsel's manner is courteous and conciliatory, the witness will soon lose all fear. Many members still sneer at trial by jury. Such men, however, when not among the unsuccessful and disgruntled, will, with but few exceptions, be found to have had but little practice themselves in Court or else to belong to that ever-growing class in our profession who have relinquished their court practice and are building up fortunes such as were never dreamed of in the legal profession but learners in the law as a profession, and who through opportunity, combined with rare commercial ability, have come to apply their learning, especially their knowledge of corporate law to great commercial enterprises, combinations, organizations, and reorganizations, and have thus come to practise law as a business

A race of experience

it is a race of experience. The experienced advocate can look back upon those less advanced in years of experience and rest content in the thought that there are just so many cases behind him that if he keeps on, with equal opportunities in Court, they can never overtake him. Some day, the public will recognize this fact. But at present, what does the ordinary litigant know of the advantages of having counsel to conduct his case which is "at home "in the courtroom and perhaps even acquainted with the very panel of jurors before whom his case is to be heard, through having already tried one or more cases for other clients before the same men? How little can the ordinary businessman realize the value to himself of having a lawyer who understands the habits of thought and of looking at evidence the bent of mind of the very judge who is to preside at the trial of his case? Not that our judges are not eminently fair-minded in the conduct of trials, but they are men for all that, often very human men, and the trial lawyer who knows his judge starts with an advantage that the inexperienced practitioner little appreciates. How much, too, does experience count in the selection of the jury itself, one of the "fine arts" of the advocate? These are but a few of the many similar advantages one might enumerate. Were they not apart from the subject, we are now concerned with the skill of the advocate in conducting the trial itself once we have chosen the jury. When the public realizes that a good trial lawyer is an outcome, one might say of generations of witnesses, when clients fully appreciate the dangers they run in intrusting their litigations to so-called "office lawyers "with little to no experience in Court, they will insist upon their briefs being entrusted to those who make a speciality of court practice, advised and assisted, if you will, by their private attorneys. The chief will eliminated, speedy trials will clear the court calendars, and justice will be speedier.

It is absurd to assume any witness who has sworn positively to a particular set of facts, even if he has inadvertently stretched the truth, is going to be readily induced by a lawyer to alter them and acknowledge his mistake. People, as a rule, do not reflect upon their meagre opportunities for observing facts and rarely suspect the frailty of their powers of observation.

Expert witnesses

Witnesses can only give evidence of what they know from the sense of what they saw, heard, smelt, touched or tasted. But experts are in a class of their own. An expert can give evidence of opinion. That opinion must be in a field of specialised knowledge, and the witness must have gained expertise in that field through training, study or experience. We must identify facts on which an expert gives an opinion.

Before you cross-examine an expert, you will need to do a great deal of preparation. With a lay witness, you can use your knowledge of human affairs and your courtroom experience. With an expert, it is quite different. The advocate starts from an inferior position. Without careful preparation, the advocate will not be able to detect fallacies, oversights, exaggerations, evasions or distortions. With diligence, you will be able to master sufficient expertise. To put it another way, if the advocate with perseverance cannot follow the expert's propositions, neither will the court.

It is critical to research the expert's qualifications, community standing in the expert's field, and prior testifying experience. Perhaps the most crucial place to look for helpful information is in the expert's prior testimony. Finding a similar case in which the expert gave conflicting expert testimony is effective ammunition for cross-examination. It is also essential to identify and read the expert's prior writings. Many experts maintain their web pages, and the contents can be used for cross-examination.

Biased experts

Biased expert witnesses pose a distinct challenge to the legal system. In the criminal sphere, they have contributed to several wrongful convictions, and in civil cases, they can protract disputes and reduce faith in legal jurisprudence. The data suggests that an increase in the frequency of challenges related to expert biases did not noticeably affect the proportion of experts excluded. This suggests that the exclusionary rule did not significantly impact the practical operation of expert evidence law as it pertains to bias. Kazi Karimuddin usually concluded by recommending that one way for courts to address the problem of biased experts better is to recognize the issue of contextual bias.

One of the most formidable hurdles in generating and conveying knowledge is curbing one's own biases; we often see what we want to see can occur unintentionally and even unconsciously. In law, many wrongful accusations and convictions are a product of biased expert judgments (we will parse the term "bias"). This is known as the bias blind spot and has been demonstrated explicitly by both forensic science experts and forensic psychology experts.

The biases of experts studied the biases of forensic experts and how to limit them. Despite the detrimental effect expert bias has on legal proceedings, courts around the world have traditionally refrained from excluding experts for non-independence, partiality, or prejudice. Instead, courts have let concerns of bias affect the weight ascribed to an expert's testimony system. This has inspired a great deal of legal-psychological research studying expert biases and how to mitigate them. In response to the problem of biased experts, courts have historically employed procedural mechanisms to manage partiality but have generally refrained from using the exclusionary rule.

The manner of cross-examination

It needs but the simple statement of the nature of cross-examination to demonstrate its indispensable character in all trials of questions of fact. No cause reaches the stage of litigation unless there are two sides to it. If the witnesses on one side deny or qualify the statements made by those on the other, which side is telling the truth? It is not necessarily which side is offering perjured testimony; there is far less intentional perjury in the courts than the inexperienced would believe, but which side is honestly mistaken? On the other hand, the evidence itself is far less trustworthy than what the public usually realizes. The opinions of which side are warped by prejudice or blinded by ignorance? Which side has had the power or opportunity to observe correctly? How shall we tell? How can we make it apparent to a jury of disinterested men who are to decide between the litigants? Obviously, by the means of cross-examination. If all witnesses had the honesty and intelligence to come forward and carefully followed the letter as well as the spirit of the oath, "to tell the truth, the whole truth, and nothing but the truth," and if all advocates on either side had the necessary experience, combined with honesty and intelligence, had similar swearing to develop the whole truth and nothing. Still, the truth, of course, is that there would be no occasion for cross-examination. The occupation of the cross-examiner would be gone. But as yet, no substitute has ever been found for cross-examination as a means of separating truth from falsehood and of reducing exaggerated statements to their actual dimensions.

The system is as old as the history of nations. Indeed, to this day, the account given by Plato of Socrates's cross-examination of his accuser, Miletus, while defending himself against the capital charge of corrupting the youth of Athens may be quoted as a masterpiece in the art of cross-questioning to discover the weak point in the witness under examination. One has to deal with a prodigious variety of witnesses testifying under an infinite number of differing circumstances. It involves all shades and complexions of human morals, human passions, and human intelligence. It is the mental duel between counsel and witness. In discussing the methods to employ when cross-examining a witness, let us imagine ourselves at work in the trial of a cause and the close of the direct examination of a witness called by our adversary.

The first inquiry would naturally be, Has the witness testified to anything that is material against us? Has his testimony injured our side of the case? Has he made an impression with the jury against us? Is it necessary for us to cross-examine him at all? Before dismissing a witness, however, the possibility of incorporating new facts that may favour plaintiffs should be explored. If the witness is truthful and candid, plain, straightforward questions are needed. If, however, there is any reason to doubt the willingness of the witness to help develop the truth, it may be necessary to proceed with more caution and possibly to put the witness in a position where it will appear to the jury that he could tell a good deal if he wanted to, and then leave him. The jury will thus draw the inference that, had he spoken, it would have been in our favour. But suppose the witness has testified to material facts against us, and it becomes our duty to break the force of his testimony or abandon all hope of a jury verdict. How shall we begin? How shall we tell whether the witness has made an honest mistake or has committed perjury? The methods in his cross-examination in the two instances would naturally be very different.

Some people call it the language of the eye, or the tone of the voice, or the countenance of the witness, or his manner of testifying, or all combined, that betrays the wilful perjurer. It is difficult to say what it is, except that constant practice seems to enable a trial lawyer to form a pretty accurate judgment on this point. A skilful cross-examiner seldom takes his eye off an important witness while his adversary is examining him. Every expression on his face, especially his mouth, every movement of his hands, his manner of expressing himself, and his whole bearing all help the examiner arrive at an accurate estimate of his integrity. Let us assume, then, that we have been correct in our judgment of this particular witness and that he is trying to describe the occurrences to which he has testified but has fallen into a severe mistake through ignorance or blunder. Oversight needs to be taken care of in the minds of the jury. How shall we go about it?

Best lawyers are withdrawing from court practice

It is often honestly said that many of our best lawyers are withdrawing from court practice because the nature of the litigation is changing.

To such an extent, this change is taking place in some localities, where the more critical commercial cases rarely reach a court decision. Our merchants prefer to compromise their difficulties or to write off their losses rather than enter into litigations that must remain dormant in the courts for upward of three years, awaiting their turn for a hearing on the overcrowded court calendars. The sympathies of the jury are invariably on the side of the witness. They are quick to resent any discourtesy toward him. They are willing to admit his mistakes if you can make them apparent, but they are slow to believe him guilty of perjury. A good advocate should be a good actor.

This congestion is not wholly due to lack of judges or that they are not capable and industrious men, but is large, the fault of the system in vogue in all American courts of allowing any lawyer, duly enrolled as a member of the Bar, to practise in the highest courts. In the United States, there is no distinction between barrister and solicitor; we wear all barristers and solicitors by turn. One has but to frequent the courts to become convinced that, so long as the ten thousand members at the NewYork County Bar all avail themselves of their privilege to appear in Court and try their own clients' cases, the great majority of the trials will be shoddily, and much valuable time wasted. The conduct of a case in Court is a peculiar art for which many men, however, learned in the law, are not fit. Where a lawyer has but one or even a dozen experiences in Court each year, he can never become a competent trial lawyer.

One experienced in the trial of causes will not require, at the utmost, more than a quarter of the time taken by the most learned, inexperienced lawyer in developing his facts. His case will be profoundly prepared and understood before the trial begins. The presentation will be clear and presented to the Court and jury with brevity. He will, in this way, avoid many of the erroneous rulings on questions of law and evidence, which have been upsetting so many verdicts on appeal. He will not only complete his trial in a shorter time, but he will be likely to bring about an equitable verdict in the case, which may not require appeal and will have good chances of success by a higher court instead of being sent back for a retrial and the consequent consumption of the time of another judge and jury in doing the work all over again. These facts are becoming more and more appreciated each year. In our local courts, there is already an ever-increasing coterie of trial lawyers who are devoting the principal part of their time to court practice. A few lawyers have gone so far as to refuse direct communication with clients except as they come represented by their attorneys.

It is absurd to suppose that any witness who has sworn positively to a particular set of facts, even if he has inadvertently stretched the truth, is going to be readily induced by a lawyer to alter them and acknowledge his mistake. People, as a rule, do not reflect upon their meagre opportunities for observing facts and rarely suspect the frailty of their powers of observation. They come to Court, when summoned as witnesses, prepared to tell what they think is known to them in the beginning, resent an attack upon their story as they would upon their integrity. If the cross-examiner allows the witness to see, by his manner toward him at the start, that he distrusts his integrity, he will straighten himself in the witness chair and mentally defy him at once. If, on the other hand, the counsel's manner is courteous and conciliatory, the witness will soon lose the fear all witnesses have of the cross-examiner and can almost imperceptibly induce to enter into a discussion of his testimony in a fairminded spirit, which, if the cross-examiner is clever, will soon disclose the weak points in the testimony. The sympathies of the jury are invariably on the side of the witness, and they are quick to resent any discourtesy toward him. They are willing to admit his mistakes if you can make them apparent, but they are slow to believe him guilty of perjury. Alas, how often is this lost sight of in our daily court experiences? One is constantly brought face to face with lawyers who act as if they think that everyone who testifies against their side of the case is committing willful perjury—no wonder they accomplish so little.

Brow-beating style of law practice

By their shouting and brow-beating style, the cross-examiners often confuse the wits of the witness. It is true, but they fail to discredit him with the jury. On the contrary, they elicit sympathy for the witness they are attacking. Little realize that their "vigorous cross-examination," at the end of which they sit down with evident self-satisfaction, has only served to close the mind of at least one fairminded juryman against their side of the case effectually, and as likely as not, it has brought to light some critical fact favourable to the other side which remained unrevealed in the examination-in-chief. A good advocate should be a good actor. The most cautious cross-examiner will often elicit a damaging answer. Now is the time for the most excellent self-control. If you show by your face how the answer hurts, you may lose your case by that one point alone. How often does one see the cross-examiner somewhat staggered by such an answer? He pauses, perhaps blushes, and after he has allowed the answer to have its full effect, he finally regains his self-possession but seldom his control over the witness. With the really experienced trial lawyer, such answers, instead of appearing to surprise or disconcert him, will seem to come as a matter of course and will fall perfectly flat. He will proceed with the following question as if nothing had happened, or even perhaps give the witness an incredulous smile as if to say, "Who do you suppose would believe that for a minute?"There is an anecdote apropos to this point. He suffered the witness go through his statement and then, as if he saw in it something of great value to himself, requested him to repeat it carefully so that he might take it down correctly. He carefully avoided cross-examining the witness and, in his argument, made not the least allusion to his testimony. When the opposing counsel, in his close, came to that part of his case in his argument, he was so impressed with the idea that he had discovered that there was something in that testimony which made it in his favour. However, he could not see how he contented himself with merely remarking that though he had seemed to think that the testimony bore in favour of his client, it seemed to him that it went to sustain the opposite side and then went on with the other parts of his case."

It is the love of combat that every man possesses that fastens the jury's attention to the progress of the trial. The counsel who has a pleasant personality; who speaks with apparent frankness; who appears to an earnest searcher after truth; who is courteous to those who testify against him; who avoids constantly delaying the progress of the trial by innumerable objections and exceptions to perhaps incompetent but harmless evidence; who seems to know what he is about and sits down when he has accomplished it, exhibiting a spirit of fair play on all occasions. it is he who creates an atmosphere in favour of the side that he represents, a powerful though unconscious influence on the jury in arriving at their verdict. Even if, owing to the weight of testimony, the verdict is against him, the amount will be far less than the client had schooled himself to expect. On the other hand, the lawyer who wearies the Court and the jury with endless and pointless cross-examinations, who is constantly losing his temper and showing his teeth to the witnesses, who wears a sour, anxious expression, who possesses a monotonous, rasping, penetrating voice; who presents an untidy, unkempt personal appearance; who is prone to take unfair advantage of witness or counsel, and seems determined to win at all hazards soon prejudices a jury against himself and the client he represents, entirely irrespective of the sworn testimony in the case.

Cleverness of cross-examiner

The evidence often seems to be going all one way, when in reality, it is not so at all. The cleverness of the cross-examiner has a great deal to do with this; he can often create an atmosphere that will obscure much evidence that would otherwise tell against him. This is part of the "generalship of a case "in its progress to the argument, which is of such vast consequence. There is eloquence displayed in the examination of witnesses as well as in the argument. "There is matter in the manner? I do not mean to advocate that exaggerated manner one often meets with, which divides the attention of your hearers between yourself and your question, which often diverts the attention of the jury from the point you are trying to make and centres it upon your peculiarities of manner and speech. As the man who was somewhat deaf and could not get near enough to Henry Clay in one of his finest efforts, exclaimed, "I didn't hear a word he said, but, great Jehovah, didn't he make the motions!" The very intonations of voice and the expression on the face of the cross-examiner can influence the jury and enable them to appreciate a point they might otherwise not take into consideration,

It is one thing to have the opportunity to observe or even the intelligence to observe correctly. However, it is still another thing to be able to retain accurately, for any length of time, what we have once seen or heard, and what is perhaps more problematic is still to be able to describe it intelligibly. Many witnesses have seen one part of a transaction and heard about another part, and later on, become confused in their minds, or perhaps only in their modes of expression, as to what they have seen themselves and what they have heard from others. All witnesses are prone to exaggerate, enlarge, or minimize the facts to which they take oath. A prevalent type of witness met with almost daily is the man who, having witnessed some event years ago, suddenly finds that he has to be a court witness. He immediately attempts to recall his original impressions. Gradually, as he talks with the attorney who is to examine him, he amplifies his story with new details, which he leads himself to believe are recollections. Which he finally swears to be facts. Although perfectly honest in intention, they are apt, in consequence, to complete their story by recourse to their imagination. And few witnesses fail, at least in some part of their story, to entangle facts with their own beliefs and inferences. All these considerations should readily suggest a line of questions, varying with each witness examined, that will, if closely followed, be likely to separate appearance from reality and to reduce exaggerations to their proper proportions. It is fresher then and has a more lasting effect than if left until the summing up and then drawn to the attention of the jury. The experienced examiner can usually tell, after a few simple questions, what line to pursue. Picture the scene in your mind; closely inquire into the sources of the witness's information, and draw your conclusions as to how his mistake arose and why he formed his erroneous impressions. Exhibit plainly your belief in his integrity and your desire to be fair with him, and try to seduce him into being candid with you. Then, when the particular fault that affected his testimony comes to mind, he could quickly tell the jury. His mistakes should often be drawn out by inference rather than by direct question because all witnesses have a dread of self-contradiction. Suppose he sees the connection between your inquiries and his own story. In that case, he will draw upon his imagination for explanations before you get the chance to point out to him the inconsistency between his later statement and his original one.

One must avoid the mistake, so common among the inexperienced, of making many trifling discrepancies. There is a witty remark that "juries have no respect for small triumphs over a witness's self-possession or memory." Allow the loquacious witness to talk on; he will be sure to involve himself in difficulties from which he can never extricate himself. Some witnesses prove altogether too much; encourage them and lead them by degrees into exaggerations that will conflict with the common sense of the jury. Under no circumstances can a false construction be made on the words of a witness; there are few faults in an advocate that are more offensive in a jury.'s impression. If, perchance, you obtain a really favourable answer, leave it and quietly pass it on to some other inquiry. The inexperienced examiner, in all probability, will repeat the question with the idea of impressing the admission upon his hearers instead of reserving it for the summing up and will attribute it to bad luck that his witness corrects his answer or modifies it in some way so that the point is lost. He is indeed a poor judge of human nature who supposes that if he triumphs over his success during the cross-examination, he will not quickly put the witness on his guard to avoid all future favourable disclosures.

A strategy where the witness won ferret the whole truth

It is well, sometimes, in a case where you believe that the witness is reluctant to develop the whole truth, so to put questions that answers you know will be elicited may come by way of a surprise and in the light of improbability to the jury. I remember a recent incident, illustrative of this point, which occurred in a suit brought to recover the insurance on a large warehouse full of goods that had been burnt to the ground. The insurance companies were unable to find any stock book that would show the amount of goods in stock at the time of the fire. One of the witnesses to the fire happened to be the plaintiff's bookkeeper, who, on direct examination, testified to all the details of the fire but had nothing to say about the books. The cross-examination had few pointed questions."I suppose you had an iron safe in your office, in which you kept your book of account?" "Yes, sir."

"Did that burn up?" "Oh, no." "Were you present when it was opened after the fire?" "Yes, sir." "Then won't you be good enough to hand me the stock book that we may show the jury exactly what stock you had on hand at the time of the fire on which you claim a loss? ("I haven't it, sir." "What, haven't the stock book? You do mean you have lost it?" "It wasn't in the safe, sir." "Wasn't that the proper place for it?': "Yes, sir." "How was it that the book wasn't there?" "It had evidently been left out the night before the fire by mistake." Some of the jury at once drew the inference that the all-important stock book was being suppressed and refused to agree with their fellows against the insurance companies. Presented by The Law Offices of Eric Michael Papp, Corona, California - www.ca-nvlaw.com

The average mind is much wiser than many suppose. Questions can be put to a witness under cross-examination, in argumentative form, often with far more significant effect upon the minds of the jury. The juryman sees the point for himself as if it were his discovery and clings to it all the more painstakingly. During the cross-examination of Henry Ward Beecher in the celebrated Tilton-Beecher case, and after Mr Beecher had denied his alleged intimacy with Mr Tilton's wife, Judge Fullerton read a passage from one of Mr.

Beecher's sermons are to the effect that if a person commits a great sin, the exposure of which would cause misery to others, such a person would not be justified in confessing it, merely to relieve his conscience. Fullerton then looked straight into Mr. Beecher's eyes and said, "Do you still consider that sound doctrine?" Mr. Beecher replied, "I do." The inference a juror might draw from this question and answer would constitute a subtle argument upon that branch of the case.

8. KAZI KARIMUDDIN'S TIPS FOR A SKILLFUL CROSS-EXAMINER

An expert in the dock

These days, when it is impossible to know everything, but it becomes necessary for success in any avocation to know something of everything and everything of something, the expert is more and more called upon as a witness in both civil and criminal cases. In these times of specialists, their services are necessary to aid the jury in their investigations of questions of fact relating to subjects with which the ordinary man is not acquainted.

The cross-examination of various experts, whether medical, handwriting, real estate or other specialists, is a subject of growing importance. Here are a few illustrations of specific methods that can give more or less success in the examination of this class of witnesses.

It has become a matter of common observation that not only can the honest opinions of different experts be obtained upon opposite sides of the same question, but dishonest opinions may also be suppressed when the same question has different facets.

Attention is to the distinction between mere matters of scientific fact and mundane matters of opinion. In opinion, the experts differ so much among themselves that mere expert opinion becomes a conjecture beat around the bus bush, which is unlikely to produce any concrete pah or conclusion and will only lead to the wilderness. It is unwise for the cross-examiner to attempt to cope with a specialist in his field of inquiry. Lengthy cross-examinations along the lines of the expert's theory are usually disastrous and need caution.

Drift, debate, and division are the inevitable aftermath of significant political and financial scams, and it will take time and leadership- to discover, create and build upon a viable consensus that can arise from the confessions. Cross-examination is the most effective device for testing the veracity of witnesses. Great faith is placed in the capacity of the skilful cross-examiner to expose dishonest, mistaken or unreliable witnesses and to uncover inconsistencies and inaccuracies in oral testimony. The objective of cross-examination is to elicit information that is favourable to the cross-examiner and to cast doubt on the accuracy of the evidence given by the witness.

Kazi's approach to criminal law

Kazi Syes Karimuddin was one of the most versatile criminal lawyers in Central India, and his legal bandwidth and canvas extended his expertise to a vast range of legal matters, both civil and criminal. Kazi Karimuddinn relied on his phenomenal memory and rarely had assistants. He believed in developing insights into the minds of witnesses, handling and addressing them with mesmerising gestures and questions. The testimony contains ha so many diversions, evasions, and conflicts, which are sometimes inadequate to reveal the truth. Here, you need a remarkable cross-examiner.

The great American Watergate was a titanic, but Kazi Karimuddin handled many smaller titanics with great finesse. His juniors admit that hidden trials conjure up the image of the cross-examiner decimating the expert witness in the witness box. Total deconstruction of expert evidence in court occurs only rarely. In reality, lawyers who cross-examine experts are often at a disadvantage as they do not possess sufficient in-depth knowledge of the specific field. This is where Kazi Karimuddin overturned his adversaries.

The importance of skilful questioning during cross-examination

When it comes to criminal defence attorneys, the ability to ask skilful questions during cross-examination is an art form that can make or break a case. It is an essential tool in the arsenal that criminal defence attorneys use. No one understands this better than the attorneys at the Law Offices of Richard J. Fuschino Jr. Read on for more information on the significance of skilful questioning during cross-examination and how it can be the difference between success and failure in a criminal trial, especially when facing complex cases like white-collar crimes.

The art of cross-examination

Cross-examination is a pivotal phase in a trial as the defence attorney gets the opportunity to question the prosecution's witnesses. It is a battle of wits, strategy, and knowledge of law. The attorneys know that the questions they ask witnesses can shape the narrative of the case and influence the jury's perception of their client.

A series of prosodic questions can become a tool for circumventing institutional constraints which police the boundary between evidence and interpretation. By asking leading questions that project their expected answers, framing the questions as statements of fact that invite the witness's agreement, and painstakingly building the propositions step by step, the lawyer is able to simulate a monologue and control the trajectory of the flow of confession of the witness. The lawyer takes the witness through the entire trajectory, giving him no hint of the various contours that will pose challenges he will need to surmount the lawyer, which will make the task of ferreting out the truth. Medical experts will reliably agree to correct statements of decontextualized medical principles without attempting to apply the principles to the facts of the case, with the lawyer using prosodic questions which have embedded in them subtle hints based on principles that are juicy to the judges who are predisposed to hear his questions as an attack on the witness's testimony—with a point-by-point narrative critique and counterversion of the witness' conclusions. This clairvoyant can produce the witness' agreement with this critique and counterversion. The lawyer thus achieves a narrative transformation of the evidence in which the witness' damaging conclusions substitute benign explanations through the production of a multilevel discourse that controls what both the witness and the jurors hear. The witness's confessi clinches the case in the plaintiff's favour.

Uncovering the truth

One of the main objectives of cross-examination is to uncover the truth. The best white-collar crime attorneys know that behind every witness statement is a jumble of hidden facts that contain a heap of inconsistencies that throw up the pathway to facts. This is why skilful questioning can reveal these hidden truths, potentially leading to a better outcome for the defendant in a case.

Challenging credibility

In a court of law, credibility is everything. Criminal defence attorneys are well aware of this fact. Through skilful questioning, attorneys can challenge the credibility of the witness. This is especially important when it comes to cases involving white-collar crimes, where complex financial transactions and paper trails can give odour and create opportunities for misinterpretation or manipulation.

Creating doubt

Creating reasonable doubt is the foundation of criminal defence. This means that skilful questioning during cross-examination is an essential tool for attorneys to use to cast doubt on the prosecution's case. A skilful attorney will understand that even a single well-placed question can plant the seed of doubt in the minds of jurors, which can potentially lead to an acquittal.

Protecting the rights of the accused

The United States legal system places a very high value on the rights of the accused. Criminal defence attorneys take their role seriously in ensuring that the rights of clients get priority at all times. This is why they strive to create the most skilful line of questioning during cross-examination so that they can protect their clients from wrongful convictions and unjust penalties and sentences.

A strategic approach

Cross-examination is not an easy thing to do. It requires a very strategic approach, and this is where the expertise of a top-notch criminal defence attorney shines. Attorneys must carefully plan their questions, anticipate the responses, and have a backup plan in case things take an unexpected turn.

Expertise will enable them to cross-examine the witnesses

A necessary prerequisite of cross-examination is that the cross-examiner should reach a clear understanding of the issues involved in the trial. The trial lawyer should determine, in the first instance, whether his case will be served best by cross-examination. However, where it is to take place, lawyers should not be that they are overwhelmed by opposing experts and before submitting in deference to him - consider the following: Those who profess expert knowledge do not always possess it, and those who have it are not always correct.

I had accompanied my grandfather, Kazi Syed Karimuddin, in several bank cases. The insights gleaned from his expertise helped me when I became a banker. Examination of experts when examining a witness in a bank case, the order of examination is as follows:

- **Examination-in-chief**: The witness is first examined.
- **Cross-examination**: The adverse party can cross-examine the witness if they wish.
- **Re-examination**: The party calling the witness can re-examine them if they want to.

Here are some things to consider when examining a witness:

- The witness can be cross-examined on previous written statements that are relevant to the matter. The writing does not need to be shown to the witness.
- The order in which witnesses are examined is regulated by law and practice. If there is no law or practice, the court has discretion. The Supreme Court of India does not allow the recalling of witnesses to fill in gaps or cover remaining aspects.

Many lawyers, for example, undertake to cope with a medical or handwriting expert.

Many lawyers cope with a medical or handwriting expert on his ground—surgery, correct diagnosis, or the intricacies of penmanship. In some rare instances (more especially with poorly educated physicians), this method of cross-questioning produces results. More frequently, however, it only affords an opportunity for the doctor to enlarge upon the testimony he has already given and to explain what might otherwise be entirely overlooked by the jury. Experience believes experts should not be cross-examined on his speciality unless convinces him that he can expose the doctor's erroneous conclusions, not only to himself but to a jury who will not readily comprehend the abstract theories of physiology upon which even the medical profession has divergent views.

On the other hand, some careful and judicious questions seeking to bring out separate facts and points from the knowledge and experience of the expert will tend to support the theory of the attorney's side of the case and usually produce good results. In other words, the art of the cross-examiner should be directed at bringing out such scientific facts from the knowledge of the expert as they will help his case and thus tend to destroy the weight of the opinion of the expert given against him.

No broad question should be put to an expert to afford him a chance in his answer to give his reasons in his way, for his opinions, which counsel calling him an expert might not otherwise have fully brought out in his examination.

A practical guide for the future is to study how juries have discredited expert witnesses in the past. The whole effect of the testimony of an expert witness may sometimes effectually be decimated by putting the witness to some unexpected and offhand test at the trial [as to his experience, his ability and discrimination as an expert so that in case he fails to meet the test he will be ridiculed before the jury. Thus, the laughter at his expense will cause the jury to forget anything of weight that he has said against you.

A very prominent physician, president of one of our leading clubs at the time, but now dead, had advised a woman who had been his housekeeper for thirty years and who had broken her ankle as a consequence of stepping into an unprotected hole in the street pavement, to bring suit against the city to recover $40,000 damages. There was very little defence to the principal cause of action: the hole in the street *was* there, and the plaintiff ha*d* stepped into it, but her right to recover substantial damages was vigorously contested.

Her principal, in fact, was her only medical witness, and her employer was a famous physician. The doctor testified to the plaintiff's sufferings, described the fracture of her ankle, explained how he had himself set the broken bones and attended the patient, but affirmed that all his efforts were of no avail as he could bring about nothing[89] but an imperfect union of the bones and that his housekeeper, a most respectable and estimable lady, would be lame for life. His manner on the witness stand was exceedingly dignified and frank and evidently impressed the jury. The intimate personal acquaintance between the cross-examiner and the witness can be another embarrassment.

The cross-examination began by showing that the witness, although a graduate of Harvard, had not immediately entered a medical school, but on the contrary, had started in business on Wall Street, had later been manager of several business enterprises, and had not begun the study of medicine until he was forty years old. The examination then continued in the most amiable manner possible, each question in a tone almost of apology.

Counsel. "We all know, doctor, that you have a large and lucrative family practice as a general practitioner, but is +++it not a fact that in this great city, where accidents are of such common occurrence, surgical cases are usually taken to the hospitals and cared for by experienced surgeons?"

The doctor, amid roars of laughter from the jury, in which the entire courtroom joined, hastily readjusted the bones and sat blushing to the roots of his hair. Counsel waited until the laughter had subsided and then said quietly, "I think I will not trouble you further, doctor."

This incident is not the least bit exaggerated; on the contrary, the impression made by the occurrence is challenging to present adequately on paper. Counsel on both sides proceeded to sum up the case, and upon the part of the defence, no allusion whatsoever was made to the incident. The jury appreciated the fact and returned a verdict for the plaintiff of $240. The next day, the learned doctor wrote a four-page letter of thanks and appreciation stating that the results of his "stage fright" had not been spread before the jury in the closing speech.

An estimate of the susceptibility of occasional juries drawn from some country panels to have their attention diverted from the facts in a case by their fondness for entertainment has, at times, induced attorneys to try the experiment of framing their questions on cross-examination of medical experts so that the questions themselves will amuse the jury. It will overlook the damaging testimony given by a serious-minded and learned opposing medical witness.

An illustration of this was afforded not long ago by a case brought by a woman against the Trustees of the New York and Brooklyn Bridge. The plaintiff, while alighting from a bridge car, stepped into the space between the vehicle and the bridge platform and fell up to her armpits. She claimed that she had sustained injuries to her ribs, lungs, and chest and that she was suffering from resultant pleurisy and intercostal neuritis. A specialist on nerve injuries, called by the defence, had testified that there was nothing the matter with the plaintiff, as he had tested her with the stethoscope and had made a thorough examination, had listened at her chest to detect such "rales" as are generally left after pleurisy and had failed to find any lesions or injuries to the pleural nerves whatsoever.

Judicial resistance to expert testimony

A skilful cross-examination is a technique used by lawyers to challenge the credibility of a witness and discredit their testimony. Expert testimony on eyewitness identification is one of the most controversial issues in evidentiary procedure today. With false identifications recognized as a leading cause of wrongful convictions ., numerous commentators have urged courts to expand the use of expert testimony to educate jurors about the shortcomings of eyewitnesses and recently heightened the stakes of the debate, identifying the availability of specialist testimony among its reasons for refusing to strengthen judicial filters against admittedly unreliable identifications. Yet admission of expert testimony on eyewitness identifications remains the exception rather than the rule. 6 Because the unreliability of eyewitness testimony is a matter of "common knowledge" among lay jurors, courts insist juries are competent to evaluate eyewitnesses without the benefit of any specialized expertise — to impeach faulty evidence "using their common-sense and faculties of observation" alone.

Among courts today, for example, only two circuits actively favour the admission of eye-witness expert testimony, while eight favour exclusion in the absence of certain narrowly defined circumstances, and one exercise a per se exclusionary rule.

While courts formally justify their exclusion of experts based on the sufficiency of the jury's common-sense authority over eyewitness evidence, even judges who acknowledge the dramatic deficiencies in jurors' knowledge of eyewitness identifications resist admitting expert testimony on the subject. Instead, these judges insist on addressing the limitations of lay juror knowledge through traditional safeguards, most notably cross-examination by opposing counsel9 and cautionary jury instructions issued by trial judges. 10 Especially in light of emerging research on the substantive shortcomings of such procedures, courts' insistence on the inability of scientific experts to contribute meaningfully to the trial process presents a marked contrast to courts' typical humility about their institutional competencies. Big defaulters are well-connected tycoons and have the money to employ legal eagles who can play the judicial system. Here, the law flounders. India has some of the most draconian laws in books; they are ineffective against mighty dodgers. We keep producing new rules when the existing ones are adequate and need more teeth to obtain results.

The reluctance of courts to admit expert testimony on eyewitness identifications has been attributed primarily to one concern: defending the competence of lay jurors to evaluate witness credibility against intrusion from self-identified experts. Despite a general trend toward admitting expert evidence on factual matters and mounting scientific research challenging jurors' ability to assess eyewitness evidence reliably, courts continue to affirm the sufficiency of the jury's lay knowledge in order to deny the utility of more rarefied knowledge on eye-witness identifications.

India's mounting destructive debris

A mounting pile of troubled loans beleagues the Indian banking system. The proportion of bad debts, where the borrower is not making interest payments or not repaying any principal, has surged to such horrifying levels that the banks are creaking under the strain. Several financial storms have rumbled on in the economic system, a third of which is on crutches. The perverse behaviour of promoters of ailing businesses has led to a situation where the precious money of taxpayers has to be used to clean the poison that has leached the financial system.

The question is ~ why should ordinary people bear the burden of the fat cats? These freeloaders are remorselessly winnowing scarce bank capital. The government has to dress up the balance sheets of banks to make them apparently healthy so that they can lend again. Ironically, instead of being chastised, the wayward borrowers are lauded as captains of the industry. Most borrowers seem to have a deep aversion to repaying bank loans. In several cases, they have adequate assets and capital to redeem the debt but avoid doing it. Things have turned so bad that whether it is an individual or institution, getting back any money at all is a reason for celebration.

We have seen several business leaders splurging on lavish extravaganzas and misdirecting capital into expensive vanity projects but reneging on loan promises. The reason why we have been trying to protect the borrower against the creditor so far is that the cruel moneylender has always loomed large in our collective psyche. The scene now is totally different. Large borrowers are not like helpless illiterate villagers, and the lender today is not the chukar or predatory lender who charges stratospheric interest rates. Banks now offer pretty affordable loans. Added to this is the government subsidy.

We can distinguish between unscrupulous debtors who invest unwisely or selfishly and general debtors and suitable remedial measures undertaken. The latter group may have genuinely tried to use their loans sensibly. Still, they cannot make repayments, either because of the economic downturn or because they have no choice but to take on such debt, such as by having to pay for essential medical care. A willful default takes place when a loan amount is outstanding even though he has resources and uses them for purposes other than the designated purpose or if a property is due without informing the bank. One wouldn't like to resurrect the "genuine "versus "wilful" trope, but a blanket, no-questions-asked write-offs can hardly be helpful in solving such complex problems.

Exploitation of weak government structures

Borrowers turn into wilful defaulters by exploiting weak governance structures. When borrowers become insolvent, their concurrent loans get compounded to an existing mountain of debt. Each time that happens, banks have to make heavy write-downs, sloughing the dud loans like rotten potatoes and wiping off profits, thus weakening their balance sheets. The net result is that most banks are suffering from the consequences of bad lending and have become opposed to any lending-related risk. Instead of taming the loan dodgers, the government is hounding bankers for so-called wrong credit decisions. The entire financial sector is wary of lending.

Most big defaulters are well-connected tycoons and have the money to employ legal eagles who can play the judicial system ~ it is here the law flounders. India has some of the most draconian laws in books; they are ineffective against mighty dodgers. We keep producing new rules when the existing ones are adequate and need more teeth to obtain results. Noble Prize-winning French economist Jean Tirole writes in his book Economics for the Common Good: "The state often fails. There are many reasons for these failures. Regulatory capture is one of them. We are well aware of the friendships and mutual support that create collaboration between a public body and those who are supposed to be regulating it."

Repayment ethics have been deeply ingrained in Indian culture but have become foul words on account of the perverse behaviour of borrowers. The sanctity of repayment and its moral obligation is part of the philosophy since the time of Manu ~ no matter how deceitfully the debt was contrived and how cruel the costs were. Manu listed 18 main categories of law for the king to decide on. Of those, wrote Manu, "The first is non-payment of debts." He held: "By whatever means, a creditor may be able to obtain possession of his property, even by those means may he force the debtor and make him pay." What about disputes and debt recovery?

Manu specified that the punishments should be in the case of the 18 types of disputes arising from loan repayment. When a creditor sued the debtor for recovery of money, it was the duty of the king to ensure that the creditor got his money back. Manu permitted the king to employ all means, fair or foul, to recover the dues, which included killing the debtor's wife, children and cattle or obstructing his movements. Manu emphasized that a defaulter could not absolve himself of his debt burden, even by death. The great statesman Chanakya believed that sons should pay with interest the debt of a deceased person or co-debtors or sureties.

Was a spouse responsible for the debts incurred by a person to whom they were married? Yes and no. A wife was exempted from the debt burden of her husband if she had not consented to his borrowings. However, for the debt incurred by a wife, her husband was liable for repayment. Crony politicians are equally guilty of undermining the stability of banks. They have used public banks as political milch cows and stacked the decks with populist sops. Banks became spigots for burnishing election credentials and have been sure to shovel considerable loans to the buddies of politicians.

The nexus of politicians and creative business schemers has stoked a forest fire that spread quickly, singeing many in the financial sector. In every business venture, the equity holders take the risks. In India, lenders take the risks while the promoters have much less skin in the game and are essentially playing with other people's money. The cosy nexus between tycoons, few bank executives and politicians have held back a much-needed shake-up of a moribund, scandal-prone sector. Scams are a product of greed and immorality. However, abuse of the financial system has been made possible because of the system's weaknesses.

One of the most challenging tasks I had to handle in my long career as a banker was handling the recalcitrant defaulters who made us literally beseech and supplicate before them when they refused to pay up the loan. I had to make regular appearances in the witness box whenever we filed a lawsuit against any tough loan defaulter. The experience followed a familiar narrative. Lawyers thrive on promises, and defaulters prefer paying heavy fees to lawyers rather than honouring their debts.

It is strange that repayment ethics, so deeply ingrained in Indian culture, have been made foul words. The sanctity of repayment, no matter how deceitfully the debt was contrived and how cruel the costs, has been drilled into the Indian consciousness since the time of Manusmruti. Manu listed eighteen main categories of law for the king to decide on. Of those, wrote Manu, "The first is non-payment of debts." Manu held: "By whatever means a creditor may be able to obtain possession of his property, even by those means may he force the debtor and make him pay."

In the hallway of the court where I made my first testimony in a loan default case, a diverse crowd of rich, poor and middle-class had begun to gather. I entered the courtroom and sat just below the judge's bench. Four dirty fans on long stems circled slowly above my head, with the subdued hum produced by low voltage. Lawyers wearing their traditional black-and-white costumes came and went from the courtroom, bowing according to custom as they entered, filling several rows of chairs behind the front row, where they would wait all day long for their case to get hearing. Light green folders and crowded dockets were everywhere—stacked high on the judge's desk, piled on the litigant's table, stuffed into shelves on the wall. A long bulb glowed dimly in the hall, threatening to switch off anytime, casting surreal shadows on the walls.

My encounter in the witness box

My encounter in the witness box left my ideals evaporating. As I took my place in the dock, my lawyer, pulling on his robes, hurried into the court. He saw me and raised his thumb. A dizzying number of exhibits—notices, bank vouchers, signed cheque correspondence—were placed before me as my lawyer and the defendant's lawyer sparred over legal issues.

The lawyer defending the defaulter proceeded to grill me in near-perfect theatrical slang with a cannon fire of questions: "Did the borrower sign in your presence?"; "Were the contents of the documents explained to him?"; "Can you produce any witnesses in support of your argument?" He tried to play an intelligent game and questioned every simple line of logic. Painfully aware of how words skate over and around truth, never having quite enough nuance to grasp it completely, I contested him equally forcefully, testifying in blunt terms. At stake was a loan of Rs.25,000, and the lawyers were battling as if the country's sovereignty was at stake. He was gesturing with ferocious gravitas. He reminded me of the famous aphorism: If the facts are against you, pound on the law. If the law is against you, pound on the facts. And if both are against you, pound on the table!

My lawyer couldn't respond suitably. He kept skirting around the law. His usual refrain would be, "Your Lordship, this is a leading question." It appeared his strategy was to wear out the defending lawyer or elicit some favourable response from the Magistrate, who kept on overruling the objections. The judge pronounced: "The court found no violations." Perhaps an individual judge may be biased, I thought at the time, but the judicial system as a whole can't ignore both the law and self-evident facts. My lawyer tried to inject some hysteria in the courtroom in order to impress me. He would keep banging the table while making his point. This is not surprising. The law deals with the same sort of questions as politics.

I tried to reason with the Magistrate that if I had known that each loan could generate a thriving cottage industry of litigation, I would have moderated my enthusiasm and sense of commitment. He had a passion for helping people experiencing poverty, and now I have found that I have become trapped in multiple helices in chasing this vain chimaera. My humble, polite voice chimed oddly amid the thundering perorations of top-rank lawyers. The Magistrate seemed to have been offended by my remark as if he sat on Vikramaditya's throne and lesser mortals like me dare not use his court for moral philosophizing. In front of me sat the philosopher king, the flag-bearer of the cloistered virtue that is justice, holding the court in its majestic grandeur, and I was a supplicant who dared to dispense his version of wisdom.

He was conscious of being a deity in his tiny kingdom, in which he exercised unbridled authority. He appeared pretty patronizing, dispensing justice the way a modern saint dispenses benedictions. For him, everyone who entered the witness box was someone who stood in obeisance before his stern tribune of justice. The judge grimaced at my audacity in explaining my understanding of the law, and his mouth was a straight, grim line as if to say, "We know the law better." The regulations of the judiciary are broad enough to be used punitively by small-minded judges. It was a field day for the Magistrate, slamming people from the banking fraternity to the undisguised delight of the chattering lawyers.

Standing in the hallowed precincts of the temple of justice, I shuddered, wondering whether the Magistrate would frame me for lowering the dignity and prestige of the court. Looming in front of me was the lofty majesty of law in whose shadow stood a puny creature. I felt as if the loan defaulter was the king and I was the supplicant.

Expert witness

I realized that giving expert testimony, including depositions, experience, compelling language, and credibility, along with the importance of testifying only within the scope of reasonable and accepted scientific knowledge and staying clearly within the boundaries of your professional expertise., An expert witness is an individual who possesses specialized knowledge through skill, education, training, or experience beyond that of the ordinary person and can, during a legal case, provide the court with an assessment, opinion, or judgment within the area of their area of expertise. They are 'servants' of the court. An expert witness report addresses condition and prognosis, breach of duty, and causation.

The law of evidence was forged over the centuries as ancient legal traditions progressed to modern standards for the resolution of legal disputes. An expert testimony is necessary to address matters outside of the common knowledge of the judge and jury. With the development of partisan expert testimony, concerns regarding the need for expert testimony versus its potential for abuse became apparent. As expert testimony in the courtroom became more commonplace, calls for its regulation proliferated. Legal standards have been developed for the admissibility of expert testimony to keep pace with legal challenges to expert testimony.

The Indian legal system is quite well known for its Dickensian delays. Despite repeated proclamations from the throne of the government and the lofty pedestals of courts for dispensation of inexpensive and timely justice, the legal system continues to be dear and mired in interminable delays. The cost to Indian society due to its sclerotic legal system is steep.

In an age which heralds technology as the silver bullet, we should not overlook the most critical source of competitive advantage ~ the people. Compliance and controls are dependent on the people running them. A process is only as good as the people managing it. The most agile auditors will also have to struggle to stop managers who are determined to hide their dirty laundry from view. In several cases, the bankers themselves fudged the accounts and contributed to the malaise. The turmoil has prompted calls for improvising risk management models, which seem to have created an illusory sense of security.

However, models and machines cannot act as a surrogate for human expertise. Money management is no longer a sophisticated world. In a prophetic warning, way back in 1913, John Maynard Keynes wrote in Indian Currency and Finance: "In a country so dangerous for banking as India, (it) should be conducted on the safest possible principles." Our departure from the time-honoured metrics has come at a heavy cost. The government has already decided to set up a bad bank to spin off stressed loans to experts who can focus on recovery. However, a bad bank is not a magic wand that will resolve the issues of India's soured loans.

Finance is a wild animal and made up of so much human drama and passions that it needs the most sophisticated minds to read and leaven the nuances that shape its contours. The biggest misconception about banking is that people think one should have a degree in business or finance to do well in this industry. Banking is a generalist profession dealing with diverse sectors. An educational background in economics or finance may help one understand banking concepts in the beginning. However, in the long run, it is the person with the right mix of personal qualities and leadership skills who will rise above the rest.

These include the ability to learn quickly and continuously, openness to new challenges, a disciplined professionalism, an outgoing and inquisitive nature, an analytical and systematic mind, negotiating savvy and personal integrity. Any achieving banker will soon find himself thrust out of a comfortably known field into an unfamiliar one. He must be open to challenges. He must learn the ropes by himself before he can guide others. A banker must master and micromanage details.

A banker knows the surface of many disciplines but the depths of none; he should be ready to unlearn certain theoretical assumptions if his life experience warrants him to do so. India's financial community has a lot on its plate: demographic changes, structural changes, and operational changes. It is now all playing out. The most important thing at this juncture is financial stability. It has become challenging to assess which parts of the loan book could develop into default hotspots. We need a new generation of bankers with vigilant eyes and firefighting abilities to ensure the robust and resilient financial health of the system. This alone can keep the economy continually perked up.

9. INDIAN MUSLIMS AND THE CONSTITUTION

India's Muslim population of some 172 million is the third largest in the world – after those of Indonesia and Pakistan – and forms the most significant religious minority in India. Indian Muslims are far from homogenous, divided by factors including language, ethnicity and caste, amongst others. The great majority are Sunni Muslims, and the remainder are Shi'a and various other sects such as Bohras, Isma'ilis and Ahmadis. Muslims form a majority in the state of Kashmir, while elsewhere, they are in particularly sensitive areas. The vast numbers are in the states of Uttar Pradesh, Bihar, West Bengal, Kerala, and Assam.

While the majority of Muslims reside in Western and Eastern Uttar Pradesh, and primarily in urban areas, there remain a number of differentiating factors – for example, identification as marginalized (officially called 'Other Backward Class' or OBC) or as belonging to a specific occupational group – which have a bearing on an individual's socio-economic and political position.

In the north of India, most Muslim communities speak Urdu, which is not a recognized official language, primarily because of the lack of a distinct majority population in a specific area. Apart from Kashmir, Muslims are everywhere in a minority in India. Uttar Pradesh, the state with the largest population in India, did not recognize Urdu as an official language before 1989. Muslims campaigned for Urdu to receive the status of an official language alongside Hindi. There were clashes between Hindu and Muslim students in which at least twenty-three people died. Urdu has also received official language status in Bihar, Jharkhand, Telangana, West Bengal, and Delhi, the national capital territory.

Notwithstanding the large Muslim population of India, Muslims are strikingly under-represented in the civil service, military and institutions of higher education. Beneath this pattern lies the issue of access to education and the general problem of large numbers of Muslims not being adequately trained or equipped to compete on equal terms in the marketplace.

Indian Muslims are also not granted the same constitutional safeguards as the scheduled castes and scheduled tribes, and they are not entitled to reservations in employment and education, except for a small segment included within what is called the Other Backward Class (OBC) section. Although Hinduism is the majority religion, it is not an official or state-sponsored one; India is a secular state, and complete freedom of religion is guaranteed. Following the adoption of the National Commission for Minorities Act (1992), the body was renamed the National Commission for Minorities. It monitors the position of non-scheduled caste and non-scheduled tribe minorities such as Muslims, although it has no power to implement changes. Nor are Muslims entitled to reserved constituencies in central or state government assemblies, although all have Muslim parliamentary representatives. There have been several Muslim chief ministers, and two Presidents have been Muslim, although the latter position has little real power despite high visibility. Overall, Muslims are not proportionally represented in legislative bodies, including the national parliament and state assemblies,

The great secular Muslims

- Abul Kalam Azad, Sheikh Abdullah, and Abdul Ghaffar Khan return parity to its richer, two-pronged definition of commonality and difference between Hindus and Muslims to challenge both exclusionary Pakistani nationalism and the threat of Hindu majoritarianism
- Muslim political thought in India could embrace the loss of older forms of monarchical and communitarian power to

channel a politics of democratic sovereignty global intellectual history understands the modern problem of minority in the age of partitions and identitarian sovereignty

- Sheikh Abdullah and Abdul Ghaffar Khan as political thinkers with ambitions beyond Kashmir and the North-West Frontier
- by anchoring Islam in their Muslim-majority regions, these nationalists settled the minority question. They counterintuitively appropriated a secular nationality for all Indian India, which, by its constitution, is considered to be a secular state.

However, the Indian government's reason for the differing opinions was that Indian legal jurisprudence on religious personal laws should keep in mind a 1951 judgment in the case of State of Bombay v Narasu Appa Mali, which held that codified personal laws are subject to constitutional scrutiny, whereas uncodified laws are not. Kazi got the Shar'aht codified through the Muslim Personal Law (Shar'aht) Application Act of 1937 and that the triple talaq practice violated the right to equality under Article 25, which grants individuals the freedom and right "freely to practice, profess and propagate religion." He added that "the stature of 'personal law' is that of a fundamental right."

"Sovereignty is always limited": the constituent assembly discusses the inclusion of a fundamental right on personal laws.

The fundamental rights do not currently include a right to practice personal laws. On 2 December 1948, the Constituent Assembly expressly rejected a motion to include a fundamental right to "follow the personal law" of religion under Article 19, which lists six freedoms that the constitution confers to Indian citizens. In the following extract from that discussion, Muslim members of the assembly discuss their strong desire to include the right to follow personal law under Article 19. At the same time, BR Ambedkar and M Ananthasayanam Ayyangar express their opposition.

Mohammad Ismail Khan: Sir, I move that after sub-clause (g) of clause (1) of Article 13 [Article 19 of the present constitution], the following new sub-clause be added: "(h) to follow the personal law of the group or community to which he belongs or professes to belong."

Personal law is part of the religion of a community or section of people [who] professes this law. Anything that interferes with personal law will be taken by that community and also by the general public, who will judge this question with some common sense as a matter of interference with religion. It is a question of difference of opinion as to what a religion should or should not do. People differ, and people holding different views on this matter must tolerate the other view. Some religions omit altogether dealing with the question of personal law, and other religions like Hinduism and Islam deal with personal law. It is not only Muslims but also Hindus who think that this is a religious question and that it should not be interfered with. The personal law of one community does not affect the other communities. Therefore, sir, what I urge is the freedom to follow the personal law for each community, and it will not interfere with the rights of any other community.

Mr Munshi stated that Muslim countries like Egypt or Turkey did not have any provision of this sort. Turkey was under a treaty obligation. Under that treaty, non-Muslim minorities can have questions of family law and personal status regulated in accordance with their usage. That is the obligation under which Turkey provides for minorities. With regard to Egypt, no such question of personal law arose in that country. However, what is to be understood is whether the minorities in that country got what they wanted,

Kazi: The people outside and the members of the Constituent Assembly must realize that a Muslim regards the personal law as part of the religion, and I really assure you that there is not a single Muslim in the country—at least, I have not seen one—who wants a change in the mandatory provision of religious rights and personal laws, and if there is anyone who wants a change in the compulsory principle, or religion as a matter of personal law, then he cannot be a Muslim. Therefore, if you really want to protect the minorities—because this is a secular state, it does not mean that people should have no religion—if this is the view of the minority Muslims or any other minority that they want to abide by personal law, those laws have to be protected.

Maulana Hasrat Mohani: I would like to say that any party, political or communal, has no right to interfere in the personal law of any group. More particularly, I say this regarding Muslims. There are three fundamentals in their law, namely, religion, language, and culture, which have not been ordained by human agency. Their law regarding divorce, marriage and inheritance has been derived from the Qur'an, and its interpretation is recorded therein. If there is anyone who thinks that he can interfere in the personal law of the Muslims, then I would say to him that the result will be very harmful. Mussalmans will never submit to any interference in their law, and they will have to face an iron wall of Muslim determination to oppose them in every way.

M Ananthasayanam Ayyangar: Amendments were moved that unless there is a provision in the fundamental rights, there is no safety, and the majority community may introduce its law or flagrantly violate the personal law of any community. Let us take the communities. There are three main religions. Let us take Muhammadanism [an archaic term used to refer to Islam]. There is absolutely no provision in the Fundamental Rights that you ought to ride rough-shod over their law. The law of the land as it exists today gives sufficient guarantee so far as that is concerned. But our friends who moved the amendments wanted a double guarantee that their law ought not to be interfered with.

My submission is that it is impracticable, for, in an advanced society, even the members who belong to a particular community may desire their law to be changed. Let us take the Muhammadan law. I would only refer to two or three amendments that have been made to that law as set out in the Shari'ah. As recently as 1939, the central legislature passed a law enabling the dissolution of Muslim marriages under certain circumstances. You will be pleased to note that under Muslim law, a man has the unilateral right to declare a marriage void by pronouncing the word talaq, and there is another form of divorce called kulamp. [A] woman usually has no right to dissolve a marriage. She has to go to a court of law, and various matters have to be set out, such as impotence and soon. All that has been made easy now.

Another consideration is that a woman who cannot lead a family life with the husband in the same household has, under certain conditions, the right to separation. These have hitherto not been envisaged nor provided for in the Dissolution of Muslim Marriages Act. As a member of the Assembly, I was a member of one of the committees that considered this question. We left the question entirely for the Muslim members concerned to settle.

A time may come when members of a particular community may feel that they need to act in the interests of the community. But if we make a provision here that the personal law shall not be interfered with, there will not be any right for the members of that community itself to modify that law. Therefore, it is not necessary to introduce it as a fundamental right. There is absolutely nothing in this Constitution which allows the majority to override the minority. This is only an enabling provision. Without the consent of the minority that is affected, no such law will be framed. I therefore feel it is unnecessary to include it in the fundamental rights.

BR Ambedkar: Coming to the question of saving personal law... "If such a saving clause were introduced into the Constitution, it would disable the legislatures in India from enacting any social measure whatsoever. The religious conceptions in this country are so vast that they cover every aspect of life, from birth to death. There is nothing which is not religion, and if personal law is to be saved, I am sure that in social matters, we will come to a standstill. I do not think it is possible to accept a position of that sort".

There is nothing extraordinary in saying that we ought to strive hereafter to limit the definition of religion in such a manner that we shall not extend beyond beliefs and such rituals as may be connected with essentially religious ceremonials. It is not necessary that the sort of laws, for instance, laws relating to tenancy or regulations relating to succession, should be governed by religion. In Europe, there is Christianity, but Christianity does not mean that Christians all over the world or in any part of Europe where they live shall have a uniform system of law of inheritance. No such thing exists.

There is no understanding of why religion should be given this vast, expansive jurisdiction so as to cover the whole of life and to prevent the legislature from encroaching upon that field. After all, what are we having this liberty for? We have this liberty in order to reform our social system, which is so full of inequities, so complete of inequalities, discriminations and other things which conflict with our fundamental rights.

All that the state is claiming in this matter is the power to legislate. There is no obligation upon the state to do away with personal laws. It is only giving power. Therefore, no one needs to be apprehensive of the fact that if the state has the power, the state will immediately proceed to execute or enforce that power in a manner that is objectionable to Muslims, Christians or any other community in India.

We must all remember—including members of the Muslim community who have spoken on this subject, though one can appreciate their feelings very well—that sovereignty is always limited, no matter even if you assert that it is unlimited because sovereignty in the exercise of that power must reconcile itself to the sentiments of different communities. No government can exercise its power in such a manner as to provoke the Muslim community to rise in rebellion. I think it would be a mad government if it did so. But that is a matter which relates to the exercise of the power and not to the power itself.

The Indian Constitution protects the freedom of religion, which includes the right to practice, propagate, and profess religion. However, Muslims in India are governed by several laws that relate to marriage, inheritance, and other matters, including:

- *Muslim Personal Law (Shar'aht) Application Act, 1937: Governs marriage, succession, inheritance, and charities among Muslims*
- *Dissolution of Muslim Marriages Act, 1939: Deals with the circumstances in which Muslim women can obtain divorce*
- *Muslim Women (Protection of Rights on Divorce) Act, 1986: Protects the rights of Muslim women whose husbands have divorced*
- *Muslim Women (Protection of Rights on Marriage) Act, 2019: Protects the rights of Muslim women in marriage*
- *Special Marriage Act, 1954: Allows Muslims to register their marriage under this act*
- *Other laws that apply to all family matters in India, including those of Muslims, include the Dowry Prohibition Act and the Domestic Violence Act.*

10. THE BATTLE FOR INDIA'S FOUNDING IDEALS

While secularism has been integral to India's democracy for more than fifty years, its conceptual framework is being examined anew. Signs of a crisis in the relations between state, society, and religion include the violence directed against Muslims in Gujarat in 2002 and the precarious situation of India's minority religious groups more generally; the existence of personal laws that vary by religious community; the affiliation of political parties with fundamentalist religious organizations; and the rallying of a significant proportion of the diasporic Hindu community behind a resurgent nationalist Hinduism. There is a broad consensus that a crisis of secularism exists, but whether the state can resolve conflicts and ease tensions or is itself part of the problem is a matter of vigorous political and intellectual debate. In this timely, nuanced collection, twenty leading Indian cultural theorists assess the contradictory ideals, policies, and practices of secularism in India.

We have to explore the nature of secularism in India and discuss the difficulties into which it has run. There are three basic assumptions. First, secularism as an anti-religious or non-religious ideology has universal applicability but has culturally specific expressions. Second, secularism will be welcomed by all right-thinking persons, for it shows the way to the making of rational plans for social reconstruction and state action, placing ultimate faith in the adequacy of human agency. Finally, with appropriate corrective measures, ideological secularism can still be made to succeed in India, notwithstanding all the faltering of the last fifty years. This chapter also considers Mahatma Gandhi's views on secularism as a backdrop for a discussion of Jawaharlal Nehru's ideology of secularism and his views on religion and politics, secularism and the constitution, and the majority-minority conundrum.

The British social reformer George Jacob Holyoake (1817–1906) coined the word 'secularism' to describe his this-worldly approach to personal morals, philosophy, and society and politics. A modern definition, provided by scholar Jean Baubérot, sees secularism as made up of three parts: separation of religious institutions from the institutions of the state and no domination of the political sphere by religious institutions; freedom of thought, conscience, and religion for all; and no state discrimination against anyone on the grounds of their religion or non-religious worldview. 'What is secularism?' considers these three parts in more depth and also explains that the idea of secularism is much older.

Scholars who have mainly studied secularism in the West suggest three alternative criteria: (1) a state claiming to adhere to secular principles guarantees and protects the freedom of conscience, expression, and worship of citizens who hold religious beliefs;2 (2) religions and religious communities are all equal;3 and (3) the state remains neutral in religious matters, which rules out the existence of a state religion or any official faith. After India's independence in 1947, secularism became so well established there that the adjective "secular" was finally enshrined in the preamble to the Constitution in 1976. But India has developed its version of secularism. The Indianization of this "ism" coined by the West and transplanted via colonization first occurred by partially discarding the third pillar of the previous definition: neutrality. The state does not acknowledge any official religion. Still, it does not refrain from regulating religious practices, whether it comes to banning animal sacrifice or having temples open to untouchables.5 This transgression of the standard definition of secularism was of little consequence—even the West has considerable trouble complying as the other two criteria were observed and in India's particular way, unlike the Western model that emphasizes strict separation, Indian secularism uniquely permits state involvement in religious matters to promote equality and social justice. The constitutional mandate for secularism is crucial in maintaining harmony within India's diverse society. However, challenges such as communalism, political exploitation of religion, judicial inconsistencies, radicalization, and rising. Intolerance threatens this fabric. State policies often blur governance and religion, complicating the secular framework. This chapter suggests strengthening secularism through interfaith dialogue, impartial governance, social reforms like the Uniform Civil Code, and secular politics. Additionally, combating extremism, protecting minority rights, and enhancing constitutional literacy are vital. Education plays a pivotal role in fostering mutual respect and reducing prejudices, ultimately enabling India to uphold the delicate balance of secularism essential for its unity and social cohesion. The eventual outcome of reposing their "trust" in the majority is that Muslims have never had anything like representation in the legislature in proportion to their share of the population. The share has now, alas, sunk in the Lok Sabha to an abysmal 4 per cent, under a third of their ratio to India's population. The Sikhs have fared marginally better largely because Punjab has been reconstituted, and Sikhs are the dominant political force there. And suppose the Christians have done somewhat better than the Muslims. In that case, it is mainly owing to their geographic concentration in parts of Kerala, some central Indian tribal communities, and the north-eastern hill States. Yet, the complex and sad fact is that minorities are hopelessly under-represented in our electoral system.

In the services too, as well as in corporate ownership and governance, non-governmental organizations, academia, or journalism, Muslim representation has been far below their share of the population. Perhaps the one exception is the top places in Bollywood and the arts generally. Some (but not all of this) is deliberate; principally, the cause, except in legislatures, is that in education and general living standards, the Muslims have tended to fare worse than even the Scheduled Castes, as the Justice

Sachar report of 2006 revealed. This, in turn, is explained by the leadership of the Muslim community, particularly in northern and western India, having decamped to Pakistan, leaving behind to India's tender mercies the Pasmanda Muslims, that is, the economically, educationally and culturally deprived elements of the Muslim community.

While the minorities are expected to "trust" the "good sense and goodwill" of the majority, the argument over what is the definition of "secularism" and the manner of implementation continued to be played out inside but mainly outside the Constituent Assembly. It was primarily outside because Hindu rights were virtually unrepresented in the House, with the notable exception of Syama Prasad Mookerjee, Minister for Industry. He was constrained by being a member of the Cabinet.

So K.R. Malkani, displaced from Sindh, where the Hindu population of Karachi shrank from 51 per cent on the eve of Independence to 2 per cent by the first Pakistani census in 1951, took up cudgels against any "appeasement" of the Muslim minority. He thundered in the *Organiser*, which he edited, concerning the Bharatiya Jana Sangh, which was then in the offing: "[T]he new party must adopt Hindu ideals and Hindu festivals, Hindu shrines and Hindu sacred cities, Hindu philosophy and Hindu culture, Hindu ceremonies and Hindu pujas, Hindu history and Hindu race experience—as its root foundations."

In another article, under his pseudonym "Kamal" (lotus), Malkani proclaimed: "The story of Islam is the story of violence, hate, murder, loot and rape."

Meanwhile, the Hindu Mahasabha, condemning the "unscrupulous zealots of Western secularism", asserted that: "Hindus have not only learned it (secularism) but practised it with success for centuries." However, another contributor to the *Organiser* demurred (while implicitly accepting that Hinduism was secular): "Equal respect for all religions has been the bane of Hinduism."

What the Hindu Mahasabha aimed for was the "welding of conflicting elements in the state population into *one homogenous nationalistic state based on the ancient culture of the land*" (emphasis added).

Thus, Indian secularism, according to this school of thought, was to be secured through adherence to Hindu culture, which was essentially "secular" and aimed eventually at making the nation "homogenous" and founded in the "ancient culture" of the land.

Mahatma Gandhi's clarity

The most clear-eyed in the secular camp was Mahatma Gandhi. We have already seen that for him, secularism meant inalienable "rights" for the minorities for which they must "fight unto death". For him, this meant "India would be a land where the people of every religion would live with *equality*, practice their religion *fearlessly*, and *fully belong*" (emphases added). To date, the three key requirements for minorities to live in India are to have their *identity* intact, their *dignity* unimpaired, and their *security* assured. These three requirements are so much part of our composite nationhood. The minorities, of whom Muslims were sizeable, will not feel they "belong" as they sense they are "not wanted". That is the dilemma facing minorities everywhere in South Asia. Hence, this book. Gandhiji reinforced his perception with the injunction: "I would not allow the Mussalmans to crawl on the streets in India. They must walk with *self-respect*."

In contrast to the wholesale denigration of Islam that characterized his ideological opponents on the Hindu Right, he held that "Islam stands for the unity and brotherhood of mankind, not for disrupting the oneness of the human family" (*Harijan*, 6/10/1946). While, therefore, emphasizing "equal regard for all religions" (*Ishwar Allah Tero Naam*) as the definition of secularism and holding that "the preservation of pluralism was a public good" (Rochona Bajpai), Gandhiji elaborated that it "entailed the freedom to practice religion, all religions, *publicly*".

The makers of the Constitution, on the other hand, while accepting this, stressed the right to freely practice religion, all faiths, "privately"—as the State had no business to involve itself in religion. In opposition, others (even many within the ruling party) held that secularism "did mean the separation of religion from politics", even if it was only the saffron who went further to assert that "it most certainly did not mean equal respect for all religions".

In consequence, both in theory and in practice, the author finds, there was a "steady chipping away at minority rights in the course of the drafting of the Indian constitution...political safeguards were whittled down and removed from the final draft of the Constitution". It leads her to the somewhat exaggerated conclusion that in the end, "little" remained to "distinguish between the Congress and the Hindu Right on their attitudes towards the Muslim minority problem"—somewhat exaggerated because while the Hindu Right sought to "nationalize" the minority in the name of "integration", the Congress sought to reassure the minorities that the innate secularism of Indians, and particularly the Congress party, guaranteed an honourable and equitable place for the minorities in the life of the nation—an assurance that has often been breached and increasingly so since 2014.

The "minority problem" in Pakistan

Nair moves, fascinatingly, to compare and contrast the process of dealing with the non-Muslim "minority problem" in united Pakistan (and, subsequently, in Bangladesh after the secession of East Pakistan in 1971).

It was Quaid-e-Azam Muhammad Ali Jinnah himself who kicked off the debate with his inaugural address to the Pakistan Constituent Assembly on August 11, 1947, with a speech that Nehru might have written: "You are free; you are free to go to your temples, you are free to go to your mosques or any other place of worship in this State of

Pakistan. You may belong to any religion or caste or creed—that has nothing to do with the business of the State.".

Had Pakistan lived up to that proclamation, it would have become the poster boy of secularism in South Asia. Instead, over the last 75 years, the Quaid's words have been censored and perverted. It only ignited a controversy that remains alive to this day: should Pakistan be an Islamic state with only a Muslim as head of state; if so, where do the non-Muslim minorities fit in? And now that the bulk of Pakistan's Hindu community is Bangladeshi, how has Bangladesh dealt with its minorities?

In a word, the minorities in Pakistan and Bangladesh have been treated in their respective Constitutions and laws much as in India: few specific, clear, concise, and justiciable Constitutional safeguards, especially concerning representation in State/provincial and national legislatures proportionate in some measure to their population; some Constitutional measures such as protection to community personal laws and the running of minority educational institutions; some pro-minority legislative and administrative steps but offset by others blatantly aimed at the minorities; some backing to the minorities from the courts, especially when the legislative branch flinches from taking an unambiguous stand, preferring to hide behind the skirts of court judgments; and much discrimination in practice. In India, in a generalized sense, however, Chief Justice Gajendragadkar "and others...pointed out that the spirit of secularism permeated every page of the Constitution".

Few of us Indians remember now that East Pakistan returned a number of Hindus to the Pakistan Constituent Assembly, and West Pakistan returned some very important members of the Christian community, including the Deputy Speaker of the House, C. E. Gibbon.

They fought a valiant rearguard action in the debate on the Objectives Resolution (the equivalent of our Preamble), tabled in March 1949, against the labelling of Pakistan as an "Islamic state" in which only a Muslim could be "President". The debate went on until the short-lived adoption of the 1956 Constitution—and has continued almost uninterrupted since then.

In the first phase, the most articulate of the minority representatives were the two Dattas, Bhupendra Kumar and Dhirendra Nath, and Basanta Kumar Das, ably supported by a host of others—Raj Kumar Chakravarty, Kamini Kumar Dutta, Sris Chandra Chattopadhyay, Bhabesh Chandra Nandy, Manoranjan Dhar and, from the Scheduled Caste Federation, Gour Chandra Bala, Rasa Raja Mandal, and Akshat Kumar Das.

The non-Muslim members were not so quickly taken in about the validity of the essential philosophy of the idea of Pakistan as set out in the Objectives Resolution. Bhupendra Kumar Dutta argued that "if Pakistan is declared an Islamic republic", it would "assign the near about a crore of non-Muslims in the State to a subordinate position to the limit of obliteration...To the common people, both Muslims and non-Muslims, 'Islamic State' has only one meaning. It has no place for non-Muslims".

P.P. Gomez, a Christian representative from East Pakistan, poignantly asked: "Am I not a child of this soil?" Basant Kumar Das bemoaned that the Quaid-e-Azam's inaugural address of August 11, 1947, was a "forgotten document". He continued, "Is not Pakistan also the homeland of the persons who follow other religions? Do not the Muslims of India claim India as their homeland?" Dr. S.K. Sen asked, "tartly perhaps", says the author, whether "the President would perform the duties of the imam of a mosque"; else what was the need to reserve the post only for a certified Muslim?

Gibbon's impassioned opposition

Perhaps the most impassioned opposition came from the West Pakistan Christian member, C.E. Gibbon, whose intervention lasted several hours. He began by denouncing the "betrayal" of the "contract" between Jinnah and the Christian community, underlining that non-Muslim minorities could enjoy their rights in Pakistan only if, in separate electorates, they could elect representatives "who can reflect their deepest thoughts and feelings their entirety and with the utmost sublimity, without let or hindrance from any quarter." Poignantly describing the Christians as "a community within a nation"—an expression that we might appreciate applied equally to India's minority communities—he conceded that while Pakistan might not be a theocratic state, it was an "experimental state" that should be "brought in line with the conception of political representation in an ordinary secular state".

Significantly, virtually all East Pakistan non-Muslim League members, led by A.K.M. Fazlul Huq of the Krishak Sramik Party, H.S. Suhrawardy, who became Prime Minister in 1957, and, notably, Sheikh Mujib-ur-Rahman, the future Bangabandhu, were supportive, albeit initially subdued in the first phase of the debate but subsequently vocal, especially after the Awami (Muslim) League trounced the Muslim League in East Pakistan in the provincial elections of 1954. "It is their habit," said Mujib in 1956 of Muslim League majoritarianism, "to give bluff to the people in the name of Islam".

Another Awami League member, Ataur Rahman, raised a pertinent point while requesting the House "not to fall into the trap laid by the mullahs". He pointed out "that there were seventy-two sects in Pakistan, and each called the others non-Muslim and *kafir*." (A glancing reference to the anti-Ahmedia riots of 1953 that had rocked West Pakistan and the persisting Sunni-Shia differences.) He further argued that "the ideology of Pakistan was not the creation of an Islamic State… nor intended to make it impossible for the others to live in this State". He held "the great ideology of a State" to be "the improvement of a lot of the common people".

Mian Abdul Bari, who led the debate from the Muslim League, described as "terrible allegations" the claim "that we want to get rid of non-Muslims in the Muslim State of Pakistan". Nur Ahmed of the Muslim

League added that Pakistan was not going to be a "theocratic state" for "there is no priesthood, no Pope in Islam, and there is no mediator between God and Man in Islam". A Minister, Pir Ali Mohammad Rashdi, supported Bari and Nur Ahmed in arguing that Islam was not being invoked "to worry them (the minorities) or to put them in a lower position".

He added: "If the name of Islam is taken away, then there will be nothing common between East Pakistan and West Pakistan...we have put that word in to keep the whole fabric together". Yet the fabric was to be ripped apart a few years later.

The approach of Pakistan's clerics

Maulana Maudoodi of the Jama'at-e-Islami had initially opposed Jinnah and his Muslim League as Westernised secularists incapable of creating a genuine Islamic state. However, once Pakistan had come into existence, Maudoodi moved his headquarters from Pathankot (which had remained in India) to Lahore, the capital of Pakistani Punjab. Once there, he fought with increasing tenacity for an Islamic state.

He prevailed when the Basic Objectives resolution was put before the Constituent Assembly. He then asserted his belief that, in making the Constitution, Muslim members should remember that "sovereign in Islam" means God, "not man" as possessing "the real power of legislation", the Objectives Resolution as drafted "assumes the complexion and characteristics of an Islamic state". That is why he endorsed it.

For Altaf Husain, the editor of *Dawn*, however, it was "the (Muslim) League's enemies (i.e., Maudoodi and his ilk) who had raised "the bogey of a theocratic state". He went on to categorically affirm that "the application of Qur'anic principles does not mean the theocratisation of a state". A joint editorial published simultaneously in several newspapers at the instance of the establishment argued that "the danger of a theocracy has been eliminated because no priesthood had been entrusted with any special authority". At the same time, the Resolution reflected the "basic ideals which are common ground between all schools of Islamic thought", thus ensuring that "Pakistan will develop an Islamic society free from dissensions and controversies". That proved no more than a pious hope.

Javed Iqbal, son of the great litterateur Allama Iqbal, president of the seminal session of the Muslim League in 1930, shone a pretty different light on the 1956 Constitution and its Basic Objectives Resolution. He held that the position of Islam in the 1956 Constitution "reflected the attitude of hypocrisy and vagueness of the Muslim framers of that Constitution". Pakistan, he stated, "came into being because the Muslims of the Indian subcontinent sought for a State in which to implement the social order of Islam". And as the "ultimate aim of Islam" was to establish "a spiritual democracy…the modern Islamic State should offer more security to believers in other faiths than a secular state". He concluded, "Only if minorities are preserved can the true ideal of the Islamic State be attained". He believed it is "obligatory" for true Muslims "not only to tolerate non-Muslims but also to protect them and to defend their places of worship".

S.K. Patil of the Congress (Syndicate) said Nehru had brought in the word "secularism" to enable all communities "to live together as brothers" and not to bring religion into their everyday activities. He also invoked Acharya Vinoba Bhave to plead for extending the "same respect for every religion" (*sarva dharma samanta*). Sushila Nayyar of the same party (and Gandhiji's close associate as his physician) remarked that it mattered little who had started the riots; the pertinent question to ask was, why would the Muslims start communal riots knowing that "if they provoke the majority, nothing but death awaits them".

The communist viewpoint

S.A. Dange of the CPI likened Vajpayee's speech to "a manifesto calling for a civil war of the Hindus against the Muslims". Dange sought to isolate the RSS and the Jana Sangh "by ideological, political, social and moral propaganda". The socialists—Nath Pai, George Fernandes, and Acharya

Kripalani—attacked both the Congress and the BJP. Regretting that the "communal problem" had been reduced to a "quarrel between the prime minister and Vajpayee", Kripalani demanded that the government rise to its responsibility of "seeing that the flag on which we have emblazoned secularism is respected, is upheld".

George Fernandes criticized the Congress party's attempt to claim a monopoly on secularism. He asked Vajpayee, on the other hand, to "examine the vitriolic speeches" of the BJP leaders of riot-struck Bhiwandi. Kripalani went so far as to describe Vajpayee as *aloof* (fool) while, at the same time, being "scathing" at the Congress's failure to see the hand of the Shiv Sena behind the riots because the Congress was "afraid" of the new party. (Does that ring a bell today?)

Muslim Congressmen were among the most vocal and articulate. Bakar Ali Mirza of Secunderabad asked why "Hindus of India are more loyal to the Hindus of Pakistan than they are to the Muslims of India". Chaudhri Randhir Singh of Rohtak decreed "Indianisation" as a "form of casteism" and warned that such slogans were "more dangerous than China or Pakistan".

Bangladeshi secularism

The 1971 War of Liberation was a turning point in the lives of minorities in India, Pakistan, and Bangladesh. The 1971 war in Bangladesh, also known as the Bangladesh War of Independence or Liberation War, was a brutal nine-month conflict that led to the creation of Bangladesh. The war resulted in millions of refugees fleeing to India and the deaths of an estimated 500,000 to over 3 million people. The war was a significant episode in Cold War tensions, and the majority of UN member states recognized Bangladesh as a sovereign nation in 1972.

Perhaps the most profound change was in East Pakistan, now in the throes of becoming Bangladesh. It is also important to remind ourselves that Sheikh Mujibur Rahman's party was named the Awami Muslim

League before it was called the Awami League. But as Mujib himself had pointed out in the Pakistan Constituent Assembly, Hindus and Muslims had voted together in local body elections for over a hundred years. In Mujib's absence, under arrest in Rawalpindi, the interim leader and future Prime Minister, Tajuddin, surrounded by an overwhelming majority of Hindus among the 10 million Bangladeshi refugees milling around him in Mujibnagar and elsewhere in India, decided that it was time to remove all ambiguity and declare the Bangladesh that was still to come into actual existence as an explicitly "secular" state.

Thus, "secularism" came to be formulated as one of the founding principles of the new state. Later, Kabir Choudhry, the education secretary of Bangladesh post-liberation, was to claim at a seminar in Kolkata that the "seed of secularism is inherent in the soil of Bangladesh".

The challenge was to reconcile in substance that "secularism" in practice would be compatible with Islam in Bangladesh in contrast to what had happened in united Pakistan. Mujib articulated this challenge in his famous speech on March 7, 1971, when he desisted from declaring independence. However, that was expected by many in his audience and apprehended by the West Pakistan authorities. Instead, Mujib emphasized that "the seventy-five million people—Hindu, Muslim, Bengalee or non-Bengalee—all are our brothers". That sentiment reflected the inclusion of "Fraternity" as a founding principle of the Indian Republic in the Preamble to the Indian Constitution.

This clarity on the meaning and implications of "secularism" was carried forward in the Bangladesh Constitution, which included "secularism" in the fundamental principles of State policy and went all the way in Article 12 to define "secularism" as comprising the "absence" of "communalism in all its forms"; no grant of "political status" to "any religion"; no "abuse of religion for political purposes"; and no "discrimination against, or persecution of, persons practising a particular religion". Moreover, Bangladesh was an "Islamic state," and the post of head of state was not exclusively for a Muslim. It was the boldest and clearest effort to define and elaborate the meaning and implications of "secularism" in any South Asian constitution—way ahead of India.

Mujib crowned this by declaring at the non-aligned summit in 1973 that "the Qur'an described Allah as Rabbu'l-alamin, the head of all creation, and not as Rabb'ul Muslimin, the head of only Muslims. This is the spirit which underlies our secularism".

This period of enlightened, explicit secularism did not last—and perhaps could not have lasted. After the army coup of August 1975, in which Mujib and his family were gunned down in jail, The "secularism" in the Constitution became "absolute faith and trust in the almighty Allah".

The vivisection of Pakistan

In Pakistan, the vivisection of the country in December 1971 was traumatic. Initial confusion was assuaged by several Pakistani intellectuals (particularly Javed Jabbar, who Nair does not mention) claiming that as Bangladesh had not merged with Hindu-majority India, the "two-nation theory" stood vindicated. In any case, the defection of Bangladesh had converted the "nearly one crore" Hindus of Pakistan into a tiny minority of Hindus, isolated in pockets of Upper Sindh, in villages along the Thar desert that divides India from Pakistan territorially in Rajasthan/Sindh; and in some parts of Balochistan. The minorities covered were the Christians and, to a lesser extent, the Parsis. For the representation of all religious minorities, the eventual solution found was to nominate them (and women) to reserved places in the National and provincial assemblies. The post-war leader of Pakistan, Zulfiqar Ali Bhutto, averred that "secularism, in the sense of tolerance and the rejection of theocracy, is inherent in Islamic political culture" when he dethroned by Zia-ul-Huq, who had no time for such niceties, "Islamisation" became the drumbeat to which Zia's "Nizam-e-Mustafa" (The Rule of the Prophet) marched.

Indira Gandhi

Indira Nehru was the only child of Jawaharlal Nehru, who was one of the chief figures in India's struggle to achieve independence from Britain, was a top leader of the powerful and long-dominant Indian National Congress (Congress Party), and was the first prime minister (1947–64) of independent India. Her grandfather, Motilal Nehru, was one of the pioneers of the independence movement and was a close associate of Mohandas ("Mahatma") Gandhi. She attended, for one year each, Visva-Bharati University in Shantiniketan (now in Bolpur, West Bengal state) and then the University of Oxford in England. She joined the Congress Party in 1938. Indira Gandhi appeared (perhaps unfairly) to be softening her hard line on secularism after being re-elected in January 1980. She not only conveyed the impression of personal religiosity in her dress and general behaviour, but, in her Second Coming, she also seemed politically inclined towards emphasizing that Congress secularism was not pro-Muslim or anti-Hindu.

On Shastri's sudden death in January 1966, Gandhi was named leader of the Congress Party—and thus also became prime minister—in a compromise between the party's right and left wings. Her leadership, however, came under continual challenge from the right wing of the party, led by former minister of finance Morarji Desai. She won a seat in the 1967 elections to the Lok Sabha (lower chamber of the Indian parliament), but the Congress Party managed to win only a slim majority of s

During the early 1980s, Indira Gandhi faced threats to India's political integrity. Several states sought a more significant measure of independence from the central government, and Sikh separatists in Punjab state used violence to assert their demands for an autonomous state. In 1982, a large number of Sikhs, led by Sant Jarnail Singh Bhindranwale, occupied and fortified the Harmandir Sahib (Golden Temple) complex at Amritsar, the Sikhs' holiest shrine. Tensions between the government and the Sikhs escalated, and in June 1984,

Gandhi ordered Operation Blue Star, in which the Indian army attacked and ousted the separatists from the complex. Sikh estimates of the death toll were considerably higher than those of the government, suggesting that the number of soldiers and civilians killed may have been in the thousands. Five months later, in her garden in New Delhi, Gandhi fell to a fusillade of bullets fired by two of her own Sikh bodyguards in revenge for the attack in Amritsar. She was succeeded as prime minister by her son, Rajiv Gandhi, who served until 1989. eats, and Gandhi had to accept Desai as deputy prime minister.

Decimation of BJP

Notwithstanding the massive defeat suffered by the BJP in the December 1984 election, following the sympathy wave for Indira Gandhi, which reduced their presence in the Lok Sabha to just two seats, responding to "hurt Hindu sentiment" has since been the *leitmotif* of Indian politics. This extends to the entire spectrum of "secularists". Non-Congress secularists joined hands with the BJP in opposing Rajiv Gandhi's Muslim Women (Protection of Rights on Divorce) Act, 1986, legislation that has stood the test of time over decades of non-Congress governments but has also secured complete endorsement by the Supreme Court in 2001. Worse, the "secularists" entered into an unholy, if unstated, alliance with the BJP to defeat Rajiv Gandhi in the elections held in November-December 1989, the principal issue being the Babri Masjid-Ram Janmabhoomi

The unspoken alliance of the "secular" National Front with the BJP in 1989 lubricated the way to the BJP extending "outside support" to the minority V.P. Singh government—before withdrawing this support on the Mandal-Kamandal issue and launching Advani's Rath Yatra that brought down the V.P. Singh government in just eleven months.

After the wanton destruction of the Babri Masjid on Black Sunday, December 6, 1992, the leaning away from hard secularism by the Rao government, whose Minister of State for Home Affairs, Rajesh Pilot (otherwise among the most secular of Congress ministers), categorically refused, to define Indian "secularism" on the floor of the House. The political battle lines were drawn by opposing "Muslim appeasement" with "Hindu appeasement", both to accommodate "hurt sentiment". It explains how perceptive and prescient Law Member Thomas Babington Macaulay was in underlining in 1837 that "Indians' propensity to be easily offended" requires the government "to allow fair latitude for religious discussion" but not extending to "intentional insults" or "wounding with deliberate intention the religious feelings of his neighbours by words, gesture or exhibition".

That is what has led to Narendra Modi's rule, during which Hindu majoritarianism has overtaken traditional non-denominational secularism, leaving the Indian Muslim minority feeling unwanted in their own country despite seventy-five years of proven patriotism. Mahatma Gandhi had anticipated this when he stressed that Indian secularism must make the Indian Muslim believe that he "fully belongs".

11. THE DUE PROCESS OF LAW

Due process is one of the tremendous legal principles, which, under that name or another of similar value, is an essential part of all States of law to prevent arbitrary power. Its function is to ensure that possible offenders, according to a procedure previously established by law, which enables them to receive a fair trial before an impartial judge (right to a fair trial in criminal law cases; right to a fair trial in civil law cases; right to a fair trial in administrative law cases). (right to a fair trial in criminal law cases; right to a fair trial in civil law cases; right to a fair trial in administrative law cases).

This cardinal principle of limited government of great antiquity forms clause 39 of the Magna Carta (1215). 'No free man shall be taken or imprisoned, or dispossessed, or outlawed, or banished, or in any way destroyed, except by the legal judgment of his peers or by the law of the land.' Subsequently, this right was extended to all subjects and 'law of the land' became synonymous with 'due process of law'. It is this terminology that appears in key amendments to the United States Constitution. The Fifth Amendment (1791), one of those that comprise the so-called Bill of Rights, was designed to ensure that the federal government did not deprive citizens of their 'life, liberty, or property, without due process of law'.There is Identical wording in the Fourteenth Amendment (1868), which provides Americans with similar protection against the governments of the states. This clause has played a dramatic part in the judicial activism of the Supreme Court since the 1950s, notably in civil rights cases.

Kazi Syed Karimuddin's caution

Constituent Assembly debated in depth over the drafting of Article 15which finally became Article 21 of the Indian Constitution in the background of the many amendments that were moved over Article 15. Karimuddin moved an amendment with the aim of protecting Indians from unreasonable searches and seizures. He criticised the absence of the 'due process' clause in the fundamental rights, which he feared could lead to misuse of state power and infringe on the citizen's right to life and liberty. He further cautioned that if the words 'according to procedure established by law' are retained, it would open a sad chapter in the history of constitutional law.12 The Advisory Committee on Fundamental Rights appointed by the Constituent Assembly had endorsed Kazi SayedKarimuddin's opinion by suggesting that no person shall be deprived of his life or liberty without due process of law.13 Kazi S stated that if the words 'according to procedure established by law' are enacted, then there will be very significant injustice to the people and nation. Once the legislature lays down the procedure by enacting the law, the authority complies with such procedure. When the courts cannot question the decision of the authority even though that decision is unjust or a result of malicious intention, he suggested that the words 'except according to procedure established by law ' should be replaced by the words 'without due process of law. There is a pretty vague notion in the average citizen's mind as to what rights and privileges are secured to him by constitutional guarantees of "due process of law." Most men, we fancy, associate the phrase with the right to trial by jury or some other such palladium of the liberties of the English-speaking race.

Due process of law is the administration of justice in accordance with established rules and principles. It is a fundamental principle of limited Government that ensures that all people are treated fairly and tried according to previously established legal procedures. The function is to ensure that all persons have to undergo according to the system previously established by law, which enables them to receive a fair trial before an impartial judge (right to a fair trial in criminal law cases; right to a fair trial in civil law cases; right to a fair trial in administrative law cases). Due process is a concept in international law that refers to the minimum standards of justice necessary for foreign visitors. Due process includes the right to a fair trial, being informed of rights if suspected of a crime, and prohibiting the arbitrary deprivation of life, liberty, or property. Due process prevents arbitrary power by ensuring that people are tried somewhat before a trial. It guarantees the right to a fair trial and prohibits arbitrary or discriminatory treatment by government agencies. Due process is the administration of justice in accordance with established rules and principles. It is a fundamental principle of limited Government to have an impartial judge.

Due process of law is a legal principle that ensures the state respects a person's legal rights by applying all relevant legal rules and principles to a case. It also protects individuals from the power of the law.

Critical aspects of the due process of law

Origins

The due process of law originated in Chapter 39 of King John's Magna Carta, which stated that no freeman could be harmed, dispossessed of their property, or seized except "by the law of the land".

- **United States Constitution**

The Fifth and Fourteenth Amendments of the United States Constitution guarantee that no person can be deprived of life, liberty, or property without due process of law.

- **Judicial review**

Courts have the authority to review whether the law is fair and just, as well as whether the Procedure prescribed by law was followed correctly.

- **Individual rights**

Due process protects individual rights and ensures that the law is not arbitrary or unjust.

Due process requires that the Government respect the rights of the accused and create a fair system against the accused. The concept of due process appeared as far back as the Magna Carta, which held that no noble would be exempt from the rule of law. Magna Carta's origins in the troubled reign of King John are examined, and the significance of the role Magna Carta played after that as a symbol of the subject's right to protection against the absolute authority of the sovereign is enforced. Magna Carta – Latin for the Great Charter – is perhaps the most famous document in English history. It laid the legislative foundations of personal freedom in the English-speaking world.

The Charter was agreed at a meeting held at Runnymede in June 1215 to end the civil war brought about by King John's misrule. Paradoxically, however, instead of ending the war, it simply started another - the war of Magna Carta. By the time of King John's death in October 1216, the Charter seemed a failure,. Yet, in the minority of the reign of John's son and successor, Henry III, it was to experience an extraordinary revival. Dusted down, abbreviated and reissued by the Regent, William Marshal, and the papal legate, Guala, it was to form the basis for a new political dispensation, a new style of kingship. In its final form, agreed when the young king came of age in 1225, the Charter became, in effect, England's fundamental law, its essential statute.

Such was the Charter's prestige and importance that in the late Middle Ages, whenever there was a political crisis, the first demand of any opposition was for its reissue. Over time, however, the Charter's relevance was to become less. As the nature of political life changed, and as new issues came to the fore not addressed in its clauses, its status became increasingly symbolic. Stage by stage, parliamentary legislation took the Charter's place as the most effective means to curtail arbitrary kingship. It was only in the political crises of the early 17th century, in the reigns of James I and Charles I, that the Charter was once again to take centre-stage in the nation's political life. The formidable lawyer Sir Edward Coke, champion of the 'ancient constitution', found in the Charter's terms precisely the text that he needed to legitimize his assault on what he considered Stuart tyranny. Since the 17th century, the Charter has never really looked back. The celebrations staged in 2015 to mark the 800th anniversary of its making, culminating in a visit to Runnymede on anniversary day itself by HM the Queen, reaffirmed its central position in English national life.

Due process is a course of legal proceedings according to rules and principles that have been established in a system of jurisprudence for the enforcement and protection of private rights. In each case, due process contemplates an exercise of the powers of Government as the law permits and sanctions under-recognized safeguards for the protection of individual rights.

Due process derives from early English common law and constitutional history. Due process is considered the minimum standard for administering justice. It is projected over the three powers of the state: the. Due process has derived its meaning from the word 'the law of the land' used in Section 39 of the Magna Carta of 1215. Due process is

- **Fairness**: Most countries agree that foreign visitors should be guaranteed a basic level of fairness and justice.
- **National treatment**: Some countries argue that they should grant no more rights to foreigners than they do to their citizens.
- **Expropriation**: International law recognizes that states have the right to confiscate foreign property, but expropriation is lawful if it meets due process requirements.
- **International investment agreements**: These agreements play a significant role in outlining the elements of due process.
- **Lack of due process**: A lack of due process doesn't always violate international law.

According to Oxford sources, due process is a legal principle that ensures people are treated somewhat and tried according to established laws:

Due process is embedded in clause 39 of the Magna Carta (1215). The first concrete expression of the due process idea embraced by Anglo-American law appeared in the 39th Article of Magna Carta (1215) in the royal promise that "No freeman shall be taken or (and) imprisoned or disseised or exiled or in any way destroyed...except by the legal judgment of his peers or (and) by the law of the land." In subsequent English statutes, the references to "the legal judgment of his peers" and "laws of the land" are treated as substantially synonymous with due process of law

The meaning of due process as it relates to substantive enactments and procedural legislation has evolved over decades of controversial interpretation by the Supreme Court. Today, if a law can reasonably promote public welfare and the means selected to bear a reasonable relationship to the legitimate public interest, then the law has met the due process standard. If the law seeks to regulate a fundamental right, such as the right to travel or the right to vote,

The principle is that the Government must respect all of the legal rights that are available to a person according to the law. The due process holds the Government subservient to the law of the land and protects individuals from the excesses of the state. Due process is either procedural or substantive. The procedural due process determines whether the governmental entity has taken an individual's life and liberty without the fair Procedure required by the statute.8 When a government harms a person without following the exact course of the law, it constitutes a due process violation that offends against the rule of law. It may involve the review of the general fairness of a procedure

Indian scholarship and expertise

The noted Indian lawyer and researcher Abhinav Chandrachud elucidates the due process of law in great depth. His thesis discusses the exciting and chequered history of "due process of law" from the emphatic denial of "due process" in A.K. Gopalan v. State of Madras to its acceptance in Maneka Gandhi v. Union of India. The author also explains the scope and applicability of the due process doctrine in regard to executive and legislative actions. He identifies its practical application in three spheres of Indian constitutional law: i) articulation of fundamental structure doctrine; ii) application of arbitrariness test derived from Article 14; and iii) recognition and creation of several unenumerated rights relating to life and personal liberty. The elusive nature of due process, as explained by Frankfurter J, has also been analyzed.

His work traces the origins of due process of law, taking into account its expanded scope and ambit from merely procedural due process to substantive due process. The difference between the two has been lucidly explained and analyzed.

Some justices have adhered to the proposition that the framers of the Fourteenth Amendment intended the entire Bill of Rights to be binding on the states. They have asserted that this position would provide an objective basis for reviewing state activities and would promote a desirable uniformity between state and federal rights and sanctions. Other justices, however, have contended that states should be allowed considerable latitude in conducting their affairs so long as they comply with a fundamental fairness standard. Ultimately, the latter position substantially prevailed. Due process comprises those principles of justice that are "so rooted in the traditions and conscience of our people as to be ranked as fundamental." In fact, however, almost all of the Bill of Rights has by now been included among those fundamental principles

The court is concerned with the constitutionality of the underlying rule rather than the fairness of the process of the law. Therefore, every form of review other than that involving procedural due process is a form of substantive review. This interpretation of due process is also a command that the Government shall not be unfair to the people. Various countries The process of Government, which deprives a person of life and liberty, must comply with the due process clause. However, 'due process' is not a term with a clear definition.

The dispute concerning Article 21 centres on the expression "procedure established by law."While having distinct structures, its significance nearly corresponds to the due process provision of the 5th Amendment of the American Constitution. Dr B.R. Ambedkar, the mastermind behind the Indian Constitution, clarified that the objective was to safeguard freedom through proper legal procedures, although deliberately excluding the word 'due process'. The Constituent Assembly encountered the task of reconciling theoretical fairness

with the necessity for societal transformation and governmental protection throughout the deliberations.

The exclusion of the due process provision

The public criticism was severe, especially over the exclusion of the due process provision. Dr. Ambedkar established Article 15A (now Article 22) as a means of providing reparation for the perceived detriment. He contended that this inclusion preserved a significant portion of what was omitted by the absence of the due process language in Article 21. The discussion highlights the importance of the phrase "procedure established by law." The deliberation inside the Constituent Assembly revolved around the authority of the court to examine the substance of a case, specifically in relation to the use of the terms "due process of law" and"procedure established by law." The ultimate incorporation of the current phrase "procedure established by law" happened after a protracted deliberation and several proposed revisions.

In addition, the Constituent Assembly deliberated on the right to privacy, akin to the Fourth Amendment in the United States, via a resolution proposed by Kazi Syed Karimuddin. The purpose of this resolution was to safeguard individuals from unjustified searches and confiscations. Nevertheless, although Ambedkar agreed with its merits, it couldn't pass muster. Conversely, Article 20(3) of the Constitution ensured the entitlement to protection from self-incrimination. To summarise, the discussions in the Constituent Assembly demonstrated the careful equilibrium between personal liberties, societal factors, and the procedural protections outlined in Article 21 of the Indian Constitution. The debate pertaining to the fundamental right to privacy and the selection of language in the Constitution continues to be essential elements of India's constitutional history.

Indian experience of due process revolution

The due process development in India has been enriched mainly by two principal spheres: First, the concept of 'Procedure established by law under Article 21 is required to be just, fair and reasonableness because of the interactions of Articles 14, 19 and 21; secondly, interrelationships among Articles 20, 21 and 22, as a result of development under Article 21, has furthered this phenomenon to a considerable extent. 10 Article 21 of the Constitution provides that: "No person shall be deprived of his life or personal liberty except according to Procedure established by law". Although Article 21 does not explicitly prescribe any quality or standard for the

Constituent Assembly debated in depth over the drafting of Article 15, which finally became Article 21 of the Indian Constitution in the background of the many amendments that were moved over Article 15. Kazi contended that if the words 'according to procedure established by an amendment with the aim of protecting Indians from unreasonable searches and seizures. He criticized the absence of the 'due process' clause in the fundamental rights, which he feared could lead to misuse of state power and infringe on the citizen's right to life and liberty.

The Advisory Committee on Fundamental Rights appointed by the Constituent Assembly endorsed Kazi Syed Karimuddin's opinion by suggesting that no person should be deprived of his life or liberty without due process of law. Kazi cautioned that if the words 'according to procedure established by law' are enacted, then there will be very significant injustice to the people and nation. Once the legislature lays down the Procedure by enacting the law, such Procedure should complied with by the authority. Then, the courts cannot question the decision of the authority even though that decision may be unjust or has apparently hostile intent. Therefore, he suggested that the words 'except according to procedure established by law' should be replaced by the words 'without due process of law'. On the other hand, B.N. Rao, the Constitutional Advisor to the Constituent Assembly, believed that due process would provide excessive powers to the courts. He stated that: "The courts, manned by an irremovable judiciary not so sensitive to public needs in the social or economic sphere as the representatives of a periodically elected legislature, will, in effect, have a veto on legislation exercisable at any time and at the instance of any litigant."

Limitations on the powers of the state, both executive and legislative

The doctrine implied by 'without due process of law' has a long history in Anglo-American law. It does not lay down a specific rule of law, but it implements the fundamental principle of justice. Due process means that the substantive provisions of the law are fair and just and not unreasonable, oppressive, capricious, or arbitrary. That means that the judiciary is empowered to review legislation. In America, the judiciary has that kind of power that undoubtedly leads to a conservative outlook on the part of the judiciary and uncertainty in legislation. The due process phase guarantees a fair trial in terms of both Procedure and substance. The Procedure should be in accordance with and should be appealable to the civilized conscience of the community. It also ensures a fair trial in substance, that is to say, that substantive law itself should be just and appealable to the civilized conscience of the community. The various decisions of the American Supreme Court, when analyzed, will stress the four.

Fundamental principles

First, each one must get a fair trial; second, the court or agency which takes jurisdiction in the case needs authorization by law to such prerogative; third, the defendant must be allowed an opportunity to present his side of the case; and fourth that certain assistance, including legal counsel and the confronting and detailed examination of witnesses, must be made available. These four fundamental points guarantee a fair trial in substance.16 Shri K.M. Munshi also supported the words 'without due process of law' because it would strike a balance between individual liberty and social control. Even

Shri Alladi Krishnaswami Ayyar lent his support for 'due process'. Mr Z.H. Lari said that it is necessary not only in the interest of individual liberty but in the interest of proper working of legislatures that such a clause as due process of law should find a place in the thConstitution.18Even Dr B.R. Ambedkar confessed that he was in a somewhat difficult position with regard to the words 'Procedure established by law' and 'due process'. One point of view was that due process of law must be present in this Article; otherwise, the Article would be worthless. The other point of view is that the existing phraseology is quite insufficient for the purpose. He further commented on the question.

The Constitution grants legislation to the particular legislature. The 'due process' clause would give the judiciary the power to question the law made by the Parliament on another ground. That ground would be whether that law is in keeping with certain fundamental principles relating to the rights of the individual. In other words, the judiciary would have the authority to question the law not merely on the ground of whether it was in excess of the authority of the legislature but also on the ground of whether the law was good, apart from the question of the powers of the legislature making the law. The law may be perfect and valid as far as the authority of the legislature is concerned. But it may not be a good law. That is to say, it violates certain fundamental principles, and the judiciary would have the additional power to declare the law invalid. We do not doubt the judiciary's power to examine the law made by different legislative bodies on the ground and whether that law is in accordance with the powers given to it. The introduction of the phrase due now raises the question.

There was discussion on whether the judiciary should empowered additionally to question the laws made by the state on the grounds that they violate certain fundamental principles. There are two views on this point. One view is that the legislature may be trusted not to make any law that would abolish the rights of a man. Another view is that it is not possible to trust the legislature; the legislature is likely to err, is expected to be led away by passion, by party prejudice, by party considerations, and the legislature may make a law which may abrogate what may be the fundamental principles which safeguard the individual rights of a citizen. We are, therefore, placed in two difficult. Positions. One is to give the judiciary the authority to sit in judgment over the will of the legislature and to question the law made by the Parliament on the ground that it is not good law in accordance with fundamental principles. Is that a desirable principle? The second position is that the legislature ought to be trusted not to make bad laws. It is tough to come to any definite conclusion. There are dangers on both sides. Further, Dr Ambedkar opined that it is not possible to omit the possibility of a legislature packed by party men making laws that may nullify or violate what we regard as certain fundamental principles affecting the life and liberty of an individual. At the same time, he expressed another view of how five or six.

Provisions of the Act have imposed unreasonable restrictions on the exercise of those rights. Further, the petitioner contended that freedom of movement is part of the right to personal liberty protected under Article 21. Therefore, the law under Article 21 has to be just and not lax. The majority of judges held that Articles 19 and 21 are independent and exclusive—Kania, CJ., joined by Mukherjee, J., propounded the doctrine of the directness of legislation. Kania, CJ., observed that if any bill does not directly violate any article but indirectly encroaches upon any articles of the Constitution, then that does not mean that legislation is ultra vires. The proper approach is only to consider the directness of the legislation and not what the result of the detention will be.23 Once the majority of the judges arrived at a conclusion about the non-application of Article 19 into the sphere of Article 21

The new approach

The 1978 Maneka Gandhi v. Union of India was a landmark case that expanded the scope of Article 21 of the Indian Constitution, which guarantees the right to life and liberty by establishing that due process of law is a fundamental part of the Procedure established by law. The case's ruling also linked Articles 14, 19, and 21, making them inseparable and requiring any procedure to meet the requirements of all three articles to be valid.

The ruling in Maneka Gandhi established that:

- The Procedure established by law must be fair, just, and not arbitrary. The content of the Procedure established by law must meet the substantive tests of Articles 14 and 19
- The Procedure must be "right and just and fair, and not arbitrary, fanciful or oppressive."
- The ruling in Maneka Gandhi has led to a broader interpretation of fundamental rights, which has protected citizens from the arbitrary exercise of state authority. It has also paved the way for the Supreme Court to include other rights in the scope of the Article, such as the right to clean water, the right to education, and the right to a fair trial.

Maneka Gandhi questioned the constitutional validity of Section 10(3)(c) of the Passport Act, 1967, which empowered the authority to impound the passport of a person in the public interest. She contended that this section gives discretionary power to the authority to impound the passport without being heard, which is an unjust process and violates the right to equality and is suitable for personal liberty. The seven-judge bench of the apex court upheld the contentions of the petitioner that the Procedure established under Article 21 should be just, fair and reasonable. Further, such Procedure should be tested under Articles 14 and 19 of the Constitution. Krishna Iyer, J., observed that the law prescribing a procedure for deprivation of life and personal liberty in Article 21 could not be any Procedure. Still, it had to be one that was neither arbitrary nor unfair nor unreasonable.41 Thus, the due process concept is read under Article 21 by articulating that 'procedure established by law' must be fair, just and reasonable. Krishan Iyer, J., in Sunil Batra v. DelhiAdmistration42, conceded that: "True, our Constitution has no 'due process' clause, but in this branch of law, after Cooper and ManekaGandhi, the consequence is the same" and added that Article 21 is the counterpart of the procedural due process in the United States.43The apex court in Ranjan Dwivedi v. Union of India44 reiterated the ratio of Maneka Gandhi case by expressing that it is difficult to hold that the substance of the American doctrine of due process has notes introduced in the conservative text of Article 21 of the Constitution. which would be no procedure at all, and the requirements of Article 21 would not be complied with. The object of substantive law is to provide justice to people, and that is the end of law. On the other hand, procedural law offers a means to achieve justice. The end and means are interrelated. Justice cannot be valid unless the means governing the process are fair. The means also cannot be justified unless the end is fair. The relation between the end and means is in Article 21 of the Constitution. Ascertaining the true meaning of life, personal liberty, and Procedure established by 21 is the mode of expansion, particularly after Maneka Gandhi.

Interpretation in Gopalan case

The narrow interpretation of Articel 21 of the Supreme Court in the Gopalan case has gradually been watered down and has finally faced a burial. The liberal interpretation of Procedure established by law in ManekaGandhi marks the beginning of a new dimension of procedural due process, especially in the criminal justice system under Article 21 of the Constitution. Now, the courts do not hesitate to quash the law if such law offends due process requirements. The re-interpretation of Article 21 and Article 14 after 1978 by the court marks a watershed in the development of Indian constitutional law. The vast extent of public law and public interest litigation and the court's routine intervention in administration, which is seen in Indian courts today, is the result of the due process of law in the Indian Constitution. It has judicial review has been aptly defined as always a function, so to speak,=of the viable constitutional law of a particular period. The viable constitutional law of India since 1978 has been the concept of 'due process' of law in the Constitution.

12. MASS SURVEILLANCE IN INDIA

It is necessary to address the ethics of placing large groups of people under mass surveillance to ascertain who, amongst them, is planning to take part in rights violations at the behest or on behalf of foreign actors. It reviews contemporary mass surveillance practices as described by Edward Snowden and mounts the best possible case in their favour. Of all the objections levelled against mass surveillance, two stand out: the claim that it violates the right to privacy and the claim that it is parasitic and entrenches unfair inequalities. The chapter argues that the privacy objection is not as decisive as it seems and that the fairness objection, though contingent on extant practices, is compelling. In the world as it is, it concludes, mass surveillance is morally wrong; highly complex forms of terrorism require States to take adequate measures to defend themselves, including mass monitoring of communications, unlike "targeted" surveillance (covert collection of conversations, telecommunications and metadata by technical means – "bugging"), "strategic" surveillance (or mass surveillance) does not necessarily start with suspicion against a particular person or persons. It has a proactive element aimed at identifying a danger rather than investigating a known threat. Herein lay both the value it can have for security operations and the risks it can pose for individual rights.

It is necessary to address the ethics of placing large groups of people under mass surveillance to ascertain who, amongst them, is planning to take part in rights violations at the behest or on behalf of foreign actors. It reviews contemporary mass surveillance practices as described by Edward Snowden and mounts the best possible case in their favour. Of all the objections levelled against mass surveillance, two stand out: the claim that it violates the right to privacy and the claim that it is parasitic and entrenches unfair inequalities. The chapter argues that the privacy objection is not as decisive as it seems and that the fairness objection, though contingent on extant practices, is compelling. In the world as it is, it concludes, mass surveillance is morally wrong.

Nevertheless, Member States do not have unlimited powers in this area. Mass surveillance of citizens is tolerable under the Convention only if it is strictly necessary for safeguarding democratic institutions. Taking into account the considerable potential to infringe fundamental rights to privacy and freedom of expression enshrined by the Convention, Member States must ensure that the development of surveillance methods resulting in mass data collection has the simultaneous development of legal safeguards securing respect for citizens' human rights.

Kazi Karimuddiin's amendment

Kazi Syed Karimuddin moved the amendment to embed safeguards against arbitrary search and seizure in the Indian Constitution.4 The proposed text read as follows:

Amendment 512, moved by Kazi Syed Karimuddin, "The right of the people to be secure in their persons, houses, papers and effects against unreasonable searches and seizures shall not be violated, and no warrants shall issue but upon probable cause supported by oath or affirmation and particularly describing the place to be searched and the persons or things to be seized"

Ambedkar was willing to accept Karimuddin's proposal.6 He pointed out that this clause was already in the Criminal Procedure Code and was, therefore, a part of Indian law, but also acknowledged that it may be desirable in the interest of personal liberty to 'place these provisions beyond the reach of the legislature'.7The chaos during voting over the proposal suggests that it was contentious. The Vice-President attempted twice to put the Karimuddin text to vote.8 Although he declared the amendment as having been accepted both times, Mr Krishnamachari objected, saying both times that the majority vote was for those who were not in favour of the amendment. The records of the day's debates suggest that there was unrest in the house. Jawaharlal Nehru supported a proposal to postpone the vote, which was dome.

The European case law

According to the case law of the European Court of Human Rights, it would be counter to government efforts to keep terrorism at bay if the terrorist threat were substituted with a perceived threat of unfettered executive power intruding into citizens' private lives. It is of the utmost importance that the domestic legislation authorizing far-reaching surveillance techniques and prerogatives provides for adequate safeguards in order to minimize the risks to the freedom of expression and the right to privacy, which the "indiscriminate capturing of vast amounts of communications" enables. The standards related to targeted surveillance identified in the case law of the Court have, therefore, been adapted to apply to strategic surveillance.

While not doubting the power of imperialism, by the early twentieth century, it no longer constituted the sole or even most important enemy for a number of Muslim intellectual and political movements. Instead, it was the coming dominance of the nation-state as a political form that inspired these movements, for they often tended to see it in Hegelian terms as representing the simultaneous fulfilment and transformation of the colonial order. At the time, these movements were frequently accused by their nationalist enemies of being secessionists hand-in-glove with imperialism, and today, they are seen as being anti-national and global in their arena of operations. But I am concerned with the way in which they sought to undo the categories of majority and minority and, with them, the nation-state. The Indian government's mass surveillance systems present a new threat to the right to Privacy. Mass interception of communication, keyword searches, and easy access to particular users' data suggest that the State is moving towards unfettered large-scale communication monitoring. This is particularly ominous given that our privacy safeguards remain inadequate even for targeted surveillance and its more familiar pitfalls. This need for better safeguards became apparent when the Gujarat government illegally placed a young woman under surveillance for obviously illegitimate purposes, demonstrating that the current system is prone to egregious misuse. While the lack of proper safeguards is problematic even in the context of targeted surveillance, it threatens the health of our democracy in the context of mass surveillance. The proliferation of mass surveillance means that vast amounts of data are collected easily using information technology and lie relatively unprotected. This paper examines the right to Privacy and surveillance in India in an effort to highlight more clearly the problems that are likely to emerge with mass surveillance of communication by the Indian Government. It does this by teasing out our privacy rights jurisprudence and the concerns underpinning it, considering its utility in the context of mass surveillance, and then explaining the kind of harm that might result if mass surveillance continues unchecked.

Privacy and the Indian Constitution

The Oxford Dictionary of Law defines Privacy as the right to be left alone and to have a private life. The right to privacy is not explicitly stated in the Indian Constitution. Still, the Supreme Court has ruled that it is a fundamental right that is protected by Article 21 of the Constitution. The Supreme Court has also ruled that the right to privacy is "intrinsic to life and personal liberty".

Here are some other details about the right to privacy in India:

- The right to privacy includes the right to be protected from unlawful interference with one's privacy, family, home, or correspondence.
- The right to privacy also consists of the right to be protected from illegal attacks on one's honour and reputation.

- The right to privacy is legally binding under customary international law.
- The Union Government has argued that privacy is multifaceted and cannot be treated as a fundamental right.

2017 has been a big year for constitutional development in India. In a historic and landmark decision, a 9-judge bench of the Supreme Court pronounced that the right to Privacy is a constitutional right which is not only rooted in the right to life and liberty but also enshrined in all other fundamental rights, including the right to equality and the essential freedoms.

Surveillance in terms of safety is an essential activity by any nation's national security force. It is done with the proper mechanism to figure out the hidden activity of the intruder. It is true that in many developing or underdeveloped countries, the country's prevailing laws are not being executed. Hence, personal rights and privacy issues can occur. occured.

Similarly, in India there, mass surveillance is prevalent to protect the nation from foreign aggression, internal disturbance, etc. In addition, at a prima facie, it is a protection initiative for the welfare of the citizens. Still, citizens, but due to proper execution and other issues, are hampering the rights to privacy. There needs to be a legal and political role in maintaining the mechanism of the surveillance project and making a balance between personal liberty and the right to privacy. This paper delves into how mass surveillance is hampering the rights to Privacy and ways to create balance between them.

The right to dignity has been the focus of the Court for the development of the right to Privacy. The Court held that the right to live with dignity includes the right to autonomy and to make decisions about one's life choices. Justice Chandrachud eloquently stated, "…The best decisions on how life should be lived are entrusted to the individual. …… The State must safeguard the ability to make decisions – the autonomy of the individual – and not to dictate those decisions." He went on to hold that dignity permeates the core of the rights guaranteed to the individual under Part III of the Constitution and that Privacy assures dignity to the individual.

Specific references to the protection of one's sexuality, sexual orientation and gender identity became part of one's intimate life choices that need to be protected under the rubric of Privacy. The Court referred to several critical decisions around women's autonomy over their bodies and sexuality as part of the right to privacy, including the right of women to work at night, protection of reproductive rights, the right to bodily integrity, the rights of unwed mothers, the right against forced sterilization and the right to decide on marriage, procreation and the choice of family life. These, the Court held, were matters of one's most intimate and personal decisions and essential in the pursuit of happiness, which is founded on autonomy and dignity.

The Court also declared that the right to sexual orientation and gender identity were inherent in the right to life. Justice Chandrachud went as far as to hold that the Court's previous reasoning in Suresh s Koushal was flawed and held "That "a minuscule fraction of the country's population constitutes lesbians, gays, bisexuals or transgender people" (as observed in the judgment of this Court) is not a sustainable basis to deny the right to Privacy. ......Discrete and insular minorities face grave dangers of discrimination for the simple reason that their views, beliefs or way of life do not accord with the 'mainstream'. Yet in a democratic Constitution founded on the rule of law, their rights are as sacred as those conferred on other citizens to protect their freedoms and liberties." It held that the rights of the LGBT community were inherent in the right to life and constituted the essence of liberty and freedom. It held that "[s]exual orientation is an essential component of identity" and that "[e]qual protection demands protection of the identity of every individual without discrimination."

The judgment is fascinating in the way in which several judges refer to the right to gender identity and other rights relating to one's intimate life in a very outspoken manner. J. Bobde held that the right to Privacy is confined not only to intimate spaces such as the bedroom or the washroom but also to a person wherever they are. Interestingly, the Supreme Court has addressed these issues because washrooms and toilets are the sites where current battles for recognition of the rights of the trans communities are being fought and could pave the way for the future.

How is privacy defined?

Privacy is The right to be left alone and to keep certain matters secluded from public view, as recognized in Article 8 of the European Convention on Human Rights and the Human Rights Act 1998. The right includes privacy of communications (telephone calls, correspondence, etc.); privacy of the home and office; environmental protection (including freedom from excessive noise the protection of physical integrity; protection from unjustified prosecution and conviction of those engaged in consensual nonviolent sexual activities; and protection from being photographed and described in circumstances where the individual has a reasonable expectation of privacy.

Yet, public authorities have a limited but positive duty to protect privacy from interference by third parties. Arrests took place without warrants and searches without justification. Lawless laws are governing us, and there is no remedy for grievances that got redressal on account of unauthorized arrests and searches."Dr Ambedkar pointed out that this clause was already in the Criminal Procedure Code and was, therefore, a part of Indian law, but also acknowledged that it may be desirable in the interests of personal liberty to 'place these provisions beyond the reach of the legislature'. Despite Ambedkar's support, the Amendment failed.

We must ponder on the action for breach of confidence as it relates to commercial secrets. It first considers the jurisdictional basis of the action for breach of trust and then discusses the elements for establishing a breach of confidence. The first element is that there must be confidential information; the second element is that the defendant comes under an obligation of confidence; the third element of a breach of confidence requires an unauthorized use of the information to the detriment of the person communicating it.

The horizontal application of the right to privacy

Artificial intelligence has been at the centre of the global conversation in recent days, with a major summit in the U.K. and a new executive order coming down from the White House. The broad contours of the rights encompassed within the framework of Privacy given by the Supreme Court paved the way for full recognition of rights, specifically for women and sexual minorities. This judgment is already witnessing the vast potential it has for the advancement of women's rights, as it is being used to challenge the criminal law exemption to child marital rape and to challenge the constitutionality of outdated family laws that restrict women's rights. It will also have a significant impact on the rights of the LGBT community as it has the potential to overturn the Suresh Koushal decision. The horizon of new rights for protection under the rubric of the recognition of privacy remains undone.

However, petitioners have argued that if Privacy is to be elevated to a fundamental right, its sub-species would also have to be granted the same status. At the time of drafting the Indian Constitution, there were limited examples of codification of the right to Privacy. Everyday law, for instance, did not clearly articulate the privacy doctrine.3 The European Convention on Human Rights, which contains one of the most powerful articulations of the right to Privacy, was not in force at the time. However, the United States of America used a patchwork of law to protect Privacy in different contexts, and the principles from this law almost made their way into the Indian Constitution in the form of an amendment based on the U.S. Fourth Amendment.

The Constituent Assembly did not take the right to privacy as seriously as it should have whilst crafting the Fundamental Rights. This might have been because of the relative scarcity of material on the right to privacy at the time. This resulted in some initial reluctance on the part of the Supreme Court to read this right into the Constitution. However, the Supreme Court of India eventually read the right to privacy into fundamental rights and has been tracing it through the different cases that implicate this right.

Convinced of its necessity, the Criminal Procedure Code offered adequate safeguards but its provisions were not respected. He argued that similar principles inserted in the Constitution would, be dropped.. In a speech riddled with inconsistencies, he made the very curious argument that the liberties granted to the people prior to independence would be unsustainable after independence and that fettering the parliament's discretion with the procedure in the context of law and order would be wrong. It is unclear whether this reasoning prevailed or whether concerns during the Constituent Assembly's sessions influenced the vote. Apart from privacy in the context of search and seizure, the need for the right to privacy in the context of correspondence was also highlighted to the Constituent Assembly. Communication surveillance was addressed in an amendment moved by Somnath Lahiri. This was to include a clause protecting the Privacy of correspondence within the fundamental right of liberty (which later became Article 19) in the ConstitutionThe House resolved to take up the Lahiriproposal towards the end of the discussion on the basic rights instead of in the context of the right to liberty. It appears, however, that the proposal was never seriously considered or even put up for vote.

Exclusion of iPhone

The records of the Constituent Assembly debates are, therefore, disappointing. The iPhone is seeking powerful reasoning to explain the omission of the right to Privacy. Some members made a robust case for the inclusion of this right on more than one occasion, but for reasons that are not entirely clear, the arguments were not sustained.

B. The Supreme Court of India Traces Out Citizens' Rights Against Illegal SurveillanceWhile the Constitution, and the choices made about the Fundamental Rights were still fresh in public memory in 1954, the apex court refused to read the right to Privacy eight into the Indian Constitution. This was in A.P. Sharma v. Satish Chandra, where the Supreme Court declared that it could not import the right to Privacy analogous to the U.S. Fourth Amendment into a different fundamental right given that the constitution makers had not thought to recognize this right toprivacy.19However, the apex court gradually moved away from this position, to acknowledging that other rights and liberties guaranteed in the Constitution would be seriously affected if the right to Privacy was not protected. This process began in Kharak Singh v. State of U.P.20, where the Court discussed the relationship between surveillance and personal liberty (personal liberty being guaranteed by the Constitution) and found that unauthorized intrusion into a person's home would interfere with her right to individual freedom. The right to privacy was conceived around the house, and unauthorized intrusions into homes were interference with the right to personal liberty. The Court recognized "the right of the people to be secure in their persons, houses, papers, and effects". It declared that their right against unreasonable searches and seizures was not to be violated. However, this right did extend to the shadowing of citizens outside their homes. In a dissenting opinion that exhibited extraordinary foresight, JusticSubba Rao maintained that broad surveillance powers put innocent citizens at risk and that the right to Privacy is an integral part of personal liberty. In Gobind v. State of A.P.23, the Supreme Court said that the Constitution makers 'must be deemed to have conferred upon the individual as again the government is a sphere where he should beet alone.'

What was implicit in the privacy cases after Kharak Singh became explicit-

Italy in Collector v. Canara Bank 28, where the Supreme Court said quite clearly that the right to privacy 'deals with persons not places', and reiterated this position more recently in Directorate of Revenue v. Mohd. Nisar Holia The doctrine has therefore expanded beyond the Kharak Singh30 majority judgment to the broader interpretation advocated by Justice Subba Rao in his dissent. Canara Bank also made it clear that inroads into the right to Privacy for surveillance.'

After a very promising narrative that recognized the role played by procedural safeguards in protecting citizens' right to Privacy, the Supreme Court regrettably accepted Kapil Sibal's argument that it could not impose prior judicial scrutiny in the absence of a statutory provision supporting such scrutiny. Had the Court declared the power to intercept communication under the Telegraph Act constitutionally untenable, this may have resulted in the introduction of robust safeguards. However, the Court opted instead to craft interim procedural safeguards for the interception of communication under the Telegraph Act. These safeguards consisted mainly of proper record-keeping and internal executive oversight by senior officers such as the home secretary, the cabinet secretary, the law secretary and the telecommunications secretary. They are opaque and rely solely on members of the executive to review surveillance requests, leaving little for third-party scrutiny or challenge by affected parties).

This was a highly inadequate and flawed process in the Telegraph Act and the Information Technology Act, as a result of which the Supreme Court of our communication interception jurisprudence has focused on targeted surveillance for years. Rapid evolution in technology has, however, enabled surveillance, which is different from targeted surveillance and its identification of particular.

Mass surveillance

The international safeguards recommended for targeted surveillance assume some prior suspicion of the target of surveillance. The clarity about the objective and the target makes it easier to 'objectively assess the necessity and proportionality of the contemplated surveillance, weighing the degree of the proposed intrusion against its anticipated value to a particular investigation'. These safeguards for targeted surveillance emerge from International Human Rights legal norms that require that there must be clear justification whenever there is any interference with the right to Privacy, such that there is a proportionality analysis that ensures that there is a compelling justification for any serious interference with protected human rights.

The protection offered under the European Convention on Human Rights

It did not clarify the specifics of what might be an acceptable set of safeguards in the context of mass surveillance. Drawing upon its past jurisprudence, the European Court insisted on reasonable procedural safeguards. It stated quite clearly that there are significant risks of arbitrariness when executive power is exercised in secrecy and that the law should be sufficiently clear to give citizens an adequate indication of the circumstances in which interception might take place. Additionally, the extent of discretion conferred and the manner of its exercise must be clear enough to protect individuals from arbitrary interference. This question is likely to be examined in more detail by the Court in the near future: London-based organizations Big Brother Watch, Open Rights Group, English PEN and Constanze Kurz have brought the U.K. government before the ECHR for the mass surveillance of data conducted by British spy agencies.

Surveillance in Infia

Our safeguards in India apply only to targeted surveillance and require written requests to be provided and reviewed before telephone tapping or intervention. India has no requirements for transparency, whether in the form of disclosing the quantum of interception taking place each year or in the form of subsequent notification to people whose communication was intercepted. It does not even have external oversight in the form of an independent regulatory body or the judiciary to ensure that no abuse of surveillance systems takes place. Given these structural flaws, the Gujarat illegal surveillance controversy is unsurprising. The complete lack of accountability for the misuse of the surveillance framework in that context bodes ill for the manner in which surveillance is likely to be used in India. In this context, mass surveillance and the Central Monitoring System (CMS) raise real concerns about the extensive misuse of power by the State. News reports in India indicate this is a move towards intercepting all communication over the Internet and scanning it for keywords like 'attack', 'bomb', 'blast', and 'kill'. Tweets, status updates, emails, chat transcripts, and even voice traffic over the Internet (including from platforms like Skype and Google Talk) will be scanned by this system. In the context of phone call surveillance, CMS is even more opaque than targeted surveillance since the State can intercept communication directly without making requests to private telecommunication service providers. This means that there is one less layer of scrutiny through which abuse of power can reach the public. There is no one to ask whether the requisite paperwork is in place or to notice a dramatic increase in interception requests. Unfettered mass surveillance does not augur well for democracy. Understanding why this is so can be difficult owing to the nature of privacy alarms arising from mass surveillance.

Different kinds of privacy harms may result from surveillance, like the disruption of valuable activity and the chilling of socially beneficial behaviour like free speech.4 Among these is the creation of power imbalances like (excess executive power) that damage the social structure. 48 These different harms tend to be acknowledged in a piecemeal fashion depending on context. For example, in Kharak Singh

49, the problem was the right to Privacy in the digital age, Report of the Office of the United Nations High Commissioner for Human Rights, A/HRC/27/3, para 41. of disruption of the target's activities as well as one of chilling socially beneficial. However, only Justice Subba Rao was willing to acknowledge that the matter was also a privacy problem. This acknowledgement of the chilling effect on speech as a privacy problem is, however, unambiguous in the PUCL case. Privacy harms in the form of power imbalances that damage the social structure are the most difficult to identify clearly. Their impact remains invisible for a large part. Solove points out that one of the problems with the identification of such harms is that privacy violations are often framed as injuries to individuals and weighed against security interests (seen as societal interests. The acknowledgement of the right to Privacy as a societal interest offers a more helpful way to frame the surveillance debate. It clarifies the need to focus on oversight and accountability mechanisms, bearing in mind the impact of unrestrained surveillance on the health of our democracy.

India's rationale for surveillance safeguards

There is no excuse for a democracy like India, which has articulated its commitment to human rights, not to put these privacy safeguards in place. However, since the safeguards essentially check the wielding of executive power, it seems unlikely that the executive will voluntarily put them in place without external pressure. One expects the Supreme Court of India to recognise the damage that unrestrained mass surveillance will wreak on our democracy and that it takes its jurisprudence forward by several steps unimpeded by its initial reluctance to create robust safeguards in the PUCL telephone tapping case.

The Indian Supreme Court faces the challenge of reconciling a long tradition of common law adjudication on administrative matters with a constitutionally entrenched Bill of Rights. This article examines the Court's jurisprudence on one aspect of judicial review that encapsulates the difficulties this challenge presents: the use of privacy issues can occur. Of uncodified administrative law "principles of natural justice" in conducting judicial review for violation of constitutional rights. I present the broad claim that the Indian Supreme Court's erratic attempts to incorporate the principles of natural justice into constitutional rights have led to an unpredictable and often erratic form of judicial review. As the distinction between standards of administrative review and constitutional review diminishes, leading to a "constitutionalized administrative law," this doctrinal confusion endangers both the consistency of administrative adjudication and the enforcement of fundamental rights. A resolution for this confusion must come from a more thoughtful and consistent jurisprudence by the Court.

13. ARE INDIA'S MUSLIMS A MINORITY

Kazi Syed Karimuddin was the first man to move for the abolition of the reservation of seats for minorities during the second reading of the Constitution. However, he had also pleaded for proportional representation. He was a straightforward parliamentarian who had a strong faith in his conviction. But his proposal for proportional representation didn't find favour

India is moving into a deplorable situation. Prime Minister Narendra Modi, however, is playing a long game. His rise to national power, on a promise of rapid development, swept a decades-old Hindu nationalist movement from the margins of Indian politics firmly to the centre. He has since chipped away at the secular framework and robust democracy that had long held India together despite its sometimes explosive religious and caste division.

Minority is a word with several meanings. In public health, it usually means a specified societal group that may be small in numbers and, therefore, considered to have limited political influence, such as homosexuals or members of certain ethnic or religious groups. A visible minority is readily recognizable because of skin colour or other distinguishing external characteristics, such as mode of dress or culturally determined behaviour. In some communities, so-called visible minority groups constitute a substantial majority. Advocating proportional representation so as to escape the "pervading evil of democracy [that] is the tyranny of the majority", Kazi Karimuddin argued that it "is not based on religious grounds and it applies to all minorities, political, religious and communal". "Without any sacrifice of democratic principle", he further argued, "representatives of communal and political minorities can be elected". Similarly, ZH Lari contended that with proportional representation, the parliament will become "the mirror of the national mind" and that "minorities will not have grievances about their representation".

Fourteen per cent of India's one billion people are Muslim. Characterized by economic and political diversity, they are further divided regionally and linguistically: Bengali, Deccani, Gujarati, Hindustani, Mappila, Oriyya, and Punjabi. Most are Sunni Muslims following the Hanafi legal tradition; about 10 per cent are Twelver Shiis, and a smaller percentage are Ismaili Shiis. Most Indian Muslims supported the partition of British India at independence, but a substantial minority supported the Indian National Congress. In independent India, Muslims have been politically active as one of the largest Muslim national communities in the world.

The 'Muslim community' in India emerged during colonial rule as a new kind of sociological category. This emergence had its relations in the designs and exigencies of British rule, including the deployment from the early years of the nineteenth century of new forms of classification like the census, which for the first time defined India's Muslims as a minority. More interesting, however, was the way in which the colonial state provided Muslims the opportunity to redefine themselves as a group. In this chapter, I will argue that rather than being territorialized by British rule as a demographic or religious minority, Muslims adopted forms of self-definition that ended up deterritorializing both India and Islam. They did so by abandoning the idea of territorial nationality, which defined them as second-class subjects in a state where they were unfree instead of free, a minority instead of a majority. What resulted from this abandonment of territoriality was a Muslim community that occupied an imagined space situated at an angle to the sovereignty of the state. Like a shadow, this community had a territorial notion of nationality while being quite distinct from it.

The religious partition

During the twentieth century, many political actors and theorists across the globe believed that the religious partition was a solution to the democratic problem of numbers c. Swimming against the tide of Pakistani nationalism, a set of eminent Muslim thinker-politicians associated with the Indian independence movement recognized the structural significance of a consenting minority to the formation of a plural democracy. Leaning on Islam's universalism to extend its ambitions beyond political separatism, they not only endorsed but deepened a uniquely Indian nationalist rendering of the secular. By remaking the Indian Muslim concept of parity, championing regional particularity, and engaging with the shifting meaning of sovereignty over historical time, the likes of Abul Kalam Azad, Sheikh Abdullah, and Abdul Ghaffar Khan charted a third way to nationalism. On the one hand, and in the hope of averting its minimization, the Muslim secular challenged the abstractions of its Hindu friends, M.K. Gandhi and Jawaharlal Nehru. On the other, it critiqued Mohammad Ali Jinnah's campaign for Pakistan since it institutionalized rather than dispelled India's identitarian animosities. Democracy is both about majority rule and minority rights.

It is vital that minorities feel secure and have equal rights. But what happens when a society bends 'too much' to accommodate the rights of minorities, be it because of religion, sex, caste or sexual orientation? In the constitutional debates, there was healthy disagreement on how to tackle 'forever discrimination' against the Dalits. No one disagreed with the goal that there must be some well-defined policy. India chose the command economy route of quota reservations rather than the more liberal and secular route of affirmative action.

More than a third of the world's 1.2 billion Muslims live as political and religious minorities. Early Islamic history yields two models for Muslim minorities to follow: the Meccan model, where Muslims facing persecution opted for emigration, and the Abyssinian model, in which the Muslim minority lived among a Christian majority in a state of tolerance and peaceful coexistence. In the modern world, Muslims living as minorities still consider themselves part of the worldwide family of Muslims.

The demand for a caste census is just the latest manifestation of a policy gone awry. How awry? As in the Supreme Court interpretation of quotas, there is a 50 per cent cap on the quota for reservations, but the quota is very elastic. At times, it can be more than 50 per cent. Our policymakers and/or their advisers, and even our lawmakers, forever think that people are stupid; if you believe that the description is extreme, substitute 'irrational' for stupid. Some time back, I had stated that the anti-liberal, anti-secular, anti-merit system would end when everyone demanded reservation. Yesterday, the Jats wanted reservations; today, it is the Marathas; tomorrow, it will be the Brahmins. You wait!

Well, wait no longer. The Bihar census yielded the estimates in Figure 1 (never mind that the implied fertility rates of some castes may be beyond comprehension or reality). You must count SCs and STs 21 percent, EBCs 36 percent, and OBCs 27 percent. Since all of them deserve reservations (a total of 85 per cent), we are as close to 100 per cent reservation as we will ever get.

One of the accepted beliefs about Modi's tenure as prime minister is that he was chief minister of Gujarat at the time the Godhra riots happened. Therefore, he and his policies are likely to be discriminatory towards Muslims.

Official consumer survey data conducted by the National Sample Survey Office (NSSO) showed that the welfare of poor Muslims in Gujarat had improved at least as fast as that of those who were not Muslim. The welfare of Muslims had increased faster in Gujarat than in other states. The Modi government has increased welfare spending via direct benefit transfer (DBT) schemes and provided free grain to all; it is now conventional wisdom that free food and DBT do not discriminate on the basis of caste or religion.

Jawaharlal Nehru, India's first prime minister, opted for the broadest possible answer. The India his Congress party advocated was, he wrote, proudly plural: "An ancient palimpsest on which are inscribed layer upon layer of thought and reverie, and yet no succeeding layer had completely hidden or erased the previous writing".

But Hindu nationalists such as Vinayak Savarkar discerned in the countless communities that populated modern-day India, Pakistan and Bangladesh an essential "Hindutva", or Hindu-ness, that persisted no matter what faith an Indian practised.

"Religious minorities will all have the right to practise their religion", Savarkar wrote of India he envisioned – but they were inescapably citizens of a Hindu "Rashtra", or nation.

Another India

Another India is the story of the world's most significant religious minority. Weaving together vivid biographical portraits of a wide range of Indian Muslims—elite and subaltern, secular and clerical, activist and apolitical—it brings the experience of the country's Muslims under a single focus and, by throwing light on the Indian Muslim condition, the first thirty years of independence, reflects on the true character of democratic India. What we have here is a somewhat different picture from received accounts of the "world's largest democracy." Challenging the traditional histories of Nehru's India, minority rights were neglected right from independence. Despite its best intentions, the Congress regime that ruled for three decades was often illiberal, intolerant, and undemocratic. Muslims had to contend with discrimination, disadvantage, deindustrialisation, dispossession, and disenfranchisement, as well as unresponsive leadership. Anil demonstrates how the Muslim elite encouraged depoliticization, taking up seemingly noble but largely inconsequential causes with little bearing on the lives of ordinary members of the community. There was no room for mass protests or collective solidarity in this version of Muslim politics. *Another India* explores this elite betrayal, whose consequences are still felt by India's 200 million Muslims today.

Muslims constitute slightly less than 14 per cent of India's total population of 1.3 billion [EPA]. Only a day after the Indian government led by the right-wing Bharatiya Janata Party leader Narendra Modi took the oath of office, Najma Heptullah, the new minister of minority affairs, made an unusual statement. While some were surprised, even shocked, by her statement, others expressed happiness over it. She said: "Muslims are not minorities; Parsis are. We have to see how we can help them [Parsis] so that their numbers don't diminish".

Currently, Parsis number about 69,000, whereas Muslims constitute slightly less than 14 per cent of the total population of 1.3 billion. In one view, based on the 2006 Sachar Committee report, which studied the status of the Muslim community, unlike Parsis, "Muslims are worse off than any other community, even the Musahar (low caste) Dalits, in terms of their socio-economic condition."

The goals of independent India of achieving the constitutional promise of an egalitarian society have primarily led by an emphatic endorsement of the right to equality on the one hand and the implementation of positive discrimination measures, such as caste-based reservations in public employment and education, on the other. The idea of redistributive justice was a common theme often visited in the Constituent Assembly Debates.1 India shares a long history of social and economic oppression with most other countries in the developing world. While the markers for such oppression are often race and socio-economic status, or both, in most parts of the world, in India, caste and tribal identity remain the most important vectors for discriminatory practices and structural inequities.

The complex perception of Islam

Westerners tend to think of Islamic societies as backwards-looking, oppressed by religion, and inhumanely governed, comparing them to their own enlightened, secular democracies. However, measuring the cultural distance between the West and Islam is a complex undertaking, and that distance is narrower than they assume. Islam is not just a religion and, indeed, not just a fundamentalist political movement. It is a civilization and a way of life that varies from a Muslim country but has a shared spirit far more humane than most Westerners' reality.

Through a variety of mechanisms, later, the Assembly scrapped all suggestions and provisions discussed for the political representation of minorities, especially Muslims, for the provision for reserved seats for the SCs was retained. Jawaharlal Nehru regarded as the architect of "secular India" but who made no efforts to institute the term "secular" in the constitution, pleasingly said: "In the very nature of things, in a democracy, the will of the majority will ultimately prevail."

Having constitutionally robbed Muslims of any representational power in future parliament and services, the Assembly offered them "minority rights", which were also vehemently opposed initially. On the obscene grounds of disruption of "national outlook" and "national unity", people such as Jay Prakash Narayan and Damodar Seth argued that language alone – not religion – should form the basis of classifying a minority. To Seth, if religious minorities were allowed to run their educational institutions, it would "promote communalism and anti-national outlook". Was not right that "any claim for the sharing of power by the minority is labelled communalism while the monopolising of the whole power by the majority is called nationalism"?

With the wings of symbolic power in future parliament and services chopped, the constitution gave minorities such as Muslims the "rights" (read compensation) to establish their educational institutions and "to profess, practise and propagate religion", of course, "subject to public order, morality and health and the other provisions".

It is within this historical context that one can understand why some felt worried over Heptullah's statement, whereas others felt happy. Those deeply concerned about it felt that even those minority protections were probably to be revised or trimmed, if not deleted.

The affirmation of India's Muslims being a minority comes from the reality that they have been consistently vulnerable to Hindu vigilantes and ideologues. Since the ruling Hindu nationalist Bharatiya Janata Party (BJP) came to power in 2014, led by Prime Minister Narendra Modi, incidents of sectarian violence targeting the Muslim minority, who make up about 14% of the population, have become increasingly frequent.

Hardline vigilante Hindu rightwing groups, emboldened under the Modi regime, have carried out sustained persecution and lynchings of Muslims and held a growing number of rallies and marches platforming anti-Muslim hate speech and genocidal calls to violence. In BJP-controlled states, Muslims have been described as "intruders", faced discriminatory policies and had their homes bulldozed.

The pervasive majority

As Andre Liebich and Abul Kalam Azad observed, if a minority existed only in relation to a majority, Heptullah's verbal erasure that Muslims are not a minority is premature because she did not question its constitutive cognate term, Hindus as the majority, which is the pervasive premise of nearly everything Indian.

MN Srinivas, the foremost sociologist in independent India, held that "the concept of the unity of India is inherent in Hinduism". According to Srinivas, the term "Hindu" includes Buddhists, Jains and Sikhs. His guru and the father of Indian sociology, GS Ghurye, held that tribes were not distinct or separate from Hindus. To him, they were "imperfectly integrated classes of Hindu society". Likewise, Nirmal Kumar Bose considered tribes as "full-fledged Hindus". Note that until 1940, the government census did not classify tribes as Hindus.

All these assertions, some also supported by the measure of the government of free India, such as the inclusion of tribes in the census as Hindus, reflect the assumption as well as the attempts to craft a Hindu majority in a democracy based on the strength of sheer numbers.

The BJP's allegation that the Congress and other political parties indulge in "minority appeasement" and use Muslims as a "vote bank" assumes and enacts the premise of a majority. During the heyday of the campaign to demolish the Babri mosque in the early 1990s to build in its place a temple for lord Ram, the BJP and its allies rejected the proposal for a constitutional settlement by arguing that the temple was ultimately an issue of people's faith. Clearly, the people here referred to the majority community.

The contemporary discourse of terrorism is deliberately rendered synonymous with the minority community and its religion in a way that assumes that people enacting political violence from the majority community are rarely called terrorists. In fact, in the ideological discourse of the BJP and its parent organisation, the Rashtriya Swayamsevak Sangh (RSS), because of their religion, Muslims and Christians can never be loyal to India. In contrast, members of the majority community naturally are.

Nothing reflected the assumption of a Hindu majority more crisply than the slogan "*Hindu ghata, desh bata*" (as the number of Hindus decreases, India will break/get divided) raised and written on public walls during the 1980s and 1990s.

International perspective on minorities

Muslims live in every country of the world. They are a majority in approximately fifty countries and territories and live as minorities everywhere else. In today's interconnected world, Muslim minorities, especially in the West, are increasingly taking on roles as advocates of justice and freedom and as ambassadors to Muslim-majority countries.

Muslims in Muslim-majority communities are also asserting their roles as global citizens, as is evident in the recent Arab upheavals taking place. Today's globalized world also means that the actions of other faiths' adherents have direct implications on the treatment and role of minorities across the globe. The recent Qur'an burning by a fringe pastor in the United States is an example of the possible extreme consequences. As a response to the Qur'an burning, violent protests in Afghanistan resulted in brutal deaths and the beheading of UN staff of other faiths.

The term "minority" in this report refers to the numerical meaning and does not indicate marginalized communities. 3 One such example is Bahrain, where the numerical majority, the Shia population, is a marginalized minority in terms of political power. 4 For example, indigenous communities may face different issues than migrant or diaspora communities. In the case of the Philippines, the indigenous Muslim community in the south is involved in an independence struggle, while the diaspora community in the north is facing integration and identity issues. 5 "The Future of the Global Muslim Population: Projections for 2010-2030,"

Questions persist about the role of culture versus religion in shaping identity, as well as about the assumed tension between Western and Muslim identities. Can Muslims be entirely Western and still live as Muslims? Some individuals and groups in the West are uncomfortable with the social expressions of Islam, generating much debate about whether Muslim communities can be part of Western society. Discussions about the difference between integration and assimilation abound. Muslim communities in the United States and Europe face similar challenges despite the fact that the responses from each government and each society have been different. In the case of the United States, the government has not imposed policies requiring complete assimilation into society. In contrast, there have been policy bans on mosque minarets in Switzerland, seven on face veils in France and Belgium, and European Muslims have struggled to establish their place in society.10 These policy bans have emboldened neighbouring governments to introduce restrictive policies in their own countries. Are these government policies detrimental to integration efforts, and will they be perceived as promoting assimilation and the dilution of religious identities? European countries like France, Germany, and Denmark are case studies that Muslim minorities must re-examine the reasons for the negative public perception of Islam and Muslims.

Minorities in Muslim-majority countries are also affected as the negative sentiment against them rises. The American government and its policymakers should not ignore its interconnectedness with today's world. As General David Petraeus recently pointed out, acts by fringe elements in the United States that denigrate Islam endanger American troops and civilians. At the same time, it is also essential to address the treatment of other faith communities in Muslim-majority countries. What are some basic standards that Muslims should use to ensure the rights of marginalized and minority communities? Interfaith relations Despite misconceptions and fear, the myriad interfaith initiatives that have emerged in these difficult times represent a more hopeful scenario. Partnerships and alliances to support marginalized Muslim communities are evolving as faith communities stand up for the values of religious freedom and tolerance that are common to all. Human dignity and the right not to be discriminated against based on identity are core values that bind faith communities together to stand up for the rights of all marginalized communities.

An example is the "Shoulder-to-Shoulder" interfaith coalition in the United States that seeks to "combat the recent increase in anti-Muslim rhetoric, hate crimes, and Islamophobia." There are also numerous interfaith efforts aimed at improving the relationship between the Muslim and Jewish communities in the United States. Collaboration between mosques and synagogues has increased multifold, and interreligious efforts are on the rise. These interfaith coalitions are crucial for Muslim Americans as they fight radicalization within their communities while facing intolerance by some segments of society. Interfaith initiatives have provided an opportunity for all communities to learn from the works of other faiths in dealing with and overcoming issues such as anti-Semitism and in improving perceptions of Islam and Muslims. Best practices in interfaith cooperation that successfully work toward peace need to be encouraged and adopted for a better-shared future, leading to a peace agenda for every faith community.

The Constitution actually conceives 'minority' as an open category to protect the interests of various religious, linguistic and culturally distinctive groups. Hence, there is no possibility to think of Muslims as a permanent minority in the constitutional schema.

Muslims - a defined national minority

As the Mandir politics built the ground for a more significant movement that ultimately led to the demolition of Babri Masjid, the Congress government initiated a package to reach out to the 'minorities' in general and Muslims in particular. The National Commission for Minorities Act (1992) was perhaps the most important initiative. It recognised the need to evaluate the reasons behind the relative marginalisation of religious communities. This law led to the establishment of the National Commission for Minorities (NCM) in May 1993.

However, even the 1992 law does not define the term 'religious minority'. Instead, it is the central government that is empowered to notify a few communities as a "minority" of this Act. Following this mandate, the Congress government notified five religious communities: Muslims, Christians, Sikhs, Buddhists and Zoroastrians (Parsis) as national religious minorities in October 1993. This list was amended in 2014 when Jains also became a national minority.

This simple administrative move, however, posed a serious challenge to the constitutional principles, which intentionally do not identify any religious or cultural group as a 'national Representing the most widespread religious affiliation after Christianity, both geographically and demographically, Islam came to constitute a significant site for the thinking of an anti-nationalist political future at a global level. Taushif Kara's article in this special issue looks at one way in which a scattered population of Indian traders in East Africa sought to escape their new status as a minority by invoking an equally novel Islamic cosmopolitanism. However, such thinking did not reflect omlu\y in Muslims, and figures like Gandhi and Rabindranath Tagore in colonial India were also critics of nationalism. The former described himself as a philosophical anarchist in his desire for a society that managed itself without the state. Indeed, anti-nationalist thinking in the early years of the twentieth century reconceptualized anarchism in the colonial world to represent its only substantial inheritance in modern history.

Victory of communalism over anarchism

The emergence of the Soviet Union ensured the victory of communism over anarchism in Europe and America. But I would like to suggest that it went from strength to strength in the colonial world, where anti-imperialism was often linked with a distrust of the modern state and nationalism generally. In Asia and Africa, however, anarchism drew not only from its European canon or ideas about village republics and other pre-modern institutions but increasingly from religion, itself a category defined by colonialism and separated by it from the state. Deprived of their pre-colonial connection to kingship, both Hinduism and Islam could be understood in terms of decentralized self-governance by way of caste for the former and a sacred law legitimized by nonstate authorities for the latter.

The exclusion of colonized peoples from political institutions and power led, in many places, to the grounding of their anti-colonial movements in society rather than the state. Indeed, even when it came to occupying the state, a number of these movements did so with grave suspicion and reservations, as was the case even when an avowedly statist party like the Indian National Congress first assumed government in the provinces in 1937. And society has remained the most authentic side of politics in a number of post-colonial countries. While religion, then, was separated from political authority and thus secularized in order to represent society's self-governance, it did not cease being a site of power. It had, in fact, come to represent a potentially universal site of nonstate politics.

When the Indian poet and philosopher Mohammad Iqbal counterposed Islam to communism rather than imperialism in the first decades of the twentieth century, it was not because he approved of the latter but saw the former as the only competitor to Islam's global future as a form of decentralized self-governance. Islam, in other words, took the place of anarchism, a dead political form by then, in relation to communism. Similarly, his compatriot, the low-caste thinker and leader B.R. Ambedkar, counterposed Buddhism to communism in the 1950s once he had abandoned hope in the transformative power of the nation-state and turned to religion as the medium of social reform. In both cases, religion represented not communitarianism but the force of moral individualism set against the universalistic imperative of Marxism.

Iqbal and Ambedkar both spoke for groups of minorities in colonial India. At the same time, Gandhi and Tagore thought that moral and so political agents could only be or at least start as minorities of various kinds. Whether social and hereditary or political and temporary, the majority, in their view, could possess no agency of its own but was constituted by the abandonment of moral individualism to collective prejudice. While both sets of men began from different political premises, they agreed on the importance of individual agency and freedom and, therefore, the virtue of the minority as the path to making such an individual. Iqbal and Ambedkar thought their minority communities could best produce such individuals as moral and political agents. At the same time, Gandhi and Tagore sought to break down but also constitute new majorities by means of them.

Today, these men are anti-colonial thinkers and nationalists of various stripes. However, while each eventually compromised with the nation-state, they remained deeply suspicious of it. Amar Sohal's article on this issue analyses the creativity of such compromise in the figure of the Kashmiri leader Sheikh Abdullah. Iqbal and Ambedkar saw it as a useful stopgap in the establishment of a national state based on the tyrannical dominance of a social majority. Ambedkar even described the colonial dispensation as a dry dock permitting the building of new and anti-national political forms. But he soon recognized the empire's weakness and reconciled himself to working within the bounds set by its successor.

Early in his career, Gandhi had also imagined the empire as the carapace for a new moral and political order. Whatever the violence of its founding, of which he was acutely aware, the Mahatma imagined the British Empire could be redeemed if it freed its subject peoples into a vast democratic concourse where neither majorities nor minorities could exist. Curiously, then, he thought that the empire would make for a democratic order because its multifarious citizenry would perforce come together to constitute temporary or political rather than permanent or hereditary majorities and minorities. Unlike the nation-state with its ethnic or social majorities and minorities, in other words, a democratized empire was alone capable of freeing the individual as its valid moral and political subject.

Such ideas had a long history in Indian political thought. As late as 1945, Rajendra Prasad, a leader of the Indian National Congress who would go on to become his country's President, was willing to entertain the possibility of India as a non-national state composed of many nationalities in order to keep the Muslim League from demanding the country's partition. Vanya Bhargav tells this story through the early twentieth-century figure of the Indian nationalist, Lala Lajpat Rai, in her article for this issue. In this way, the politics of a minority was able to defer, if not transform, nationalist thinking in the majority. This tradition continues today in the Kurdish movement, whose leader and theorist Abdullah Ocalan explicitly rejects nationalism and even the modern state while mobilizing socially for military action as well as self-government.

Non-state and anti-national politics for which majorities and minorities are irrelevant can take different forms. I have so far described its anarchist and cosmopolitan possibilities, of which Pan-Islamism is routinely either the most interesting or the most threatening. As it turns out, Gandhi was favoured to head the most extensive of all Pan-Islamist movements at the end of the First World War, when Indian Muslims sought to work through the empire as British subjects, forcing it to represent them and protect the Arab territories of the defeated Ottomans. It was a perfect example of the way in which the social focus of what I am calling anarchist politics repurposed the colonial state rather than demanding either independence or calling for some Islamic internationalism.

However, the political form that came to dominate Islamic movements worldwide from the middle of the last century to its end was what we may call a libertarian or neoliberal one. It was no coincidence that Islamism, as one version of this neoliberal vision is known, emerged with the apparent victory of the nation-state in decolonization. Compelled to operate within this state, Islamism nevertheless sought to restrict its reach into Muslim society by placing the latter under the authority of the sacred law while reserving political sovereignty for God and so expelling it from human control. Instead of interpreting Islamism only in its terms as a peculiarly theological enterprise that is part of a self-contained history, I want to suggest that, however distinctive it is, it is a much more familiar phenomenon than we imagine.

The rules-based order theory

While the market had not yet come to define Muslim society, Islamism is putatively neoliberal because it explicitly sought to reduce politics to a set of administrative interventions in what we would today call a 'rules-based order'. Its eventual aim was to do away with states altogether and usher in a caliphate that, not by accident, resembled the deferred anarchist telos of Leninism. And this comprised, of course, the withering away of the state and the replacement of rule over people by what Lenin called the administration of objects. With the beginning of the new century, y various forms of globalized militancy have overtaken Islamism. They are even more resistant to the state and, like their predecessors, condemn nationalism as nothing more than the idolatry of the majority.

Muslim minorities have provided particularly fertile grounds for such rethinking, given their international and now global affiliations. But the figure of the minority has also been deployed in Muslim-majority contexts to launch equally fulsome criticisms of the nation-state. The anarchism that I have argued characterizes so many of these movements, whether on the left or right, is not, in other words, defined by the demographic and political situation of the minority but surpasses it ideologically.

These men might well have agreed that a self-professed majority can have no authority except that of force, which is what makes political and social majorities so dangerous. Only those defined as a minority, then, possess an authority that cannot be based on force because they must work by persuasion and claim the majority's consent in some way. Sometimes, this minority is cis conceived as an aristocracy or an oligarchy, if not as a conspiracy and cabal, all negative identities from a majority's point of view. But for Gandhi, as much as Iqbal, the minority was heroic and the actual agent of change since a majority was conservative by definition.

It was the heroic character of the minority, like Lenin's vanguard, that anarchist Islam sought to recover and translate into the moral individual. Instead of serving simply as the path to such individuality, minority politics got subsumed. From Iqbal's ego ideal to the nihilistic martyrs of al-Qaeda, whose ideas and actions he would, of course, have abhorred, it is the individual who has inherited the figure of the minority. Rather than constituting the unit of a democratic majority, as is the case in political theory, the individual in this interpretation represents the minority's democratization. There is no religious communitarianism here, only left or right versions of anarchism. Islam's moral and political agent has long been a minority of one.

The most essential feature of India today is its vast urbanization. Migration, integration, and adaptation each played an integral part in the development of Indian culture. As people are relocating to cities and towns, it is essential to build an understanding of how cities will grow inclusionary. Against this background, India's marginalized communities' exclusion from the country's increasing urban extension is on the basis of religion. Muslim marginalization peculiarly forms spatialized Muslim groups across ethnic locations concentrated in specific parts of the cities.

Backwardness and minority status

The NCM did not find any contradiction between the constitutional meaning of a minority and the 1993 notification of the government. In an official note to the Ministry of Home Affairs (dated 30 July 1997), it clarified: A national-level minority shall have the status of a minority in the entire country, irrespective of its local population. This will be so even in a state, region or district where such a minority is factually not a minority in numerical terms.

Booking the constitutional commitment to affirmative action, religious minorities – like religion-based Scheduled Castes – can be treated as specific identities entitled to special protection by the state.

Most of us will never have to face living in a nation where we are oppressed merely for following a religion, yet this should not diminish our empathy for such people. Often living in poverty and lacking the resources to flee, Muslims in India have to surrender to the rule of a leader who aims to systematically dehumanise them without even the hope of a fairer future.

As India continues to grow in global influence and the West views it as a democratic counterweight to China's influence in the region, we should not forget the tragic ethnic persecution taking place before our eyes amidst the headlines of economic development. The world, unfortunately, remains silent and largely ignorant of the oppression and suffering that Muslims are facing, with hope increasingly absent in the very nation that will soon hold more Muslims than any other.

14. NEW INNOVATIONS IN LEGAL PLURALISM

The New Legal Pluralism

We live in a world of multiple, overlapping normative communities. Some of those communities—such as federal, state, and municipal governments—are formal legal entities often wielding coercive force in the service of a bureaucratically administered set of legal norms. Others, however, are nonstate communities created through religious, tribal, ethnic, or other affiliations. Scholars studying interactions among these multiple communities have often used the term legal pluralism to describe the inevitable intermingling of these normative systems. The study of plural normative systems has arisen from a variety of different scholarly traditions. Perhaps the earliest analyses of the clashes between state and nonstate authority were those penned by lawyers, philosophers, and theologians interested in the respective realms of church and state authority. en-

Scholars studying interactions among multiple communities have often used the term legal pluralism to describe the inevitable intermingling of normative systems that result from these interactions. In recent years, a new application of pluralist insights has emerged in the international and transnational realms. This review aims to survey and help define this emerging field of global legal pluralism. I begin by briefly describing sites for pluralism research, both old and new.

The phenomenon of 'legal pluralism' in India is conditioned and facilitated by the democratic state's commitment to protect religious freedom and uphold sociocultural diversity. Community-based adjudicating institutions such as the Darul Qaza (also known as Shar'ah court) function within this constitutional framework, but every citizen also has the right to approach a state court as and when they deem necessary. So far, the discourse on Islam, personal law, and the secular state has revolved around parliamentary debates, judicial activism, and legislative changes, where the focus has been on the question of the Uniform Civil Code (UCC) and gender justice. The discussion on personal law has rarely paid serious academic attention to the complexities of kinship conflicts embedded in an economic and legal matrix or, more importantly, their resolution. Drawing on an ethnographic study of the jurisprudential practices of Shar'ah courts in Uttar Pradesh, India, the paper offers a lens to understand how conflict resolution in family matters takes place in a legal plural landscape ensconced between citizenship rights and community practices. We argue that understanding this process also offers essential insights into the shifting meaning of secularism[1,2] in contemporary India.

The phenomenon of 'legal pluralism' in India is conditioned and facilitated by the democratic state's commitment to protect religious freedom and uphold sociocultural diversity. Community-based adjudicating institutions such as the Darul Qaza (also known as Shar'ah court) function within this constitutional framework, but every citizen also has the right to approach a state court as and when they deem necessary. So far, the discourse on Islam, personal law, and the secular state has revolved around parliamentary debates, judicial activism, and legislative changes, where the focus has been on the question of the Uniform Civil Code (UCC) and gender justice. The discussion on personal law has rarely paid serious academic attention to the complexities of kinship conflicts embedded in affective as well as economic and legal. Drawing on an ethnographic study of the jurisprudential practices of Shar'ah courts in Uttar Pradesh, India, the paper offers a lens to understand how conflict resolution in family matters takes place in a legal plural landscape ensconced between citizenship rights and community practices. We argue that understanding this process also offers essential insights into the shifting meaning of secularism[1,2] in contemporary India.

The coming storm over a single common law in India

In 2014, the Supreme Court decided that, as Dar ul Qazas' decisions were not legally recognised, edicts would contradict the individual rights granted by the Constitution, and the laws of India should be ignored. The court thereby recognized state courts as leg. Ally is superior to religious institutions. Madan and the Supreme Court agreed that state courts and dar ul qazis constitute distinct legal spheres and that the distinction between these spheres maps onto secular and religious normative orders, respectively. Although *Madan* viewed this aspect of Indian legal pluralism as a threat to justice and the authority of the state, the Supreme Court saw it as a helpful alternative for members of the Muslim minority. At stake in this disagreement was the question of whether authority over marriage should rest solely with the secular state courts, as Madan argued, or whether it should reside in religious

forums. Islam has become a major, even obsessive, topic of public debate over the past two decades. From efforts by Islamist groups such as the Muslim Brotherhood to gain power through the ballot box to the violent radicalism of the Islamic State (or ISIS), the dominant image of Islam in world politics has been that of a religious ideology pushed by nonstate actors who wish to see a more "Islamic" form of politics. But what about the states themselves? Cities often wield more power than formal state law (presenta-tives of other countries". But since Independence, there's been talk of a Uniform Civil Code or UCC, a single personal law for all citizens irrespective of religion, sex, gender and sexual orientation. Even the Constitution says the state should "endeavour" to provide such a law to its citizens.

But a common law - resisted both by the country's Hindu majority and Muslims, the prominent minority - has remained, in the words of the Supreme Court, a "dead letter". PM Narendra Modi's ruling Bharatiya Janata Party (BJP) is now resurrecting the idea. BJP-ruled states such as Uttar Pradesh, Himachal Pradesh and Madhya Pradesh have been talking up the UCC.

To be sure, the UCC has been one of the original campaign promises of the BJP, along with the construction of the temple at a disputed site in Ayodhya and abolishing the special status of Kashmir. Now that the temple is the challenge of secularism in the Indian subcontinent and Kashmir has lost its autonomy, the spotlight has moved to the UCC.

The Hindu right-wing rhetoric has pushed a common personal law as a counter to what they say are "regressive" personal laws of Muslims - they cite the example of triple talaq - the Muslim practice of "instant divorce" - which Mr Modi's government criminalized in 2019. The BJP's manifesto says there "cannot be gender equality till such time India adopts a Uniform Civil Code".

In other words, framing a UCC will open up a Pandora's Box with unintended consequences even for the country's Hindu majority, which the BJP professes to represent. "The UCC would disrupt the social life of Hindus as well as Muslims," he says.

Personal laws are fiendishly tricky to unify in a staggeringly diverse and vast country like India. For one, even though Hindus follow a clutch of individual laws, they also recognize the customs and practices of different communities in different states. The Muslim personal law is also not entirely uniform - some Sunni Bohra Muslims, for example, are guided by the principles of the Hindu law in matters of inheritance and succession.

There are different laws for different states when it comes to property and inheritance rights. North-eastern Christian-majority states like Nagaland and Mizoram make their laws that follow their customs and not religion. Goa has an 1867 common civil law that is applicable to all its communities but also has different rules for Catholics and other communities, including one which protects bigamy for Hindus.

Personal laws in India are a subject of common interest to both the federal government and the states. So, states have been making their laws since the 1970s. Years before a landmark 2005 amendment to an existing federal Hindu personal law allowing daughters to have an equal share of ancestral property as sons, at least five states had already tweaked their laws to enable this.

Take adoption. In Hindu tradition, adoption was undertaken for both secular and religious purposes - to have a male heir to inherit property and for a male descendant to be able to perform the funeral rituals of his parents. Also, experts wonder what the neutral principles are to adopt when putting together a common law. The UCC would have to answer some fundamental questions: What are the criteria for marriage and divorce? What are the processes and consequences of adoption? What are the rights to maintenance or just division of wealth in the event of a divorce? Lastly, what are the rules for the inheritance of property? Then there's the politics of it, which can easily lead to a blowback, says Mr Ali. How would a BJP government reconcile a uniform law that freely allows marriages between religions and communities with anti-conversion laws that it has enthusiastically supported to curb interfaith marriages? Or is the party planning to bring in laws in small states without "significantly disturbing the customary practices" of its people?

Not surprisingly, even the Supreme Court has sounded confused about the UCC. In different judgements over the last four decades, it has nudged the government to enact a standard civil code for the "integrity of the nation". In 2018, the Law Commission, a body to advise the government on legal reform, said the code was neither "necessary nor desirable".

Clearly, the UCC is not a magic bullet. Uniformity doesn't even bring any value to a law, let alone a significant value. What makes a good law is that it is just, transparent, and constitutional to address gender inequities in personal laws. Nothing comes in the way of trying to amend those rather than demanding adherence to common law, experts say. That would essentially mean adopting best practices from all personal laws.

Many BJP-ruled states may be pursuing the UCC not because it's trendy there or because it fetches more votes. "It is more to build their political capital and ensure their survivability within the new BJP structure where they have to burnish their Hindu credentials constantly.

Others wonder why the BJP has not been able to come up with the code even in states despite being in power for a long time. With general elections two years away, does the party believe that the time has come? "The UCC is a lot of noise at the moment, and the debate is not even political yet. Show us a draft of the proposed law first.

Muslims need 'relocation', not reform

We cannot judge the era of the founding of Islam by the values of our own time. Indeed, what we understand as the emancipation of women was never really considered essential by any of the great monotheistic religions. Islam highlighted and showed the world the remarkable potential of women and the rights they deserve as equal partners to men.

This optimism tends to forget that religions don't change much and that the words of scriptures can't be erased and overwritten. The verses cannot be altered, nor can their conventional understanding be changed. In any case, believers don't have any problem with either the text or its age-old meaning. They try to mould their world in accordance with the precepts of the religion. To them, stretching the definition to measure up to the present world may amount to a provocative reversal of order.

The reform, if any, has to be in one's attitude towards the religion and not in how Islam is understood and practised. The shift in focus from the transcendent to mundane, divine to human, and religious to secular has to be the basis of reform. Suppose people continue to depend on religion for inspiration and justification for their actions, and they don't graduate to the higher morality of secularism and modernity. In that case, no matter how they reinterpret their religion, they will continue to regress. In any case, when it comes to religion, the orthodox position, being of classical vintage, commands better legitimacy.

Therefore, rather than reforming Islam, its relocation and reformulation may be a better idea. Like other religions in the modern age, Islam, too, should be relocated to where religions belong — the private sphere. The longer any religion remains part of the public sphere, the higher the chances of its politicisation and radicalisation.

Religion, after all, is a way of worship. To say that one's religion is a way of life is a statement with little meaning. A way of life is the culture, of which religion is a constituent. However, little would change if the selfish motive of personal salvation continued to disregard the public welfare. Therefore, Islam needs to become a people-friendly and welfare-oriented religion that inspires its followers to do good to people here and now rather than securing paradise for them after death. Such a secularisation would make people humane rather than dogmatic and compassionate rather than fanatic.

It's alright to say that the trajectory of European history can't be the universal template for other societies, but if we were to learn from it, successive stages from the Renaissance's humanism to religious reformation to enlightenment to the rise of the liberal, secular and democratic world, would have many lessons for us. One of these could be that even the reformed religion was not good enough for the imperatives of the modern world, and it had to be sequestered to a private space in order to let reason have an unfettered movement, which, in turn, would enable the rise of higher secular morality.

The Muslims were impelled into both reform and revival by the same impetus — the shock caused by the loss of political ascendancy. Both trends had the same purpose — the restoration of the lost glory.

This could be one reason why reform gave way to revivalism so quickly, and almost all the late 19th-century reform movements, from Sir Syed Ahmad Khan's in India to Muhammad Abduh's and Rashid Rida's in Egypt, petered out, making way for the militant Islamism.

Reform is an unruly horse that can go berserk unless it is adequately saddled. The modern trend is for the acceptance of diversity. It is equally essential for the Muslim theocracy to understand its proper role, call it religious policing, cultural policing, guardian policing, family policing, and community policing.

The many names share one vision: a humane, compassionate, culturally refined system with a mindset of respect and demonstrable concern for improving the well-being of women, primarily when women have been assigned a very exalted position by both the Qur'an and its Messenger.

The unquestioned equation of religion with law, its origins

Unlike Christianity, Islam didn't have to suffer prolonged persecution. It progressed from acquiring a chieftainship to a State to an empire with lightning rapidity, which turned it into a statist ideology. This led to the unquestioned equation of religion with Shari'aht and of Shari'aht with law. Therefore, any reform in Islam had to come through the legal route. Accordingly, the revolutionary tool of reinterpretation, l called Ijtihad, was revived according to changing contexts. This terminology (coming from the same route as jihad) connotes intellectual exertion for deriving a religious ruling in such cases as the Qur'an and the *Hadith* are silent about. In contemporary Islamic discourses, Ijtihad is a noble ideal, but, for obvious reasons, there has been no substantial effort towards its realisation. Most of the Muslim States — from Indonesia, Malaysia, Bangladesh, Pakistan and Turkey in Asia to Egypt, Morocco and Tunisia in Africa — having adopted the modern legal system, pious platitudes notwithstanding, are not going back to the archaic Shari'ah laws. And those who do — the likes of ISIS or Taliban — have no use for Ijtihad.

No wonder that the modern and scientific reinterpretation of Islam has not moved an inch beyond where Sir Syed Ahmad Khan (1817-98) left it. Even though it may be possible, it's going to be a fruitless exercise and, therefore, undesirable for both the modern and the orthodox Muslims.

The poet Iqbal's most significant contribution could be the prominence he gave to the word 'Reconstruction' in the title of his collection of essays published in 1930, *The Reconstruction of Religious Thought in Islam*. This word underscored the dilapidation of religious thought in Islam. A lesser man couldn't get away with such honesty. But the orthodoxy was so mesmerised by Iqbal's stature and erudition that the import of this proposition got lost. Be that as it may, nearly a century later, despite his iconic status, his proposed 'reconstruction' remains a pipe dream. The reason is the same as in the case of Sir Syed. It will be a pointless exercise. The zeitgeist demands not the reformation but the relocation and reformulation; in fact, a veritable transcendence of religion.

The role of shari'ah courts

The religious legal institutions that play a role in practices of Indian secularism are partly a consequence of the deep plurality of the Indian legal system, which comprises numerous nonstate forums exhibiting a variety of legal bases and formal relationships to the state. For example, there is a sector of quasi- and extra-legal dispute adjudication institutions available to settle disagreements and infractions ranging from traffic violations to marital disputes. Many of these institutions originated in the colonial or precolonial era and are now present in new forms in the postcolonial state. In recent years, the Indian government has set up secular alternative dispute resolution forums such as *Lok Adalats* (people's courts), in which judges hand down binding agreements following a process of mediation. An array of religious and community organizations, some new and some with long histories in India, also intervene in marital and family disputes without any state oversight and issue judgments that the state does not have to consider binding. Among these are *panchayats* (local councils), *mohalla* (residential) committees

Religious personal law in contemporary India is most directly indebted to its colonial predecessor. It evolved as part of an effort—riven with well-documented ironies—to govern Indians according to indigenous norms. Footnote: The legal framework that would become Personal Law in independent India was first formulated in 1772 by Warren Hastings. Governor-general of Bengal, who declared that, with regard to "inheritance, marriage, cast [*sic*] and other religious usages, or institutions, the laws of the Qur'an with respect to the Mussalmans, and those of the Shasters with respect to the Hindoos, shall be invariably adhered t) as fundamentally religious institutions and names the texts relevant to addressing and regulating religious matters for Hindus and Muslims. Reference Sharaf iHistorian Mitra Sharafi (2014) posits that two distinct but simultaneous conversations between British administrators and Hindu and Muslim leaders led Hastings to include Hindu and Muslim personal laws.

Rights of Muslim women

Today, the issue of women's rights in Muslim Personal Law is highly controversial. In particular, Muslim women's rights relating to triple talaq divorce, inheritance, and maintenance have got much attention nowadays. However, the Indian Constitution has guaranteed equality and freedom from discrimination based on gender or religion, but still, there are various practices which rest on heartless conservative culture. As we know, a large part of Muslim Personal Law is still uncodified, and most of the legal decisions pronounced by the courts rest on the norms mentioned in the Qur'an and *hadith*. The central debate on the interpretation of Muslim personal laws has both positive and negative aspects. Some authors have supported that Muslim personal laws have given various rights to Muslim women, such as choice in marriage, inheritance, etc. Some are of the opinion that multiple practices are against the spirit of the Indian Constitution. In this line, this research paper attempts to analyze the ongoing debate on the implications of Muslim Personal Law in India and suggests various solutions to empower Muslim women.

Debating Muslim women's rights and the codification of personal laws in India

Muslim personal laws in India have never been systematically codified, in marked contrast both to Hindu family laws in India and to Islamic family laws in much of the Muslim-majority world, both of which have been subject to a far greater degree of codification. We examine the call by one prominent contemporary Muslim women's organization, the Bharatiya Muslim Mahila Andolan (BMMA), for the wholesale codification of Muslim family laws in India as a pathway to protecting women's rights. Following a discussion of the broader context of India's uncodified Muslim personal law system, this paper offers a commentary on the BMMA's draft Family Law Act, first released in 2014. It demonstrates how this document synthesizes discourses of women's rights drawn from a series of Qur'anic, constitutional and transnational reference points. By drawing from such diverse sources, and while legal codification in much of the Islamic world has instituted fundamentally patriarchal legal norms, the BMMA's proposed code articulates a distinctive, more gender-equal reading of Islamic family law.

Legal pluralism in India

India has an official faith-based pluralist system that is a product of an attempt to codify existing religious, customary practices that have existed for centuries. This pluralist system comprises 'Mohammedan' or Shari'a law, the official legal origin of which can be traced back to the Shar'aht Act of 1937, which codified a proportion of the *fiqh* (law that is rooted in Islamic culture). Hindu law also forms part of the broader

Indian legal system and is, in particular, applied to family disputes. However, it is arguably more inclusive than Mohammedan law since it includes Sikhs and Buddhists. Since the 2000s, Christian Law has also become recognised as a plural jurisdiction, transforming provisions for Christians on divorce, separation, maintenance, and adoption in the Indian Divorce (Amendment) Act 2001 to become more like those seen in Britain, creating an intensely interwoven system of laws.

The complexity of this law made certain regions subscribe to different interpretations of religious law and integrate it into a colonial-era framework, such as that seen in Goa. Therefore, the legal remedies available to an individual can vary depending on where they live, their religion and the predominant religion of their local area. Viewing this set-up from an English legal perspective, this undoubtedly poses rule of law issues, specifically relating to legal certainty and fair warning – people cannot plan their lives accordingly if they are not confident as to which laws to follow.

Impact on women

Although the Indian constitution guarantees gender equality and freedom from gender and religious-based discrimination, the pluralist nature of the Indian legal system remains unrealized. Muslim women, in particular, have been subject to poor treatment under religious laws. This was borne in the Shah BanoBegum case, where a Muslim woman was denied alimony from her husband under Shari'a law even though had she been a Hindu or Christian and treated under different religious laws, she would have received redress. Although the Indian Supreme Court overturned the religious court's decision and the Muslim Women (Protection of Rights on Divorce) Act 1986 to protect Muslim women following the collapse of their marriage, their rights under Shari'a law are still minimal.

Indeed, there have been a number of cases where polygamous marriages dominate in Shari'a courts, in which men have often denied money to care for children to their first wife on account that they favour their second spouse, something which is not prevalent in Christian or Hindu cases. Women must undergo months of lengthy arbitration to achieve the same result, placing them at an inherent disadvantage, mainly if she is in an abusive relationship. Lastly, Shari'a courts have also offered unfavourable property rights to Muslim women, aside from recognising the traditional *Mahr* –a gift a husband gives to his wife during their marriage. Therefore, the impact of legal pluralism on women is that they afforded fewer rights to other Indian women, creating a 'stratified citizenry'4where social cohesion is wanting.

Impact on religious tensions

Legal pluralism has had two key impacts on religious tensions. The aim of legal pluralism in a faith-based context is to empower religious groups and encourage cooperation between them. However, pluralism has caused the '*political divide between Hindus and Muslims [to] worsen*' by placing them into faith-based legal enclaves. Recent surveys have reflected an increase in tensions; legal pluralism has been a central point in cementing the differences between Hindus and Muslims. Pluralism, by its nature, leverages one group above another and never serves to develop social cohesion but instead creates harsh swathes within communities6.

Secondly, it has altered many citizens' perceptions of religion. Indeed, despite the fact that the religious groups in India are richly diverse, pluralism's insensitive categorisation of faith groups has turned them into cultural monoliths. This not only illustrates the religious divisions that have emerged through pluralism but also that the religious groups now view each other as binary opposites – they are intolerable to one another.

Recommendations

Religious freedom is a highly controversial issue in India, with a recent survey noting that it is one of the most essential values for Indians 8.

The courts and politicians have recognised this, and the Indian Attorney General himself has asserted that the issue is far too political for the courts to decide and should lie with Parliament. Thus, arguably, reform could be achieved by the Indian Parliament abolishing the current legal system and creating a single body of law to be followed – a valid 'one law for all' approach.

However, many politicians would likely be reluctant to overhaul a legal system which is otherwise workable drastically. Moreover, facing the issue head-on may only exacerbate tensions and completely undermine its purpose. The well-known jurist John Duncan Martin Derrett observed that the best way to reform the Indian pluralist system is to let it '*wither away* and gradually replace it with a uniform law, thus avoiding confrontation between religious groups. Although this is a drawn-out process, it would nevertheless achieve the aim of protecting women and reducing religious tension.

15. THE TINDERBOX OF UNIFORM CIVIL CODE

Fourteen per cent of India's one billion people are Muslim. Characterized by economic and political diversity, there is further division regionally and linguistically: Bengali, Deccani, Gujarati, Hindustani, Mappila, Oriyya, and Punjabi. Most are Sunni Muslims following the Hanafi legal tradition; about 10 per cent are Twelver Shiis, and a smaller percentage are Ismaili Shiis. Most Indian Muslims supported the partition of British India at independence, but a substantial minority supported the Indian National Congress. In independent India, Muslims have been politically active as one of the largest Muslim national communities in the world.

There are various aspects of the Uniform Civil Code. It mainly aims to replace Personal Laws based on the scriptures and customs of each major religion in India with a standard set of rules governing every citizen. A UCC would replace the various laws that currently apply to different communities, which are often inconsistent. These laws include the Hindu Marriage Act, the Hindu Succession Act, and the Indian Divorce Act. A UCC would apply to all citizens equally, regardless of their religion. It would cover areas like marriage, divorce, maintenance, inheritance, adoption, and succession of property.

The origin of the UCC dates back to colonial India when the British government submitted a report in 1835. The report stressed the need for uniformity in the codification of Indian law

Personal laws cover marriage, divorce, inheritance, adoption, succession, and maintenance—the challenges of implementing the Uniform Civil Code and the pros and cons of the Uniform Civil Code.

The paper discusses judicial activism involved in personal laws and judgments of the Supreme Court, where the court has emphasised the need for the implementation of the Uniform Civil Code. The paramount objective of this paper is to understand the concept of the Uniform Civil Code in detail, i.e., its beginning, contemporary developments, advantages, disadvantages, and role of the judiciary.

The Uniform Civil Code (UCC) is a proposed legal framework in India that would establish a national civil code that applies equally to all citizens, regardless of their religion, community, race, sex, or caste. The UCC would promote uniform laws governing various aspects of personal life. However, the Indian Constitution's articles 25-28 guarantee religious freedom to Indian citizens and allow religious groups to maintain their affairs. Some say that the quest for a UCC is a test of the true nature of democracy. Others say that a personal law system based on religious principles is unable to function under a secular democracy.

Although criminal laws in India are the same for all, different communities – the majority Hindus (966 million), the country's Muslim (213 million) and Christian (26 million) minorities, and tribal communities (104 million) – follow their civil laws, influenced by religious texts and cultural mores.

We must all understand that Islamic laws are far from being rigid injunctions or rules set in stone. Islamic law or Shari'ah (meaning "way" or "path") is an immense amalgam of texts and interpretations that have evolved along parallel paths within five primary and numerous minor schools of law.

Shari'ah is a religious code for Muslims that covers all aspects of their life, including daily routines, spiritual and familial obligations, marital affairs such as marriage and divorce, and financial dealings.

Gender-just reforms are needed to help correct gender biases, but they should be well-intentioned. The reform backers believe that the state should undertake them, to use the words of the great parliamentarian

Edmund Burke, with "the cold neutrality of an impartial judge." In Burke's own words, "No man can mortgage his injustice as a pawn for his fidelity." The state cannot expect Muslims to jettison the core tenets of their faith.

For Muslims, changes to Islamic law have to be made within the boundaries of the Qur'an's teachings if they are to be legitimate. Without the cooperation of the religious scholars, who bestow this legitimacy, the masses will not embrace change. The clerics are critical in the whole equation. The predominant hardliners among their ranks are locked in a virtual and civil war with reformers.

Islam may not always be the sole factor in the repression of women. Local, social, political, economic, and educational forces, as well as the prevalence of pre-Islamic customs, must also be taken into consideration.

In some societies, they are a pervasive influence. But, in many cases, the proper application of Islamic law remains a significant obstacle to the evolution of the position of women. Muslims are apprehensive of the state's obsession with trying to "create" a specific type of Islam rather than allowing them space to live Islam – with all its beliefs, traditions, cultures, references, and various practices.

Article 44 of the Constitution of India provides that 'The State shall endeavour to secure a Uniform Civil Code for the citizens throughout the territory of India'. After over six decades, this anticipated code has not been developed or implemented. This book provides a blueprint for alternative frameworks and courses of action, drawing on lessons from comparative context to *create* a Uniform Civil Code for India. It explores the interplay between issues of law, culture, and religion in light of various intra-community and inter-community disputes. The book proposes a series of guidelines and considerations to inform this process. The proposed blueprint derives guidance from the experience of other nations and the many ways in which they have faced the challenge of introducing a civil code and maintaining respect for local community laws and social customs. The blueprint also focuses on the relationships between religion and the state. This set of proposals should alleviate the suspicion of the Muslim community or the Hindu majority community. A Uniform Civil Code could achieve two simultaneous objectives: to maximize the sustainability of traditions and community values while also reinforcing constitutional values that prevent discrimination and, in particular, unfair practices *against* girls and women in a democratic country.UCC can't Guarantee the Empowerment of Women

Civil Code

They see the civil code as a seductively wrapped gender welfare intervention that can be a powerful salient, paving the way for further intrusion into their religious and cultural values. The depressing social conditions of Muslim women are a phenomenon prevalent mainly among the underprivileged.

In the economically improved strata of Muslims, the sort of oppressive practices talked about are a rarity. Poverty is the root cause of obscurantism in Muslim families. Economic empowerment is one tide that can lift all the boats. It enables you to provide better education, better housing, and better healthcare.

It is a virtual cycle that transforms your worldview. The biggest problems facing Muslim women today are economic. They are not likely to be solved with civil rights remedies, but they could be relieved with public and private action to encourage economic redevelopment. More than religious redemption, women need economic redemption. A standard civil code is believed a silver bullet for gender justice, which it is not. What is required urgently is draining the swamps of Muslim poverty that are breeding unrest and frustration, leading to both physical and mental violence.

Muslim gender

Human rights calamity is unfolding in Afghanistan. Since retaking power in mid-2021, the Taliban have implemented more extreme policies against women than any other regime in the world. Taliban leaders have issued over 90 edicts limiting women's rights: they have banned women and girls from attending university or school beyond the sixth grade, restricted their access to health care, prohibited them from leaving home without a male guardian, and revoked many of their social and legal protections. Every new restriction on Afghan women strengthens the Taliban's dictatorial grip on the entire Afghan population and feeds Mapping a discussion on gender and sexualities in Islam needs to move beyond an understanding of Islamic law (*shari'ah*) and its interpretations that have traditionally been made by male religious scholars (*ulamā*). It is essential to also pay attention to the lived experiences of people on the ground and move away from a homogeneous universal construct of what gender is and what sexualities are. It should include an examination of various power structures that highlight the experiences and voices of not only women but also other subjected and subaltern groups. What are the intersections and overlapping viewpoints and arguments on gender and sexuality in Islam? Who is talking on behalf of which group?

The examination of gender and sexualities within Islam is a complex topic that needs consideration of socioeconomic and political shifts as well as ongoing processes of modernization and globalization. This includes the formation of nation-states, the codification of Islamic law, the change in family relations and mobility, the increase in the level of education and wage labour, and transnational migration. Muslim women leaders believe Islam, at its core, is progressive for women and supports equal opportunities for men and women alike. They would not like to wager for a law that makes them jettison their Islamic beliefs.

Muslim women leaders are seeking accommodation between a modern role for women and the Islamic values that more than a billion people in the world follow. Some of the leading proponents are distinguished male scholars who contend that Islam was radically egalitarian for its time and remains so in many of its texts. Muslims are well integrated in Sri Lanka, where they have their law, which jurists have lauded. Singapore and Israel accept Muslim personal law.

Israel's Shari'ah court system is more efficient than the civil law alternative. At the same time, it is also evolving in conjunction with the demands of an 'open, modern, and developed' society. Israel's religious courts are part of the judicial system, with applicants having the option of choosing whether to lodge cases in the spiritual or civil courts. Shari'ah courts in Israel follow the Hanafi legal school of Sunni jurisprudence, while laws in place since the days of the Ottoman Empire also remained in force.

The many names share one vision: a humane, compassionate, culturally refined system with a mindset of respect and demonstrable concern for improving the well-being of women, primarily when women have been assigned a very exalted position by both the Qur'an and its Messenger. Muslims of today are now a progressive generation. They've very whole-heartedly embraced efforts to do away with many of their obscurantist customs and traditions that Qurán does not support.

Deeply religious, profoundly determined, and modern in every way, they are challenging not only the unjust restrictions placed on them by their societies. However, they also oppose the tired stereotypes and empty generalisations placed on them by the West. They are arguing for women's rights within an Islamic discourse. These women are combing through centuries of Islamic jurisprudence to cull out and highlight the more progressive aspects of their religion.

Despite a prominent clergy being in favour of the retention of the triple talaq, mainstream Muslims were never supportive of this obnoxious practice. Their main opposition to triple talaq was to the government's legislative intent in trying to criminalise it and instil overtly reformist legislation with a malicious agenda.

Deliberations of UCC

Kazi, the critical persona in the deliberations on the Uniform Civil Code in the Constituent Assembly, was a staunch opponent of the code. He was a very progressive and forward-looking Muslim who saw to it that his children studied in the country's premier institutions.

There is a connection between religious diversity, freedom, and growth. If there was no way to live together, religious communities could have never created a society that would function as one. Contrary to the fears of many, religious freedom has been important as a cultural and moral force. We must understand that all divine texts share common themes to preserve human spirituality.

No concept of prosperity, social advancement, or human rights will weaken the eternal influence of divine texts. Normative deviations from divine texts are transient. But the spiritual needs that divine texts fulfil are permanent. So is the Qur'an, which exerts an extraordinary moral influence in the life of an ordinary Muslim.

Proponents of a UCC argue that a modern nation does not need "dual laws" and that a standard civil code would be a step towards eliminating gender discrimination in personal laws. The BJP has, in particular, described Muslim personal laws in India as biased against women, though activists insist gender prejudice exists across civil rules followed by most communities. A UCC, its supporters insist, would also help in national integration.

Religious minorities and tribal communities fear that a uniform code would rob them of their constitutional rights to freedom of religion and culture by imposing a state-determined set of dos and don'ts. These concerns are grounded in the religious and ethnic divisions that have torn India since Modi came to power in 2014, with the mainstreaming of Hindu majoritarianism leading to increased attacks on minorities – especially Muslims.

Does India need a UCC? What could change under a standard code? Could there be any benefits? And what are the risks that shadow the proposal?

The short answer

Irrespective of the fine print of a UCC, a uniform code would fundamentally break with India's approach to secularism, which, unlike the West, has primarily allowed different communities to follow their religious practices on matters such as marriage, divorce, inheritance and property rights. Political scientists argue that while personal laws do need an upgrade, the path towards any UCC must run through consensus. Without that, they say the proposal is little more than a political move geared towards the election – with potentially dangerous consequences for the world's largest democracy.

Jawaharlal Nehru, head of India's Interim Government, Louis Mountbatten, Viceroy of India and Muhammad Ali Jinnah, President of the Muslim League, discuss Britain's plan for India at the historic India Conference in New Delhi, June 2, 1947. Nehru's approach to secularism was grounded in the wounds of partition and his belief that minority insecurities need deep examination and appropriate response.

Indian secularism and a flip-flop

The concept of a uniform civil code isn't new, and a single law governing personal relationships is present in many multicultural nations. France was a torchbearer when, in 1804, it replaced hundreds of local regulations to institute a single set of civil rules for its citizens. Italy, Spain, Germany, Portugal and Ireland in Europe, and Egypt and Turkey in the Middle East are among other countries that have established common personal laws.

Hindu nationalists led by the BJP's ideological parent, the Rashtriya Swayamsevak Sangh – which now positions itself as a champion of gender equality in its push for a UCC – at the time opposed the Hindu Code Bill, describing it as an "atom bomb" on Hindu society.

When, in 1948, the drafting committee for independent India's new constitution discussed the idea of a UCC, one member argued that it would uphold the unity of the country and the proposed constitution's secular credentials. Muslim members countered, stating that it would interfere with their freedom of religion, but faced pushback on the grounds that women's rights "could never be secured" without a uniform civil code.

Finally, the UCC was incorporated into the directive principles of the Constitution, which means that the state was not obliged to bring the provision into effect immediately and that it should only do so with the consent of all communities.

Meanwhile, after exhaustive discussions within and outside parliament, Hindu Code Bills were passed in parliament in the form of the Hindu Marriage Act in 1955, the Hindu Succession Act, and the Hindu Minority and Hindu Adoptions and Maintenance Act in 1956. These strengthened the rights of Hindu women within marriages on questions of separation, divorce, and inheritance. Hindu nationalists have long argued that exemptions to religious minorities from these norms reveal a bias against the country's majority community.

That criticism fails to acknowledge the problematic reality that newly independent India faced under its first prime minister, Jawaharlal Nehru, in the years after the bloody cleavage of partition along religious lines, said veteran historian Mridula Mukherjee, a former professor at New Delhi's Jawaharlal Nehru University.

Nehru recognised that "minorities were feeling insecure immediately after Independence", and it was "not desirable to impose anything" on them, which would add to that sense of insecurity. The Hindu Code Bills, too, were passed only after a decade of building broad consensus within and outside parliament, she said.

But the debate would resurface in 1985 with what is known as the Shah Bano case, in which the Supreme Court upheld a Muslim woman's right to seek maintenance from her husband after their divorce. Under pressure from conservative groups, the then Congress party government of Rajiv Gandhi passed a law in parliament that overruled the Supreme Court order, reviving allegations from the Hindu right that the Indian state only cared about women's rights when it involved tweaking Hindu practices. Ahead of the national elections in 2014, the BJP promised a UCC if it came to power. The Law Commission, however, stated in 2018 that a uniform code is "neither necessary nor desirable" and "secularism" cannot contradict the plurality prevalent in the country.

'Need for caution'

There is a legitimate case for the state to seek to change personal laws with the aim of fostering equality, fairness and freedom for all. But for the most part, such reforms are only justifiable on the grounds that the "principle of gender justice was necessary to walk a fine line between needed changes and the encroachment into what communities consider practices central to their cultural identity.

But the question is, does this straight away lead to a uniform civil code? There is a need for caution. There is no reason to believe that our local customs regarding marriage, inheritance, and adoption will be similar. They will be very different, and it will be challenging to erase those differences.

The BJP has tried to project itself as a saviour of Muslim women through practices like 'triple talaq', which allowed a Muslim man to divorce his wife in minutes by saying "talaq" three times. The practice was banned by law in 2019, two years after India's Supreme Court had described triple talaq as unconstitutional.

Under Muslim personal laws followed in India, women can seek divorce from their husbands in multiple ways. They have inheritance rights, are entitled to half the share of male heirs of their inherited property, and can receive half of the whole inheritance if there is no male heir to the father's property. Muslim personal laws also require the husband to pay his wife a contractual dowry – known as 'mehr' – at the time of marriage and to pay for her maintenance. This contrasts with Hindu marriages, for instance, in which the wife's family often ends up paying large sums as dowry to the husband, even though the practice is barred by law. Indian Muslim and Christian women – not political parties –have been at the forefront of the fight for reforms against patriarchy in their communities.

Yet, all sides appear to agree that, at its heart, the tension that marks the conversation over a UCC isn't about specific practices: It is about deep-rooted fears that a uniform code is a vehicle for the Modi government to try to target minority communities and weaken their identities.

Against that backdrop, the move to scrap religion-based personal laws is a political weapon the BJP wants to use against Muslims. The Hindu right has long peddled a conspiratorial narrative accusing Muslims of using polygamy to expand the community's population with the aim of overtaking the Hindu population.

Many among India's Christians – who too have been attacked over accusations of carrying out religious conversions – are also apprehensive about the code. If a UCC mirrors the anti-conversion laws introduced by many states, the "freedom" of Christians to marry anyone may "go away", said Michael Williams, founder-president of the United Christian Forum, a conglomeration of church groups that monitors hate crimes against Christians.

There are other worries, too.

For Christians, the wedding ceremony in the church is an act of faith committed in the sight of God, which is more important than a civil act committed in front of the court. A UCC might render a church wedding ceremony and disempower the clergy and the say of the church in the civil life of the community members.

A UCC that makes it harder to practice religious customs will be unacceptable. Though Sikhs (28 million) follow Hindu personal laws for the most part, several states allow them to marry under a separate, community-specific law. Members of the community, too, have been targeted by allies of Modi's party as "antinational" in their opposition to farm laws that the BJP government tried to bring. tribal communities feared that a uniform civil code would wipe away the distinct identity that their courts protected.

Political slugfest lies ahead

For the moment, the UCC has unanswered questions. Will Hindu family laws also be replaced by the uniform code? Will there be several bills or one law? Will it primarily target Muslim personal law? Will a standard code for marriages lead to the abolition of the Special Marriage Act that allows inter-religious marriages?

Yet, filling that vacuum of detail is a cauldron of politics that has erupted in recent weeks.

Multiple BJP-ruled states, including Gujarat, Uttarakhand and Assam, have said they are considering adopting a UCC in their jurisdictions. Meanwhile, opposition-ruled states like Kerala have passed resolutions against the UCC in their legislatures. And in tribal-dominated northeastern states, even BJP allies have opposed a standard code.

Why Kazi K n endorses personal law for minorities

Kazi moved an amendment with the aim of protecting Indians from unreasonable searches and seizures. He criticized the absence of the 'due process' clause in the fundamental rights, which he feared could lead to misuse of state power and infringe on the citizen's right to life and liberty.

The discourse over the implementation of the Uniform Civil Code has often stirred up a whirlwind of uproar by political advocates and religious objectors. India follows a system of legal pluralism that allows different religious communities to be governed by their codes of personal law. This is a way of protecting distinct communal identities and safeguarding the right of citizens to practice their faith, as enshrined in the Constitution.

The Constitution grants equal protection under the law to all citizens. That said, Muslims are governed by a personal law, which came into force in 1937. However, the authors of the Constitution wanted a standard set of family laws. Article 44 of the Directive Principles of State Policy in the Indian Constitution mandates that "the state shall endeavour to secure for all citizens a Uniform Civil Code throughout the territory of India."

In his stellar speech, Kazi argued that in Article 31, the country's economic pattern was a result of vague generalizations. The word 'Directive' must be deleted. He endorsed the suggestion that they should become Fundamental Principles of State Policy. His submission was that the word 'Directive' is unnecessary and meaningless. Ambedkar believed the State has no duty to interfere with religious laws, and there is no need to be aggressive about it.

Kazi K believed that the Directive Principles provisions embodied in Part IV are significant as they relate to uniform civil code, economic patterns, and many fundamental matters. Directive Principles mean that they will not be binding on the State; in any case, they would not be enforceable in a court of law. His submission was that if this Constitution does not lay down these principles for enforcement in a court of law, or if they are not binding on the State, they are meaningless. He drew the members' attention to what Dr Ambedkar had said in his book.

Dr Ambedkar said that we do not want to lay down certain principles because it would open the coming generations to have their pattern. It is only stated in Article 31 that there will be an improvement in economic, social and other things. What is the use of generalizations, as expressed in Article 31? Therefore, it is no use treating these principles as Directive; such a course will not prove to be for the good of the people and the State

The Supreme Court struck a note of caution in the Sarla Mudgal judgment. The court stated, "The desirability of uniform civil code can be hardly doubted, but it can concretize only when the social climate is properly built by the elite of the society and the statesmen, instead of gaining personal mileage, rise above and awaken the masses to accept the change."

The Commission stated in the consultation paper: "While the diversity of Indian culture can and should be celebrated, specific groups or weaker sections of society must not be dis-privileged in the process. The resolution of this conflict does not mean the abolition of difference. Commission has therefore dealt with laws that are discriminatory rather than providing a UCC."

Kazi's perspective on the Civil Code

The discourse over the implementation of the Uniform Civil Code has often stirred up a whirlwind of uproar by political advocates and religious objectors. India follows a system of legal pluralism that allows different religious communities to be governed by their codes of personal law. This is a way of protecting distinct communal identities and safeguarding the right of citizens to practice their faith, as enshrined in the Constitution.

The Constitution grants equal protection under the law to all citizens. Muslims are subjects of a personal law, which came into force in 1937. However, the authors of the Constitution wanted a standard set of family laws. Article 44 of the Directive Principles of State Policy in the Indian Constitution mandates that "The state shall endeavour to secure for all citizens a Uniform Civil Code throughout the territory of India.".

The authors of the Constitution had realized that Muslims were stubborn about retaining their laws, and the time was not ripe for the fruition of a Common Civil Code. One of the active participants in the debate who played a crucial role in shaping the discourse was Kazi Syed Karimuddin, who represented CP and Berar province in the Constituent Assembly and was a leading criminal lawyer at Yavatmal.

On this issue, the Assembly was divided into two parts: on one side, there were people like K.M. Munshi, and on the other end, Kazi and Maulana Hasrat Mohani. Muslim members of the Assembly believed that the protection of personal laws must be a priority. Consequently, a majority of 5:4 of the subcommittee on Fundamental Rights decided that UCC should not be a Fundamental Right.

KM Munshi believed there should be some limitations on religion to bring togetherness and integration as the basis of national civic identity.

Kazi argued: "The people outside and the members of the Constituent Assembly must realize that a Muslim regards the personal law as part of the religion, and I really assure you that there is not a single Muslim in the country, at least I have not seen one, who wants a change in the mandatory provision of religious rights and personal laws, and if there is anyone who wants a change in the mandatory principle, or religion as a matter of personal law, then he cannot be a Muslim. Therefore, if you really want to protect the minorities because this is a secular state, it does not mean that people should have no religion. If this is the view of the minority Muslims or any other minority they want to abide by personal law, those laws have to be protected."There were arguments by other Muslim members

- Hasrat Mohani, freedom fighter and Urdu poet who coined the iconic "Inquilab Zindabad" slogan was equally emphatic: "I would like to say that any party, political or communal, has no right to interfere in the personal law of any group. More particularly, I say this regarding Muslims. There are three fundamentals in their law, namely, religion, language, and culture, which human agency has not ordained. Their law regarding divorce, marriage, and inheritance has been derived from the Qur'an, and its interpretation is recorded therein. If there is anyone who thinks that he can interfere in the personal law of the Muslims, then I would say to him that the result will be very harmful. Mussalmans will never submit to any interference in their law, and they will have to face an iron wall of Muslim determination to oppose them in every way".
- Naziruddin Ahmad believes that approval from the community of people who will be affected by the implementation of a uniform civil code has to be obtained. Further, he said there would be a time in the future when there would be uniformity in the personal laws of every religion, but this time has not come. The authority in the hands of the State to make uniformity in personal laws is before time. Power concerning personal laws shouldn't be in the hands of the state.
- Dr Babasaheb Ambedkar believed that the State has no duty to interfere with religious laws. There is no need to be aggressive on the fact that the State has the power, and they will utilize this power, which is in contravention to the personal laws of every religion, including Muslims.
- Sir B N Rau, the constitutional advisor to the Constitution of India, believed that a uniform civil code is a part of directive principles, which is just a direction to the State to make laws and directive principles have the least educative power.

In his stellar speech, Kazi Karimuddin argued that in Article 31, the country's economic pattern had vague generalizations. The word 'Directive' must be deleted. He endorsed Mr Kamath's suggestion that they should be Fundamental Principles of State Policy. His submission was that the word 'Directive' is unnecessary and meaningless. The provisions under this Chapter become only platitudes or pious wishes, and Dr Ambedkar rightly stated that they are more or less only Instruments of Instruction. If they are an Instrument of Instruction, why should they find a place in the Fundamental Principles to be embodied in the Constitution?

Kazi Karimuddin believed that The Directive Principles provisions embodied in Part IV are significant as they relate to uniform civil code, economic patterns, and many Fundamental matters. Directive Principles mean that they will not be binding on the State; in any case, they would not be enforceable in a court of law. His submission is that if this Constitution does not lay down these principles for enforcement in a court of law, or if they are not binding on the State, they are meaningless. He drew the members' attention to what Dr Ambedkar had said in his book.

Aharon Layish wrote a paper in July 1973 on "The Shar'ah in Israel". Israel's Shar'ah court system is more efficient than the civil law alternative. At the same time, it also evolves in conjunction with the demands of an 'open, modern, and developed' society. Israel's religious courts are part of the judicial system, with applicants having the option of choosing whether to lodge cases in the spiritual or civil courts.

Reform is an unruly horse that can go berserk unless adequately saddled. The modern trend is for the acceptance of diversity. It is equally essential for the Muslim theocracy to understand their proper role, call it religious policing, cultural policing, guardian policing, family policing, and community policing. Their main opposition to triple talaq was to the government's legislative intent to criminalise it and instil overtly reformist legislation with a malicious agenda.

Contrary to the fears of many, religious freedom has been important as a cultural and moral force. We must understand that all divine texts share common themes to preserve human spirituality.

No concept of prosperity, social advancement, or human rights will weaken the eternal influence of divine texts. Normative deviations from divine texts are transient. But the spiritual needs that divine texts fulfil are permanent. So is the Qur'an, which exerts an extraordinary moral influence in the life of an ordinary Muslim.

16. THE LEGAL NUANCES OF ISLAM

The religious law of Islam is seen as the expression of God's command for Muslims and, in application, constitutes a system of duties that are incumbent upon all Muslims by virtue of their religious belief. Most of the world's nearly fifty Muslim-majority countries have laws that reference shar'ah, the guidance Muslims believe God provided them on a range of spiritual and worldly matters. The religious law of Islam is seen as the expression of God's command for Muslims and, in application, constitutes a system of duties that are incumbent upon all Muslims by virtue of their religious belief. Known as the *sharīʿah* (literally, "path leading to the watering place), the law represents a divinely ordained path of conduct that guides Muslims toward a practical expression of religious conviction in this world and the goal of divine favour in the world to come.

Two terms are used to refer to law in Islam: shar'ah and fiqh. Shar'ahh refers to God's divine law, which is contained in the Qur'an, and the sayings and doings of Muhammad (*hadith*). Fiqh refers to the scholarly efforts of jurists (fuqaha) to elaborate the details of shar'ah through investigation and debate. Muslims understand Shar'ahh to be an unchanging revelation, while fiqh, as a human endeavour, is open to discussion, reinterpretation, and change.

Scholars and jurists developed the law by combining knowledge of the Qur'an, *hadith*, and analogical reasoning with local practice. Beginning in the mid-eighth century, the primary Sunni schools of legal thought (madhhabs)—Hanafi, Maliki, Shafii, and Hanbali—and the Twelver Shii Jafari madhhab emerged. Other minor and short-lived schools also developed.

Sunnis and Shiis differed in their understanding of who held the power to interpret shari'ah. For Sunnis, the scholars had this right, as delegated by the actual ruler. Shiis initially believed that only an imam (in this case, a descendant of Muhammad) could interpret shari'ah because the imam, like Muhammad, was thought to be infallible. When the line of appropriate descendants ended, this tradition was reinterpreted to grant judicial authority to the fuqaha as the imam's representatives. In addition to the Qur'an and *hadith* of Muhammad, Shiis also use the rulings of the imams—Ijma, or consensus, which is a product of an infallible imam's opinion.

There are two types of fiqh literature: those dealing with usul al-fiqh (roots) and those dealing with fur al-fiqh (branches). Usul al-fiqh explores the four sources of the law—the Qur'an, *hadith*, consensus (ijma), and analogical reasoning (qiyas)—to provide structures for interpreting revelation. The Qur'an and *hadith* are considered to be equal in authority, although the Qur'an, as God's word, is superior in its nature and origins. Other issues include the principles of abrogation (naskh), the application, ramifications, and limitations of analogical argument, and the value and limits of consensus. Only those with sufficient educational background in the sources of the law are qualified to practice ijtihad.-reason because it carries almost an onerous divine responsibility.

Education in fiqh was a critical part of Islamic education from the tenth century forward. It provided training in systematic thought and controlled argument, serving the needs of the merchant classes and governing bureaucracies. In the modern period, exclusive training in the traditional Islamic sciences has become less relevant than legal education.

Ritual topics include purity, prayers, alms (zakah), pilgrimage, fasting, and jihad. Social relations topics include marriage, divorce, inheritance, buying, selling, lending, hiring, gifts, testamentary bequests, agency, deposit, crimes, torts, penalties, compensations for injury, judicial practice and procedure, rules relating to enslaved people, land ownership, land holding, contractual partnerships, slaughter of animals for food, and oaths and their effects. There are five categories of actions in future literature: mandatory, recommended, permitted, abhorred, and prohibited.

Summary

- Shari'ah is the ideal form of divine guidance that Muslims follow to live a righteous life. Human interpretations of shar'ah, or fiqh, are the basis of Islamic law today.
- About half the world's Muslim-majority countries have Shar'ah-based laws, and most Muslims worldwide follow aspects of shari'ah in their private religious practices.
- Debate continues to flare over Shar'ah's place in the modern world, particularly with regard to its teachings relating to criminal justice, democracy, and social equality.

What is Shari'ah?

Shari'ah means "the correct path" in Arabic. In Islam, it refers to the divine counsel that Muslims follow to live moral lives and grow close to God. Shari'ahis is derived from two primary sources: the Qur'an, which is considered the direct word of God, and *hadith*—thousands of sayings and practices attributed to the Prophet Mohammed that collectively form the Sunna. Some of the traditions and narratives included in these sources evolved from those in Judaism and Christianity, the other major Abrahamic religions. Shiite Muslims include the words and deeds of some of the prophet's family in the Sunna. However, shari'ah is primarily a result of the interpretive tradition of Muslim scholars.

The Prophet Mohammed is considered the most pious of all believers, and his actions became a model for all Muslims. The process of interpreting shar'ah, known as *fiqh*, developed over hundreds of years after he died in the seventh century and as the Islamic empire expanded outward from Mecca and Medina, where he lived and died, in modern-day Saudi Arabia.

Islamic law varies by country and hi rooted in local custom local customs in the process of its evolution. Shari'ah is also the basis of legal opinions called fatwas, which Muslim scholars issue in response to requests from individual Muslims or governments seeking guidance on a specific problem. In Sunni Islam, fatwas are strictly advisory; in Shiite Islam, practitioners are obliged to follow the fatwas of the religious leader of their choosing.

Nature and significance of Islamic law

In classical form, the shar'ah differs from Western systems of law in two principal respects. In the first place, the scope of shari'ah is much broader since it regulates the individual's relationship not only with neighbours and with the state, which is the limit of most other legal systems but also with God and with the individual's conscience. The Shari'ah is concerned as much with ethical standards as with legal rules, indicating not only what an individual is entitled or bound to do in law but also what one ought, in conscience, to do or refrain from doing. Accordingly, certain acts are classified as praiseworthy (*mandūb*), which means that their performance brings divine favour and their omission divine disfavour, and others as blameworthy (*makrūh*), which has the opposite implications. However, in neither case is there any legal sanction of punishment or reward, nullity or validity. The shar'ah is thus not merely a system of law but also a comprehensive code of behaviour that embraces both private and public activities.

The second significant distinction between the Shar'ah and Western legal systems is a consequence of the Islamic concept of the law as the expression of the divine will. With the death of the Prophet Muhammad in 632, direct communication of the divine will to human beings ceased, and the terms of the divine revelation were henceforth fixed and immutable. The overall image of the shar'ah is thus one of unchanging continuity, an impression that generally holds for some areas of the law, such as ritual law.

Since the 19th century, Westernized elites and laypeople had their monopoly. Early Western studies of Islamic law held the view that while Islamic law shaped Muslim societies, the latter did not influence Islamic law in return. However, this position has become untenable. Social pressures and communal interests have played an essential role in determining the practice of Islamic law in particular contexts—both in the premodern period and to an even greater extent in the modern era.

Why is it so controversial?

Shari'ah is a source of debate among both Muslims and non-Muslims. Among the many reasons shari'ah generates controversy is that it's often contrasted with modern legal regimes in predominantly secular countries. Shari'ah can also be problematic, depending on who interprets it. Many observers view shari'ahas as a rigid legal system that can't evolve to reflect modern Western values. Debates over shari'ah tend to centre on specific topics:

Corporal punishment. For certain crimes, such as theft, blasphemy, and adultery, traditional interpretations of Islamic law prescribe punishments that are considered draconian compared to those in most modern legal systems. Among them are the *hudud* punishments, which include stoning, lashing, and amputation. (The Qur'an never mentions stoning, which is a punishment derived from the Book of Deuteronomy in both the Hebrew and Christian Bibles.) However, applying such punishments requires meeting extensive evidentiary thresholds, so scholars say they are primarily a deterrent rather than have a punitive effect through application.

Today, most Muslim-majority countries don't administer physical punishments, though about a dozen of them have the authority to do so under state laws. Local and international backlash often dissuades authorities from following through with such sentences. However, Indonesia, Iran, the Maldives, and Qatar are among the countries where flogging prevails, and Iran, Mauritania], Nigeria, Saudi Arabia, and Sudan have in recent decades punished convicted thieves with amputations. Additionally, the Taliban implemented public executions and amputations when they ruled Afghanistan in the 1990s and have said these punishments will return under their new government.

Jihad. Many non-Muslims assume that this word, which means "to strive," only refers to an armed struggle by Muslim extremists against non-Muslims. However, as a tenet of Shar'ah, it relates to the effort to achieve a moral aim, which could be an armed struggle against injustice, the desire to better oneself morally, or the pursuit of knowledge, for example.

Religious tolerance. Some critics say that Muslim-led states that follow shari'ah are remarkably intolerant of nonbelievers or those who practice other religions. Scholars say that this intolerance largely stems from premodern restrictions applied to non-Muslim minorities in Muslim lands, which were supported by certain *hadith*s later introduced into the Muslim canon that recommend the death penalty for Muslims who commit apostasy. Nigeria and Pakistan have carried out capital punishment for blasphemy and apostasy, as did Sudan for many years.

Development of different schools of law

Different regions within the Islamic empire developed divergent regional legal traditions, which were reproduced in study circles, or *ḥalqah* (so named because the teacher was, as a rule, seated on a dais or cushion with the pupils gathered in a semicircle before him). The most active intellectual circles dominated the Hejaz (a region on the west coast of the Arabian Peninsula) and Iraq. However, those in Syria and Egypt also played a role. With the emergence of written legal culture, regional traditions faced a need to justify their doctrines systematically and engage with traditions from other regions. Encased in books, the doctrines of the regional schools became mobile, and the locus of school identity shifted from places to the individuals responsible for their elaboration and codification. In particular, the school of Medina became associated with Mālik ibn Anas (died 795), Medina's most prominent jurist in the late 8th century. It came to be known as the Mālikī school, and the school of Kūfah turned into the Ḥanafī school, named after its most outstanding jurist, Mālik's contemporary Abū Ḥanīfah (died 767).

These legal schools with regional roots had to contend with another 8th-century development: the systematic collection of reports concerning the sayings and actions attributed to the Prophet Muhammad (*Hadith*). The regional schools had already made use of such traditions. Still, their wide-scale collection and dissemination meant that the schools faced hitherto unknown prophetic traditions that contradicted their established positions. Generally speaking, the Mālikīs and the Ḥanafīs gave greater weight to their regional traditions in resolving this tension. In contrast, two school-founding jurists of the subsequent generation, Muḥammad ibn Idrīs al-Shāfiʿī (died 820) and Aḥmad ibn Ḥanbal (died 855), sought to transcend localism by granting priority to authentic traditions. Ibn Ḥanbal drew on both prophetic traditions and the opinions of early Muslim jurists throughout Muslim lands. Al-Shāfiʿī, by contrast, rejected the putative precedential authority of regional legal traditions and the early jurists in general. Instead, he proposed a system in which the Qurʾān and the Prophetic example (Sunnah) were the only authoritative sources of law and then developed a toolkit of methods for systematically deriving legal rules from the sources and extending these rules to areas not directly covered by the sacred texts. A prominent element of this toolkit was analogical reasoning (*qiyās*).

Al-Shāfiʿī's insistence on the importance of the Sunnah as a source of law prompted great activity in the collection and classification of *Hadith* reports, particularly among his supporters, who formed the Shāfiʿī school, and the followers of Ibn Ḥanbal, who formed the Ḥanbalī school. Muslim scholarship maintained that the classical compilations of *Hadith*—especially those of al-Bukhārī (died 870) and Muslim (died 875)—constituted an authentic record of the Prophet's precedents. However, Western Orientalists have traditionally been sceptical of the attribution of most alleged Prophetic *hadith*s, arguing that they represent the views of later scholars fictitiously ascribed to the Prophet to give doctrines greater authority.

Later developments

Al-Shāfiʿī's thesis formed the basis of the classical theory of the roots of jurisprudence (*uṣūl al-fiqh*), which crystallized in the early 10th century. Juristic "effort" to comprehend the terms of the Shari'ah is known as *ijtihād*, and legal theory charts the course that *ijtihād* must follow. In seeking the answer to a legal problem, the jurist must first consult the Qur'ān and *Hadith*. Suppose there is no solution in divine revelation. In that case, the jurist must employ analogy (*qiyās*) or certain subsidiary principles of reasoning, such as *istiḥsān* (juristic discretion) and *istiṣlāh* (consideration of welfare). As an attempt to define God's law, the *ijtihād* of individual scholars can result only in a tentative conclusion, termed *ẓann* ("conjecture"), which contrasts with the idea of specific (*yaqīn*) knowledge.

Shari'ah law is a candidly pluralistic system, the philosophy of the equal authority of the different schools in a putative dictum of the Prophet: "Difference of opinion among my community is a sign of God's bounty." Outside the four schools of Sunni Islam stand the minority groups of the Shiʿah and the Ibāḍīs, whose versions of the Shari'ah differ considerably from those of the Sunnis. Shiʿi law, in particular, grew out of a fundamentally different politico-religious system, in which the rulers, or imams, were held to be divinely inspired and, therefore, the spokespeople of the Lawgiver himself. Geographically, the division between the various schools and sects became reasonably well defined as qadis' courts in different areas became wedded to the doctrine of one particular school. Thus, Ḥanafī law came to predominate in the Middle East and the Indian subcontinent; Mālikī law in North, West, and Central Africa; Shāfiʿī law in East Africa, the southern parts of the Arabian Peninsula, Malaysia, and Indonesia; Ḥanbalī law in Saudi Arabia; Shiʿi law in Iran and the Shiʿi communities of India and East Africa; and Ibāḍī law in Zanzibar, Oman, and parts of Algeria.

Although the Shari'ah doctrine is all-embracing, Islamic legal practice has consistently recognized jurisdictions other than that of the qadis. Because the qadis' courts were hidebound by a cumbersome system of procedure and evidence, they did not prove a satisfactory organ for the administration of justice in all respects, particularly as regards criminal, land, and commercial law. Hence, under the broad heading of the sovereign's administrative power (*siyāsah*), competence went to other courts, known collectively as *maẓālim* courts, and the monopoly of qadis' was confined to private family and civil law. As the expression of a religious ideal, Shari'ah doctrine was always the focal point of legal activity. Still, it never formed a complete or exclusively authoritative expression of the laws that governed the lives of Muslims in practice.

Islam and the challenge of economic development

A significant challenge confronts the world of Islam: the challenge of reconstructing its economy in a way that is commensurate with its world role: ideological, political and economic. What does this demand: economic development with a view to "catch up" with the industrialized countries of the West, Capitalist or Socialist according to one's inclination and sympathy, or politico-economic dependence? Or does it demand total socio-economic reconstruction in the light of a basically different model, with its own set of assumptions, ideals and growth path, something that would be unique and value-specific?

17. INDIA'S MUSLIMS: AN INCREASINGLY MARGINALIZED POPULATION

The increasing tendency towards seeing people in terms of one dominant 'identity' ('this is your duty as an American', 'you must commit these acts as a Muslim', or 'as a Chinese, you should give priority to this national engagement') is not only an imposition of an external and arbitrary priority but also the denial of essential liberty of a person who can decide on their respective loyalties to different groups (to all of which they belong)

– **Amartya Sen,** *The Idea of Justice*

Summary

- Some two hundred million Muslims live in India, making up the predominantly Hindu country's largest minority group.
- For decades, Muslim communities have faced discrimination in employment and education and encountered barriers to achieving wealth and political power. They are disproportionately the victims of communal violence.
- Prime Minister Narendra Modi and the ruling party have moved to further limit Muslims' rights under the controversial citizenship law, which has the power to render millions of Muslims in India stateless.

Countering discrimination against Muslims

Muslims make up roughly 13 per cent of India's population of 1.1 billion, and their numbers are nearly equal to the entire population of

Pakistan, which was carved out of British India almost 60 years ago as the homeland of the subcontinent's Muslims. Soul-searching about Muslim rights and well-being in India, which has witnessed periodic outbreaks of religious violence, has been a leitmotif ever since.

Intolerance and discrimination against Muslims are not new, but manifestations of these phenomena appear to have been on the rise in recent years. Muslims might experience verbal harassment or be the targets of hate speech, violent attacks or religious profiling. The "war on terror", the global economic crisis, anxieties about national identity and the difficulties in coping with the increasing diversity in many societies have led to a growth in resentment against Muslims and Islam that has sometimes, language in media and political discourse further fuelled by intolerance,

many Muslims experience a range of discrimination, including verbal harassment, hate speech, violent attacks and religious profiling. Many face a lack of equal opportunities in employment, housing, health and education and face restrictions on the public expression of their religion.

Another significant issue is the rise of communal violence and religious hatred. In recent years, there has been a surge in violence and religious clashes, mainly targeting minorities. This has led to widespread fear and insecurity among these communities and has caused significant harm to their homes, businesses, and places of worship.

India, the 'largest democracy of the world', has also been known after 1947 for its attempts at establishing a secular regime and its success — quite exceptional — in maintaining it for decades despite ups and downs. Even though Indira Gandhi had the notion of secularism inserted in the Indian Constitution in 1976, almost twenty years after independence, the political system set up during the reign of her father, Jawaharlal Nehru, was already designed along those lines. Secularism In India designates the equidistance of the state vis-à-vis all religions and an equally positive attitude towards them all. For instance, Article 25 of the constitution emphasizes that 'all persons are equally free to profess, practice and propagate religion', and Article 30 states that 'All minorities, whether based on religion or language, shall have the right to establish and administer educational institutions', which can also receive subsidies from the state.

Muslim representation has fallen in the ruling BJP and in opposition parties, too. When Modi assumed power in 2014, the outgoing parliament had 30 Muslim lawmakers – and just one was a member of the BJP. Muslims now hold 25 out of 543 seats, and none belong to the BJP. India has gone from being a country where it marginalized Muslims but who are

Experts say anti-Muslim sentiments have heightened under the leadership of Prime Minister Narendra Modi and the ruling Bharatiya Janata Party (BJP), which has pursued a Hindu nationalist agenda since elected to power in 2014. Since Modi's reelection in 2019, the government has pushed controversial policies that critics feel ignore Muslims' rights, restrict religious freedoms, and disenfranchise millions of Muslims. Under Modi, violence against Muslims has become more common. The moves have sparked protests in India and drawn international condemnation. Some experts who follow India say that Modi's reelection in 2024 would likely sow further religious division in the country.

How did India's partition influence Hindu-Muslim relations?

Some of the animosity between India's Hindus and Muslims goes back to the British colonial era schisms and the subsequent Partition of British India in 1947, scholars say. Economically devastated after World War II, the British lacked the resources to maintain their empire and moved to leave the subcontinent. In the years before Partition, the Indian National Congress party, under the leadership of Mahatma Gandhi and Jawaharlal

Nehru, pushed for independence, organizing civil disobedience and mass protests against British rule. Meanwhile, the All-India Muslim League political group, led by Muhammad Ali Jinnah, called for a separate state for Muslims.

In 1947, a British judge hastily decided the borders for a Hindu-majority India and a Muslim-majority Pakistan (including what is today Bangladesh). The Partition sparked deadly riots, gruesome communal violence, and mass migrations of Muslims to Pakistan and Hindus and Sikhs to India. Survivors recall blood-soaked trains carrying refugees from one country to the other, towns burned to the ground, and bodies thrown in the streets. Historians estimate between two hundred thousand and two million people died.

Why communities that had coexisted for hundreds of years attacked each other remains unclear. Some experts fault the British and their "divide-and-rule" strategy, which provided some electoral privileges for the Muslim minority, about 25 per cent of the population. Others point to tensions between Hindu and Muslim political movements, which rallied constituents along religious lines. Around thirty-five million Muslims stayed in India after the Partition.

How did religion factor into India's Constitution?

The country's seventy-five-year-old Constitution enshrines egalitarian principles, including social equality and nondiscrimination. The word "secular" was added to the preamble in 1976, but the Constitution does not explicitly require the separation of religion and government.

Leaders of the Congress party who fought for independence advocated for an India that recognized all citizens and faiths as equal. Gandhi, who envisioned a unified India free from discrimination, was assassinated in 1948 by a Hindu nationalist. Nehru, India's first prime minister, believed that secularism was essential to building a peaceful society and avoiding another tragedy like what followed Partition; he saw those trying to divide India along religious lines, especially Hindu groups, as the nation's greatest threat.

How did Hindu nationalists come to power?

Yogi Adityanath—a saffron-clad monk from the right-wing, Hindu-fundamentalist Bharatiya Janata Party—was sworn in for a second term as chief minister of the Indian state of Uttar Pradesh. For two hours that morning, temple bells rang at ceremonies organized across the state to mark the occasion. It was in keeping with the image that Adityanath has sought to project: heir to Indian Prime Minister Narendra Modi and a leading figure in the BJP's attempt to turn India into a Hindu nationalist state. Hindu nationalism dates back to colonial-era writings of Indians, such as author and politician V. D. Savarkar in his book *Hindutva: Who Is a Hindu?* Hindu nationalists believe Hindus are the "true sons of the soil" because their holy lands are in India, whereas the Christian and Muslim sacred lands are outside it. They generally champion policies intended to make India a Hindu state. Many see Indian Muslims as suspect foreigners despite the fact that most are descendants of Hindus who converted to Islam. Hindu nationalists point to Partition and the creation of Pakistan as the ultimate manifestation of Muslim disloyalty.

Political tensions started to strain India's secular model in the 1980s. After suffering an electoral defeat in 1977, Prime Minister Indira Gandhi exploited religious divisions to help return the Congress party to power. Gandhi, who died to Sikh bodyguards in 1984, was succeeded by her son, Rajiv, who further favoured Hindus.

Founded in 1980, the BJP traces its origins to the political wing of the Rashtriya Swayamsevak Sangh (RSS), a Hindu nationalist paramilitary volunteer group. The BJP came to power with a coalition government in India's 1998 national elections. The party shelved its more radical goals to hold together a coalition it led until 2004 when the Congress party regained power. These goals included ending the special status of Kashmir, a disputed Muslim-majority region; constructing a Hindu temple in the northern city of Ayodhya; and creating a uniform civil code so all citizens would have the same personal laws. (There is currently a separate Muslim personal law for issues such as marriage and inheritance.)

In 2014, the BJP won a single-party majority for the first time in the Lok Sabha—the lower house of parliament and India's most influential political body—making party leader Narendra Modi prime minister. The party again secured a majority in 2019 after a divisive campaign filled with anti-Muslim messaging. Despite the BJP facing opposition in the southern and eastern regions of India, the party won three critical Hindi-speaking state elections in December 2023,

What types of discrimination do India's Muslims face?

On the whole, Muslims suffer from deprivation on almost every front. While they are doing somewhat better in certain respects in some states (for instance, in the South), they are generally extraordinarily backward and live in the shadow of vulnerability and poverty. The relatively better-off position of Muslims in south India is partly related to the fact that some of these states have remained largely undisturbed by bicommunal rioting. Indeed, while communal violence may not be a cause for Muslim backwardness, there is some evidence to argue that the expectation of recurring violence may play a significant role in depressing fortunes, fostering insecurity and increasing social and economic vulnerability [Razzack and Gumber 2002; Mishra and Singh 2002; Robinson 2005].

Demographic transition is also underway among Muslims, among others. In many parts of the world, there appears to be a tendency towards higher fertility among ethnic minorities. Promoting security and well-being could do more to depress.

An essential aspect brought out by the data is the clear discrimination against Muslims in the sphere of state provision of public services of all kinds. There is an urgent need to rectify this imbalance. Among Muslims, some groups are worse off than others. Apart from regional differences, class, caste, and gender work to produce further inequalities in access and achievement. Muslim OBCs constitute just over 40 per cent of the total Muslim population. Muslims as a whole lag behind Hindu OBCs, and the Muslim OBCs are worse off than the general Muslim population. This suggests that the benefits of entitlements for the backward classes are not reaching the Muslim OBCs. The SCR recommends that the Muslim OBCs need additional attention; Muslims have experienced discrimination in areas including employment, education, and housing. Many encounter barriers to achieving political power and wealth and lack access to health care and essential services. Moreover, they often struggle to secure justice after suffering discrimination despite constitutional protections.

Over the last two decades, the representation of Muslims in parliament has stagnated: after the 2019 elections, Muslims held just 5 per cent of seats. That's partly due to the rise of the BJP, which by mid-2022 had no Muslim members of its party in parliament.

Meanwhile, a 2019 report found that half of the police surveyed showed anti-Muslim bias, making them less likely to intervene to stop crimes against Muslims. Analysts have also noted widespread impunity for those who attack Muslims. In recent years, state and national courts and government bodies have sometimes overturned convictions or withdrawn cases that accused Hindus of involvement in violence against Muslims. States have increasingly passed laws restricting Muslims' religious freedoms, including anti-conversion laws and bans on wearing headscarves in school.

In addition, authorities have turned to extrajudicial means to punish Muslims through a practice critics call "bulldozer justice." In 2022, authorities in several states destroyed people's homes, alleging that the demolished buildings lacked proper permits. However, critics said they primarily targeted Muslims, some of whom had recently participated in protests. In response, India's Supreme Court noted that demolitions "cannot be retaliatory," though the practice has continued.

With the BJP's arrival to power, the secular face of India has received severe criticism in the international community With some other factors like relative development differences, discrimination at social and economic levels, continuous discrimination by the ruling elite, lack of political representation and voicing out grievances has become the root cause of ethnic violence in India, which can push to the generation of parochialism. Cultural genocide and deliberate unequal economic development have caused significant loss of Muslim lives and property and generated issues, including demographic reshaping and political disenfranchisement, which have further severe implications for Muslims. This paper will try to highlight the ethnic violence against Muslims in India, analyze the reasons behind the ethnic conflict and its manifestation through primordial and instrumental theoretical framework and finally provide road maps to a solution.

The religiosity of worldwide Muslims

The hijab, or the Muslim veil, has emerged as one of the most contentious articles of clothing in recent times. Scholarly literature has often limited itself to discussing the hijab in binaries of oppression and liberation. Hijab was inextricable from the varied sub-systems of the respondent's ecology. Positive responses to the veil at home, neighbourhood, and on social media promoted the hijab, while adverse reactions at work and in educational settings impeded it. Participants devised personal "rules" for hijab, adapting it to different settings after evaluating the diverse demands of the roles they occupied. The hijab was modest clothing that covered the body, not limited to a burqa. Spiritual adherence to the principles of hijab was considered as imperative as its physical adherence.

Though the degree of physical veiling fluctuated, commitment to the veil strengthened over time. The primary reason for veiling was religion, but secondary reasons were cited in favour of the practice. The veil has many meanings, including modesty, a means of connection with the Muslim community, and a symbol of resistance. It was purposefully worn to promote a positive image of Islam and exhibit the self-efficacy of the Muslim community.

Research suggests that Muslim women wearing the hijab may be particularly vulnerable to the experiences of stigmatization as the hijab represents a dominant marker of "otherness." For the hijab-wearing group, two emergent themes were evident: "Journey of my hijab" and "The two sides of the hijab." For the non-hijab-wearing group, the emergent themes included: "My name is (un)safe" and "Not Muslim enough." The development of intervention strategies to integrate the community more meaningfully by preventing "othering" and providing agency and autonomy. In Turkey, highly educated Muslim women who were highly religious tended to cover their heads more than other highly religious Muslim women. In Belgium, highly religious Muslim women who socialised with non-Muslims used the veil more than highly religious Muslim women who did not mix as much with the native population. In Muslim countries where there is great emphasis on the piety of future brides, highly religious single women who are likely to be on the marriage market or who are highly educated tended to wear the veil more than otherwise very similar but married women and those who did not leave the home as much, says the study

The disempowered

The government denied that "caste discrimination is prevalent in India." But, the government has a hard time admitting that it is an Indian variation of a worldwide phenomenon worthy of international scrutiny. Even Dalits themselves are not free of prejudice." India does not practise anything like official apartheid. On the contrary, a fifth of the seats in Parliament are reserved for members of scheduled castes and tribes. They and other lower castes have places at educational institutions and jobs in government earmarked for them. Some states have powerful political parties based on alliances among lower castes. India's quotas and job preferment have not brought equality, dignity or even safety to India's lowest castes. Dalits are barely represented among the grandees of business, one reason why some demand reservations for jobs in the private sector. They are over-represented, however, in the ranks of landless agricultural labourers and illiterates. Such humiliations as the "two-tumbler system" (separate glasses for Dalits and non-Dalits) persist in some places. In villages, the stigma can lead not just to segregation but to violence.

Dalit activists want discussion on these injustices at the UN conference, which is to discuss not only racism but "racial discrimination, xenophobia and related intolerance". Just like racism discrimination against Dalits, The government has a hard time admitting that it is an Indian variation of a worldwide phenomenon worthy of international scrutiny. Even Dalits themselves are not free of prejudice. In the matrimonial section of a website for Dalits, advertisers boast of prospective spouses' "fair complexions.

What is the future for common Muslims?

The mood among India's Muslims is despondent, and they see their position being undermined steadily in their own country. So, what should be the agenda for Muslims? There have been multiple approaches on multiple fronts, including economic, social, and educational, but the success has not been noteworthy. This is not to undermine the significance of political instruments, which have an essential role to play. But, as experience suggests, the political route has many limitations. While political leaders may continue to work for Muslim rights, Muslim institutions need to focus on specific fundamental issues that can bring speedier and more reliable gains on the economic front. This is a more stable route to the enormous empowerment of Muslims.

The burgeoning private sector, which is a fruit of globalisation, is built on a system of meritocracy where discrimination is mainly absent and talent is respected. While the vast majority of Muslims who don't have access to quality education may continue to be deprived of this new prosperity, others who are both talented and fortunate to get a good education have a reasonably assured route to achieving their life goals.

Most Muslims will continue to draw their sustenance from the informal sector. The enormous numbers of informal workers still have no formal training opportunities. Traditional craftsmanship is losing value, and the market offers poor compensation to artisans for their skills and artistry. The gap between skill training and employment has widened, leading to a situation where many youths are unable to find the employment that they are aspiring for, and many employers are unable to find trained workers.

The feedback from corporate India shows that 65-75 per cent of the 15 million Indian youth who enter the workforce each year are not job-ready or suitably employable. The vocational training system in the Muslim community needs to reconcile with the emerging reality. Imparting more relevant skill sets makes families self-sustaining.

It is also essential to ensure that specific skills are not scaled across multiple areas in the same region, as this saturates the market with limited opportunities for the trained. This is specifically true of dense Muslim localities where competition, rather than collaboration, is ruining the community economically.

Political and social scientists will have to document facts and figures to advance this agenda. Since the Constitution and the courts have ruled out religion as a criterion for assessing backwardness, minority groups may find it challenging to get the benefits of affirmative action. Experts do argue that social backwardness is a fluid and evolving category, with caste as just one of the markers of discrimination. Gender, culture, economic conditions, educational backwardness and official policies, among other factors, can influence social situations and become the cause of deprivation and social backwardness. We are seeing this transformation at a much more exponential pace than our Constitution makers may have visualised. This understanding and legislative recognition alone can enable newer groups to get the benefits of affirmative action through social reengineering. Muslims can become eligible for at least some forms of reservation among new "backward" groups.

It is thus clear that while collective efforts will have to continue, Muslim youth have to understand that the competition requires them to achieve excellence in the field they choose. Sadly, both political and religious leaders have appropriated the responsibility for collective moral and economic salvation, freeing individuals of personal accountability. We need to abandon this trend of seeking salvation in herds and assume responsibility for both our worldly and otherworldly lives; this is the distilled essence of not just our collective economic and political wisdom but also of our scriptures.

What controversial actions has the Modi government taken with regard to Muslims?

In analyses of terrorism and Islam, Indian Muslims have primarily avoided radicalisation. Theories abound about the absence of radicalisation, but one of the arguments made by the government and policy officials and members of the *'ulama* (religious clergy) is that there is something exceptional about Indian Islam. This homogenisation is in itself problematic as it overlooks the vast cultural, linguistic, regional and sectarian diversity among Muslims in India. It fails to take into account that this very diversity and some degree of political, social and economic stability has meant that political discourse amongst Muslims is rooted in the belief of an inclusive and secular India.

The world's 1.6 billion Muslims are united in their belief in God and the Prophet Muhammad. They are bonded by such religious practices as fasting during the holy month of Ramadan and almsgiving to assist people in need. But they have widely differing views about many other aspects of their faith, including how important religion is to their lives, who counts as a Muslim and what practices are acceptable in Islam,

In 2019, the parliament passed the Citizenship Amendment Act, which allows for the fast-tracking of citizenship for Hindu, Sikh, Buddhist, Jain, Parsi, and Christian migrants from Afghanistan, Bangladesh, and Pakistan. Critics say the law is discriminatory because it excludes Muslims and applies religious criteria for the first time to the question of citizenship. The BJP promised in its 2019 election manifesto [PDF] to complete a National Register of Citizens (NRC). The NRC was created in the 1950s for the unique case of the state of Assam to determine whether residents were Indian citizens or migrants from what is now neighbouring Bangladesh. In 2019, the Assam government updated its register, which excludes nearly two million Hindu and Muslim Bengali people. Critics say this process could render many Muslims stateless if implemented nationwide because they lack the necessary documents and are not eligible for fast-tracked citizenship under the Citizenship Amendment Act.

Modi has meanwhile diminished the political standing of what was India's only Muslim-majority state: Jammu and Kashmir. In August 2019, the government split the state, which lies in the mountainous border region in dispute with Pakistan, into two territories and stripped away its special constitutional autonomy. Since then, Indian authorities have cracked down on the rights of people in the region, frequently under the guise of maintaining security. They shut down the internet eighty-five times in 2021, harassed and arrested journalists, and detained prominent political figures and activists. Dozens of civilians have been killed by armed groups since the division, despite government claims that the security situation had improved. In December 2023, the Supreme Court upheld the government's decision, ruling that the territory should regain statehood in time for local elections the following year.

"The longer Hindu nationalists are in power, the greater the change will be to Muslims' status and the harder it will be to reverse such changes," says Ashutosh Varshney, an expert on Indian intercommunal conflict at Brown University.

Until recently, it may have seemed as if religion were on the way out. As people grew more affluent and more educated, the thinking went, they would begin to rely less on the solace and meaning provided by faith. That is what happened in much of Western Europe, where church membership rates have cratered over the last century. According to a 2018 Pew study, only 11 per cent of people in Western European countries say religion is a vital part of their lives. Proponents of the so-called modernization theory see religion as a defence mechanism, a hedge against chaos and depredation; religions would invariably.

Supreme Court and minority rights

India has avowed itself to be a secular state. As a result, our Constitution's spirit is secular. In India, all political leaders profess to be secular, but none of them actually implement it. In India, political parties play a prominent part in delegitimizing religious issues in order to get votes. Despite the fact that there are several difficulties of this nature, the answer lies in approaching with due consideration. Even yet, the court seems to be unable to define minority and has relied on the interpretation of the court based on the facts. Article 30 and Article 29 of the Indian Constitution have a widespread impact, and they must offer the minority portion of their entire freedom.

The Supreme Court of India has always done its best to offer minorities the guarantees provided by the Constitution. The Constitution affords the country's minorities ample safeguards for the safety and advancement of the minorities and minority institutions, all of which have access to fundamental rights. The rights supposedly conferred on the minorities are no more than rights aimed at making India a genuinely democratic secular country and to secure to its citizen's justice — social, economic, and political; liberty of thought, expression, belief, faith, and worship; equality of status and opportunity; and to promote fraternity among them all, assuring the dignity of the individual and the unity and integrity of the nation, so proudly proclaimed in the Constitution. Religion, language, and culture were the essential elements to be considered with reference to each state to determine the question of whether any section of the population was a minority.

India's slide into fascism

India is slowly sliding into fascism. The problem with "fascism" as a description of any modern political tendency is that the term is a weapon of mass destruction that flattens the landscapes that it wants to describe. Fascism is so freighted with historically specific meaning that using it for other times and places can seem sloppy and excessive. And yet, juxtaposing the politics of contemporary South Asia with fascism, in its Nazi variant, serves a double purpose: it connects modern Indian majoritarianism with one of its ideological ancestors, and it helps us name and identify the ideological kernel of fascism that survived to fight another day.

The BJP has a history of using religious fault lines as a political tool to expand its constituency. Hindu or Hindutva chauvinism continues to drive India dangerously away from its pluralistic moorings. It is trying to recast the story of India from that of a secular democracy to that of a Hindu nation that dominates its minorities, especially the country's Muslims. The core philosophy rests on a combustible idea: those only followers of the so-called Indic religions (which it will define) can genuinely be Indians. These regressive policies are seeding long-term domestic instability, undermining interfaith harmony, and tarnishing

India's reputation for peaceful coexistence. The BJP government at the centre and in the states keep targeting Muslims with incendiary messages, encouraging and emboldening vigilante violence against them. Such violence has state inaction and seeming bias.

Discrimination against minorities

The definition of the term "religious discrimination" is contested. Religious discrimination is restrictions on the religious practices or institutions of minority religions that are not placed on the majority religion. Religious discrimination can include restrictions on (a) religious practices, (b) religious institutions and clergy, (c) conversion and proselytizing, and (d) other types of discrimination. Globally, 88.5% of countries discriminate against at least one religious minority, and religious discrimination is becoming more common over time. Religious discrimination is the norm worldwide regardless of world region, government type, and majority religion.

Motivations to discriminate are multiple and complex. They include (a) differences in religious ideologies and beliefs—many religions are ideologically intolerant of other religions; (b) religious organizations seeking an institutional monopoly in a country; (c) religious beliefs and practices running counter to liberal and secular values, including human rights; (d) countries seeking to protect their national culture from outside influences, including nonindigenous religions; (e) countries having anti-cult policies; (f) countries restricting minority religious practices that are considered objectionable to the national ideology or culture; (g) a historical conflict between minority groups and the majority; (h) the perception of minorities as a security threat; (i) the perception of minorities as a political threat ; (j) long-lasting historical tensions between the majority and minority; (k) national politicians mobilizing supporters along religious lines; (l) societal prejudices against minorities leading to government-based discrimination; (m) religious identity; (n) general discrimination that is also applicable to religious minorities. Although these are among the most common motivations for discrimination, in many cases, the motivations are unique to the specific situation.

Muslims have indeed repeatedly resorted to the law to seek protection from discrimination. This includes areas such as accessing education and housing, as well as seeking to bring to court the perpetrators of violence against Muslims. In terms of the provisions of the Constitution, such redress lies in provincial courts. This is a daunting challenge for Muslims since provincial judicial action is often subject to influence by the local government.

Muslims are a distributed minority in most of India. The only Indian state where Muslims are a majority is the state of Kashmir. Kashmir's Kashmir's ability to play a leading role in Muslim development in India, however, does not exist due to the ongoing local unrest about autonomy. This has, in effect, turned Kashmir into a near-police state with no space for political or civil society action on behalf of Muslims at large.

The causes of the decline lie in the official hostility to Muslims that has led to poor state investment in infrastructure for Muslims and continuing official and private discrimination in employment and protection of fundamental rights such as safety. The standard remedies of citizens in a functioning democracy with a rule of law like India are not available to most Muslims.

The law is ineffective on their behalf owing to official discrimination within the judiciary and interference by the state. Political trends resulting from rising provincialism and the rise of lower-caste parties have hurt them. Civil society's general weakness and media apathy have also hurt Muslims.

For nearly everyone, it is essential to think that their life has a purpose. But these purposes may be various: the purpose of one person's life may be to achieve one kind of goal, and that of another person may be to achieve a very different sort of goal. There needs to be no one thing that forms the purpose of every life. (Compare: 'everyone has a mother' versus 'there is someone who is the mother of everyone'. See quantifier shift fallacy.) Similarly, for many people, it will be enough if, at each moment, there is a purpose to what they are doing, without every moment being devoted to the same purpose and without the overall pattern itself having a purpose. The view that we are put here for a purpose, rather than being in the army, is characteristic of many religious frames of mind. It leads to lousy faith when apparent certainty about what the purpose is blinds people to other possibilities and opportunities.

Civil liberty is the absence of arbitrary restraint and the assurance of a body of rights, such as those found in bills of rights, statutes, and judicial decisions. Such liberty, however, is not inconsistent with regulations and restrictions imposed by law for the common good. Political liberty consists of the right of individuals to participate in government by voting and by holding public office. Since the proletarian and socialist movements and the economic dislocations after World War I, liberty is defined in terms of economic opportunity and security.

The path ahead

In these trying times, Muslims must look to the words of Maulana Azad, who was the president of the Indian National Congress during the negotiation of independence and was a key ally of Gandhi and Nehru.

"I am a Musalman and am proud of that fact. Islam's splendid traditions of 1,300 years are my inheritance. I am unwilling to lose even the smallest part of this inheritance. The teaching and history of Islam, its arts and letters and civilisation, are my wealth and my fortune. I have to protect them.

"As a Musalman, I have a special interest in Islamic religion and culture, and I cannot tolerate any interference with them. But in addition to these sentiments, I have others that the realities and conditions of my life have forced upon me. The spirit of Islam does not come in the way of these sentiments; it guides and helps me forward.

"I am proud of being an Indian. I am part of the indivisible unity of Indian nationality. I am indispensable to this noble edifice, and without me, this splendid structure of India is incomplete. I am an essential element that has helped build India. I can never surrender this claim.

"It was India's historic destiny that many human races and cultures and religions should flow to her, finding a home in her hospitable soil, and that many a caravan should find rest here. Even before the dawn of history, these caravans trekked into India and wave after wave of newcomers followed. This vast and fertile land gave welcome to all and took them to her bosom. One of the last of these caravans, following the footsteps of its predecessors, was that of the followers of Islam.

"They came here and settled here for good."

India has been a flag bearer of pluralism and has always been a beacon of tolerance, mutual respect and peaceful coexistence. Muslims have, time and again, responded to the challenges of the nation. Our history attests to their role in building this great nation. Alienating one-fifth of this population will not help the country and will be against the spirit of its centuries-old ethos.

www.ingramcontent.com/pod-product-compliance
Lightning Source LLC
LaVergne TN
LVHW091249150826
845673LV00006B/1368

* 9 7 9 8 8 9 7 2 4 2 5 1 1 *